REFLECTIONS ON A QUIET REBEL

REFLECTIONS ON
A QUIET REBEL

Cal McCrystal

MICHAEL JOSEPH
LONDON

MICHAEL JOSEPH LTD

Published by the Penguin Group
27 Wrights Lane, London W8 5TZ
Viking Penguin Inc., 375 Hudson Street, New York, New York 10014, USA
Penguin Books Australia Ltd, Ringwood, Victoria, Australia
Penguin Books Canada Ltd, 10 Alcorn Avenue, Toronto, Ontario, Canada M4V 3B2
Penguin Books (NZ) Ltd, 182–190 Wairau Road, Auckland 10, New Zealand

Penguin Books Ltd, Registered Offices: Harmondsworth, Middlesex, England

First published in Great Britain 1997
Copyright © Cal McCrystal, 1997
The moral right of the author has been asserted

Set in 11/13½pt Monotype Bembo
Typeset by Rowland Phototypesetting Ltd, Bury St Edmunds, Suffolk
Printed in England by Clays Ltd, St Ives plc

A CIP catalogue record for this book is available from the British Library

ISBN 0 7181 3956 9

CONTENTS

INTRODUCTION

Occasionally, when my father was alive, the odd writer or broad-caster would ask if he would co-operate in compiling an account of his life. With the exception of a long interview for Irish radio twenty or so years ago, he demurred. I once remonstrated with him about this, and received a response which was unsatisfactory to me, though typical of him. Holding up a hand, fingers relaxed and slightly parted, he cleared his throat and declaimed:

> 'Friend, be not fretful if the voice of fame,
> Along the narrow way of hurrying men,
> Where unto echo echo shouts again,
> Be all day long not noisy with your name.'

He said the lines were by an Englishman, Alfred Austin, a Victorian poet laureate. Austin, my father said, frequently was derided in England for a large output of poetry containing little of merit. He was scorned also in Ireland both for having abandoned his family's Catholicism and for seeking popularity as a rabid imperialist. Never-theless, with the above consolatory lines, penned for another author who considered himself neglected, the poet had 'redeemed' himself in my father's eyes. Point then taken, I never raised it again.

But in the few years since his death, I have wondered if there might be merit in trying to catch some of the echoes from a life with its own redemptive message for the people of Northern Ireland, among whom he toiled and whose mean rages he, I do believe, transcended. And so, after a great deal of hesitation, I embarked upon this book. What finally nudged my arm was a request, relayed to me by my brother Colm, that I write an article about my own childhood for a magazine celebrating the centenary of Holy Family parish in Belfast, where I had gone to school and spent much of my youth. This task helped me to retrieve many things about him and my native province which had been lost in the divagations of my own travels and obsessions since leaving his house and its shores. I began sifting through papers written by and about my father. As I did so, things which he had said and done long ago came back to me with extraordinary clarity; recalling one of his gestures, for example, I found myself recapturing snatches of his conversation, word-for-word.

But the book is not simply a memoir about my father; it is about the Ireland – especially its northern British province – in which I grew up, *before* the outbreak of the recent Troubles. It is an attempt to gain and impart understanding of a conflict driven by base communal hatreds, yet spangled confusingly with generous impulses that occasionally have brought Ulster people together in hope and presented their true worth. To the end of his days, I feel sure, my father never lost faith in his notion that the Protestant and Catholic working classes would eventually discard their ludicrous differences. A great amount of his life's effort was devoted to such a reconciliation, even while hot blood fell in cities and towns aflame and reeling from terrorist warfare and sectarian excesses. Though he never acknowledged it, there were times when the effort was a great burden on him.

I neither shared his optimism nor lightened his burden. Our views diverged at many points, though never opened wounds (so far as I know) in our deeply affectionate relationship. His scorn for my lack of strong political commitment could be either gently mocking or coldly withering, but it never was aimed at undermining whatever convictions I did hold. So sharp was his intellect that I seldom won an argument with him. Yet I cannot remember his superior knowledge or his gift for exposition ever producing in me a sense of humiliation at my own inadequacies.

There are many things in this book with which he probably would have disagreed (or, as my brother Colm said, on reading the manuscript, 'would have made him turn in his grave'). He might even have disagreed vehemently with some of them. But I hope any errors, omissions, distortions and other failures of mine are redeemed by the niche I have attempted, with love and respect, to enlarge for his eminence 'along the narrow way of hurrying men'.

Cal McCrystal
April 1997

REFLECTIONS ON A QUIET REBEL

1

BLAZING CHALICES

I saw my father dying and I saw him dead, but I wasn't with him when he actually expired. In December 1991, a week before the end, I visited him at his north Belfast nursing home. His half-open eyes made no flicker of recognition when I spoke to him, and I realized, with a pang almost indistinguishable from that of bereavement, that I never would communicate with him again. Two cheerful nurses murmured 'Darling' in his ear as they gave him a sponge bath and coaxed liquid into his mouth from a baby-spout plastic beaker. My two brothers, Colm and Brendan, were silent beside me, and I wondered what they were thinking as one nurse raised his diminished limbs while the other went to work with the sponge. For a fleeting moment, I glimpsed, for the first time ever, his scrotum, and marvelled at how unabated it seemed in comparison with the rest of him. Outside, darkness had fallen, erasing the trees of the nursing home gardens and, beyond and below them, Belfast docks where he had spent part of his boyhood. The exterior darkness transformed the window of his room into a subdued reflection of the nurses' activities and my father's helplessness. As my eyes tried vainly to focus on something – anything – beyond the night-backed glass, I guessed he was approaching that unfathomable non-place whose name, he once told me, made him cry as a boy: 'Far, Far Away'.

He could not recall when, or where, he had first heard, or read, these words, or to what they referred. 'But,' he said, 'every time, without fail, when I have come across "Far, far away", or even think them to myself, my eyes have filled with tears and I'm unable to speak. Just can't help myself. Isn't that a funny thing?' Indeed it was, I thought, for my father always had a tight rein on his emotions. That does not mean he was not an emotional man. Many things moved him, not least the terrible events that had long distressed his country. It's just that he regarded excessive emotional displays as both unwise and undignified. He was not inscrutable by any means, but he often chided his sons with, 'All things in moderation'. Excessive emotion and immoderate behaviour have marked Belfast and its hinterland for as long as I lived there and as often as I revisited, having decided to live elsewhere. To the rest of the world, excess and immoderation have been exemplified by the Troubles, the wave after wave of terrorist violence and sectarian murder that have afflicted Northern Ireland since 1969. But these flaws existed long before the Troubles began. They surfaced in word ('He's not one of us' – meaning, Wrong religion, don't give him a job!), and in deed (the gerrymandering of electoral constituencies). More frequently they didn't surface at all, but stayed in an uneasy, hidden churn, like bile. Temper, like bile and prejudice, had to be repressed at all costs, my father said. 'Lose temper, lose face!' Often, even in my youth, I had thought that he bottled certain things up inside him which would have been better ejected with a flash of fang or fleck of froth, to relieve the tensions his singular life must have created within him. When he was a young man and his mother moved house after his father died, he picked up an old 'cut-throat' razor from a dusty shelf and opened it to inspect the blade. At the sight of the dazzling blade's edge, he felt one of his eye-teeth splitting from crown to root. When he was much older and coping badly with his second widowhood, he had a nose-bleed so torrential and prolonged that it half-drained the choroids of his eyes, inflicting permanent damage to his sight.

Because he had uttered the peculiarly emotive words, 'Far, far away', in that confiding moment years ago, I glanced at his eyes to see if they had brimmed. But he had turned his head to look out of a window of what was then our home. A few seconds later, he turned back again, and although much of his face was in shadow,

I noted that his eyes were dry – as they were dry now, in the nursing home, under exhausted lids, seeing perhaps nothing, or perhaps all, as my brothers and I watched a young nurse kiss him tenderly on the forehead, and wondered how much longer the ebbing of his life might take.

I returned to London, pleased in a way not to be trapped in my native city. I have an abiding affection for Northern Ireland, but I also have an abiding impatience with it. It is not quite the kind of impatience that Joyce or O'Casey had for Ireland (I cannot say that Northern Ireland treated me shabbily, either in my years there or afterwards). What it is, I think, is a fairly constant irritation with people of great charm and intelligence who are prone to the peculiar habit of building caves and tunnels in which they can hide themselves from the light of modern reality and torment each other with subterranean shouts in support of Irish republicanism and British loyalism. My father did not share my impatience, or even much sympathize with it. When I had been in some foreign country – working as a journalist in, say Chile, or the United States, or Egypt, or India – he would ask me on my return what differences I had detected between the people of those countries and the people of Belfast. I would search for various characteristics: exaggerated politeness, naïvety, opportunism, etc. He would press for anecdotes that might illustrate these traits. When I managed to produce them, he would say: 'But that's no different from here! Don't you remember crafty Frank So-and-So running rings round Mrs Thingummy to get the money out of her?' And so on until he had proved to me that 'people are the same the world over'. He was similarly convinced that, despite a slight cultural divergence, Northern Irish Protestants and Catholics were indistinguishable one from the other. Therefore, he would say, they could be persuaded to live together in peace and without mutual suspicion and aggravation. At first, as a young man, I believed him, sharing his faith in the ability of human nature to shrug off its heritage of intransigence and cruelty and master its manners and its morals. Over time, however, doubts have set in. I find it harder and harder to accept that a constantly

3

recurring extreme of madness which seizes my province is capable of being eradicated. Even while growing up in Northern Ireland I discerned that its divided people were 'peace-loving'; but, at the same time, tended to sustain themselves with the comfort of having an enemy to shun. Nothing has happened since that has undermined what I concede is my rather bleak view of things.

So, in December 1991, it was an escape for me to return to my newspaper office in London. That is where I was when I got word two days later that my father's ebbing had ceased. Back in Belfast, I went to O'Kane's funeral parlour in Donegall Street, and found his body in a plain rectangular room which looked like – and might well have been – the interior of a Portakabin. Three workmen outside were up a ladder, noisily doing something to the roof. This would have amused him, I thought: no nonsense, no pomp, and men gainfully employed in a city as notorious for its unemployment as for its wounding prejudices. I sat beside the open coffin, thinking; my eyes on the shrunken face, still not quite inscrutable. My thoughts zig-zagged backwards and forwards to the years before the Troubles and the years throughout them; to a Belfast where murder seldom stalked the streets and to country ditches where terrorist victims lay dead; to the eventful childhood I shared with my brothers and to lustrous lives of friends since snuffed out by assassins; to life with Charles McCrystal, whose corpse now lay before me, and to what was going on in the street outside.

Donegall Street is (if one may be permitted to stretch a point) Belfast's 'Fleet Street'. On the corner of one of its intersections, a few paces from the funeral parlour, is the *Belfast Telegraph*, a Unionist newspaper I worked for before joining the *Sunday Times* in London in 1964. Across the street from O'Kane's funeral parlour is the nationalist *Irish News*. South, beyond the *Telegraph* intersection, the Unionist *News Letter* had its Donegall Street offices until recently. At the end of the street is the building that once housed the now defunct *Northern Whig*, also Unionist but a bit more liberal about it than the *News Letter* had been. At various times, the street has also accommodated the correspondents of London papers, such as

4

the *Daily Herald* (defunct) and *Daily Mirror*, not to mention less sensational fry, such as *Shopping News*, as well as the local distributors of Pathé-Warner. Donegall Street was home to the Catholic Boy Scouts of Ireland, the Ulster Society of Women Artists, and the Irish-American Families Association. The street offered spiritual sustenance via two buildings dominating all – the Protestant St Anne's Cathedral and the Roman Catholic St Patrick's Church. Alternative sustenance was accessible for journalists, and those with whom they liked to mix, in McGlade's bar and the Duke of York bar. In his roles as a print worker and journalist (a rare combination, I think), my father had tramped this thoroughfare much of his working life. He had drunk (moderately) in McGlade's, prayed in St Patrick's, featured controversially in the newspapers and been in O'Kane's, more often than most: grieving over the coffins of two wives, identifying the remains of friends and acquaintances killed in the Second World War German Blitz, and inspecting, over a great number of years, the bodies of some who had died in the sectarian violence that has blighted Northern Ireland within my memory and the memory of my father. Some weeks later, I was sorting through some of his old books. They smelled of pipe-tobacco – *his* smell. One of them was *Poems* by John Clare, the nineteenth-century English rural poet, a labourer's son who was certified insane, never having ceased to pine for his first love, Mary. The book flopped open at a poem called 'Remembrances' and I noticed a light pencil-mark against the following lines:

> Summers pleasures they are gone like to visions everyone
> And the cloudy days of autumn and of winter cometh on.
> I tried to call them back but unbidden they are gone
> Far away from heart and eye and for ever far away.

I put my nose to the page, inhaling ancient traces of tobacco smoke. I thought that I had solved a puzzle. The poem did not say 'Far, far away', but it did say 'far away' twice in a single line. There was also that pencil-mark. But, turning to the front of the book, I discovered

I had solved nothing. It was published in 1935, years after the phrase first made my father so uncharacteristically lachrymose; when he was thirty, and I was about to be brought into the world.

In March of that year, the month of my conception, the peace of Belfast – about to become my native city – was severely disturbed. Citizens preparing to celebrate King George V's Silver Jubilee, an event scheduled for May, were anxious to prove their loyalty to the Crown with early, unbridled zeal. As so often in Northern Ireland, an act of celebration transformed itself into a lethal convulsion.

What happened, as I gathered many years later, was that Protestant loyalists had mixed an excessive dose of triumphalism with their ardour for 'Sailor George'. Triumphalism has been a heady, recurring ingredient in the social affairs of my province. It implies that those with neither a right nor a reason to triumph should have their Roman Catholic noses rubbed in the ignominy of their defeat, without demur. But a passive reaction, or lack of any response at all, is not guaranteed. On the occasion referred to, those who were reluctant subjects of the King lashed out at those who were immensely devoted to him. In the sectarian carnage that followed, on and off between then and August, thirteen people were killed, eight of them Protestants. Thousands were injured, most of them Catholics. Two thousand Catholics were driven from their homes. One particularly vicious riot was prompted by the continued defiant construction of a Catholic church – St Anthony's – in Willowfield, a neighbourhood in east Belfast. A Protestant bishop, John MacNeice, father of the great Ulster poet Louis MacNeice, appealed for tolerance. 'Forget the things that are behind. Forget the unhappy past. Forget the story of the old feuds, the old triumphs, the old humiliations.' His exhortation went unheeded. The city coroner called the deaths 'wanton and meaningless', and delivered the verdict: 'Bigotry is the curse of peace and goodwill.' Today, pondering the words of a bishop and a coroner, I have no doubt at all that, beneath all the clangour and rancour of Ulster's relatively brief existence as a political entity, theirs is the true Protestant voice of the stricken

province: a voice carrying an intensely humane anxiety to ingemi-
nate peace when all around them rage froths and gnashes danger-
ously. Today, this voice is raised often – though not often enough,
or in public, for fear of inviting reprisal from rabid 'no-Popers'.
I sometimes sense that it is an expedient voice, rather than a
morally-convinced voice; that its exhortations for peace and tranquillity reflect more a 'let us avoid that which impedes prosperity',
than a desire to abolish communal differences. This may be a cynical
view. I like to think that, at some point in the future, I shall no
longer harbour it.

The bishop's and the coroner's anxiety was the anxiety of much
(one cannot be sure *how* much) of Northern Ireland's population
in the year of my birth. It was as heartfelt in those dark days as it is
in these dark days. But it never has been sufficiently potent to
repudiate the curse and disperse the darkness. It is an anxiety
the peculiar neural origins of which intertwine with conflicting
interpretations of history. The 'interpreters' are almost never self-
doubting, and almost always self-righteous. Either side acknowledges a desideratum in the other and frets itself to incandescence
over remedial failures. Pontine gestures don't easily dislocate what
I have come to believe is a thought barrier between the Catholic
and the Protestant communities. Generally speaking, larger attempts
at compromise receive the same short shrift that is the response to
attempts at coercion; warsmoke makes it that much harder to see
the other side's point of view. I have no idea if the coroner or the
bishop ever did manage to penetrate the thought barrier – or, if
they did, to what positive effect. By and large, while I lived in
Northern Ireland, the place and its people were ruinously locked
into the rhythms of ancient prejudice. They resisted – as they
continue to resist – all attempts, some well-meaning, to free them
from the bondage because it was as comfortingly familiar as the
Permian rock of the province. Some wear their prejudice on their
sleeves or behind a balaclava. Others are not aware that they are
wearing it at all – when in fact they are.

Charles McCrystal was one of his generation who tried to break through the thought barrier. Occasionally as a young teenager, I accompanied him on evening walks. Some of these took us through a warren of streets where Protestants lived and into a warren of streets where Catholics lived. Once, in a Protestant street, he pointed to a group of children using a lamp post as a maypole and asked me: 'Would you say those wee children were Catholics or Protestants?'

'Protestants,' I replied.

'Why do you say that?'

'Because this is a Protestant street.'

We soon afterwards entered the Catholic neighbourhood, and as we passed some children playing hop-scotch on a buckled pavement, he asked me: 'What religion would you say those children are?'

'Catholic.'

'Why do you say that?'

'Because of where we are.'

'Yes, but apart from that, is there anything about the two groups of children that defines them as Protestant and Catholic?'

'No, not that I can see. They look the same to me.'

'So really, all you've done is make an assumption . . .'

And so it went on, interminably, through the duration of our walk: a discussion that wandered from rigour into silliness and back again; that jumped from a genuine attempt at philosophical exploration into little point-scoring ambushes that used to enrage me once it dawned that his primary motive was to test my powers of reasoning. Yet I can see now that his secondary motive was to warn me, in a general way, against assuming too much from circumstantial evidence, and against pigeon-holing people.

Born in an unpartitioned Ireland, in 1905, his allegiance to that entity remained devoutly unyielding throughout his life. He spoke for it, worked for it, risked his career and the well-being of his family for it. But he never harnessed his religion to it and was resolutely opposed to those who did. He practised his Catholicism as he had been taught to do, but was distrustful of those who 'performed', say, their Lenten duties with ostentation. 'I've seldom seen a man who licked the altar rails who didn't beat his wife or turn a beggar from the door,' he said. He also said: 'An awful lot of Holy Joes cock an eye at heaven while their hand's in the till.' And he would tell all who would listen that religion should play no part in the creation and maintenance of a state – particularly the all-Ireland one he wanted. Normally, his voice had a soft, slightly husky quality, but when making pronouncements, or quoting a poet or a philosopher, it became stentorian – as though he had suddenly found himself on a stage or podium. Listening to him declaim thus in an unnatural voice could be boring at times, as could his attempts to teach us 'posture' and 'co-ordination'. These sometimes entailed a competition between my brothers and me to see who could walk around the house longest while balancing a book on our heads. At quite an early age we were encouraged to play a game called 'Finger and thumb keep moving', these digits having to remain rhythmically active while we patted our heads with one hand, rubbed our stomachs with the other, and rose up from our chairs and sat down again without missing a beat. And for all his efforts to make us believe in pacifism, he talked a lot, and approvingly, of 'the Spartan approach' to life. Given that the Spartans looked upon themselves as merely a military garrison, and that all their discipline pointed to war, this was curious, though I did not realize it until years later, when I was studying ancient history.

By my own standards today, I suppose he always maintained a fairly 'Spartan' home, with more hard surfaces than soft; dark furniture; sombre pictures of Christ and the Madonna and Child; a big, chilly bathroom with Sunlight soap in the bath; and a gloomy staircase. But while I can't remember much luxury, I can't recall much discomfort either. His brand of Spartan disciplines never stopped him declaring that 'Nothing is too good for the working-man!' This did not seem to him to be inconsistent. In fact, I think he was relentless only in his belief in the struggle for a secular, socialist, republican Ireland. But while I, in time, merely dismounted from my father's horse of history, my younger brother Brendan slapped the horse's rump disdainfully. Sometime after Charles

McCrystal died, Brendan referred to 'Daddy's almost wilful determination to give no hostages to anyone – friends, relations, even family, and to leave this world with nothing but his ideology'. It is quite remarkable how siblings differ in their estimates of parents. My older brother Colm not only loved my father unreservedly, but seems, in conversation at any rate, to mirror his beliefs and applaud the paths he trod. Brendan, on the other hand, seldom bothered to hide his scepticism of some of my father's stated views, detecting even 'a touch of sectarianism in his personal relations with Protestants'.

Reflecting on my father's life, which was three-quarters over when the Ulster Troubles broke out in 1969, I am struck by the fact that the events in Ireland's history that produced the greatest exhilaration in him and provided the greatest inspiration for his actions were those painfully brief moments when Catholics and Protestants stood side by side against what he called their common enemies: English tyranny and Irish bigotry. Chief among those episodes was the 1798 (shortlived) rebellion by the 'United Irishmen', when Presbyterian and Roman Catholic stood shoulder to shoulder with pikes and pitchforks against English authority in Ireland. That fruitless alliance played a significant part in shaping my father's life and investing it with controversy. The fact that the insurrection failed did not consign it, in his mind, to a chamber of the might-have-been; rather, he regarded it as an event that had to be commemorated again and again as a reminder that Protestants and Catholics could come together as one, even in Ulster. In 1948, my father helped organize the 150th anniversary commemoration of it, causing himself considerable angst. That was the year Gerry Adams, later to be president of the IRA's political wing, Sinn Féin, was born in west Belfast. I write this within months of the bicentenary of that failed revolution, and I can almost hear the renewed din from the 1998 celebrants, with their slogans and banners, marching feet and clenched fists, sweet virtue and bitter memory, eyes and ears averted from the Ulster reality: the longevity of sectarian prejudice.

'A movement fuelled by religious fervour is doomed ultimately to fail,' my father used to say. 'Any crusade will fail if it won't bend to reason.' Sometimes he would quote Abélard: 'By doubting we come to question, and by seeking we may come upon the truth.' I can still hear the stentorian voice saying it, his forefinger wagging like a metronome. Surely, I tell myself, there must be many in my native province who share this view and try to apply it in their daily lives. But Charles McCrystal was the only one who, in my own experience of him, thought and acted according to such principles. Most of us accept that man is by nature credulous, victimized by first impressions, from which he can escape only with great difficulty. Frequently, my father was harassed by others' first impressions of him, but in that part of his life's journey on which I was a companion I became quite convinced that he managed to overcome, by and large, his own instant notions of others.

I don't think I ever learned to share his conviction that our fellow-countrymen would, in the end, 'bend to reason' and dump bigotry and the use of violence. Occasionally we talked about this contrast between us: his optimism, and my pessimism; his faith in the working class, against my doubts. He claimed that bigotry in Northern Ireland was a weapon fashioned by the ruling class and handed to the masses. Once the ruling class was despatched (I did not take this to mean to a violent end), he said, the great hoodwink would cease. In part, his assertion was true. The Protestant working class of Ulster long had been encouraged by their 'betters' to hold that breaking the law – even committing treason – was fine, so long as it was done to preserve their 'culture' from contamination by that of their Catholic neighbours. This incitement is well documented. In the early years of the twentieth century, when the recurrent theme of Home Rule for Ireland again pulsed through British politics, the [Protestant] Ulster Volunteer Force openly organized, drilled and imported arms. No prosecution was even launched. Indeed those who openly defied the government were rewarded by the government.

F. E. Smith, British lawyer, politician, Fellow of Merton College, Oxford, pillar of society, declared in 1912: 'There is no length to which Ulster will not be entitled to go – however desperate or unconstitutional.' And soon afterwards: 'Home Rule will be dead for ever on the day when 100,000 men armed with rifles assemble at Balmoral [Belfast].' He later became Lord Birkenhead.

Sir Edward Carson, British lawyer, politician, former Solicitor-General for both Ireland and England, pillar of society, told the people of Belfast the following year: 'Go on, be ready. You are our great army. It is on you we rely . . . I know a great deal of that will involve statutory illegality, but it will also involve moral righteousness . . . The Volunteers are illegal, and the Government know they are illegal, and the Government dare not interfere with them. Don't be afraid of illegalities.' He later became First Lord of the Admiralty and a Lord of Appeal. His statue and raised fist guard the entrance to Stormont, the Unionist citadel in east Belfast from which a Unionist government ruled Northern Ireland from 1921, following the division of Ireland, until 1972 when it was suspended in favour of direct rule from London.

William Joynson-Hicks, British lawyer, politician, pillar of society, linked the Conservative Party, God, and treason when he declared at Warrington in the same year: 'The people of Ulster have behind them the Unionist Party. Behind them is the Lord God of Battles. In his name and your name I say to the Prime Minister: "Let your armies and batteries fire. Fire if you dare; fire and be damned!"' He later became Home Secretary and the first Viscount Brentford.

Andrew Bonar Law, British iron merchant, politician, pillar of society, echoed him thus: 'We shall support you to the last in any steps which Sir Edward Carson and your leaders think it is necessary for you to take to defend your rights . . . We give the pledge without any condition.' He later became Chancellor of the Exchequer, Leader of the House of Commons, and *Prime Minister*.

Accordingly, I think that when my father talked about 'Spartan discipline' to us as children, he might have chosen a different analogy from the famous city of the Peloponnesus. He might have talked, for example, of the *helots*, the slaves who performed the lowliest tasks; and the *periæci*, the subject class of free men who were tradesmen and merchants, but were denied the opportunity to generate their own political clout; and the *Spartiatai*, or governing class of rulers and soldiers, descended from the Dorians, who had invaded ancient Laconia centuries earlier. He would, I feel sure, have delighted in such a comparison had it occurred to him.

Deliberate acts of incitement from society's pillars gave Ulster's loyalists all the justification they needed to take up arms against the state. They also established a trend: years later, whenever the government of the United Kingdom would attempt to introduce legislation that was not to the loyalists' liking, the Ulster 'armies' would line up and display their batteries. Their gospel had the imprimatur of the great and good of the kingdom. In other words, officers of the British state were saying to Unionists: 'You can break the law and not be outlawed'. That certainly gave compromise a bad name and chances of peace a ride into outer space.

'Of course,' my father agreed. 'But giving one section of the people the authority to defy the government by threat of arms is a message to the other section that the use of arms is not so discreditable after all.'

'So both sides can claim legitimacy in the slaughter of one another,' I said.

'Yes, but one day it'll dawn on those doing the killing that they're destroying themselves at the behest of big vested interests. Then they'll stop.'

'One day! Should I hold my breath?'

'One day. One day,' he said.

Each time he talked like this, I was almost persuaded that he was right. His positive outlook on things was quite contagious. But after we would part, doubt would again descend on me, and within a short time my pessimism would return.

What I derived from his life's journey – and have confirmed through subsequent excursions alone in Northern Ireland – is that Ulster folk resent criticism of accepted and familiar ideas more robustly than do others in these islands. Disturbance of routine is more unwelcome there than in, say, Lancashire or Limerick. I'm not certain why this is so. It cannot have much to do with intelligence, since Ulster people are among the most intelligent I have known. It may be auto-subjugation of intelligence perhaps. There is a phrase I heard once – possibly from my father – that might go some distance towards describing the malaise (if one may use that word): 'unconscious cerebration'. It is not always wise to employ scientific, or pseudo-scientific, terms in explaining human conduct. Yet 'unconscious cerebration' seems permissible as a speculative source of behaviour in which it is difficult to locate evidence of conscious intelligence being exerted. It is, I suppose, an absence of mind in which the attention is so concentrated upon a single subject or train of thought, that one loses the sense of the present situation which accompanies less intense mental activity. Consciousness runs only in one channel, and we wake up, as it were, from a dream when the concentration is relaxed. Certain sights or sounds may have the effect of blocking the rational stream of conscious thought, switching us into a channel of irrational, pre-programmed action.

As a young reporter in Belfast before the Troubles, I was approached one Orange Day in July by a bowler-hat who knew I was a Catholic. He informed me in no uncertain words that the Orange Order stood-for-liberality-of-conscience-freedom-to-worship-in-any-religion-and-brotherly-love-in-Christ. Each explosive syllable was accompanied by a thump on my shoulder which got fiercer as his instruction went on, until my clavicle ached horribly and my face was covered in spit. He was, I'm sure, unaware that he was being aggressive. I once heard of a clergyman who went upstairs intending to change his clothing in preparation for going out to dinner. After a while, his wife went up to see what had become of him, and found that he had undressed and gone to bed. In other words, two trains of thought had passed through his mind: one the subject of learned contemplation, and the other the association of ideas which connected the act of removing his upper garments with that of going to bed. Similarly, I have come across clergymen in my native province who are conditioned to praying at their fervent best while wearing Orange regalia or confronted by an IRA man's coffin.

If the problem is not unconscious cerebration, or reflex action, could it be a rejection of criticism that conflicts with the smooth workings of primitive instincts? Being no philosopher, I hesitate even to hazard explanations of these matters. But in talking to seemingly reasonable Northern Ireland loyalists and nationalists I often am dismayed by the absence of the self-detachment and self-abnegating vigour of criticism that is capable of propelling people forward towards self-discovery and communal adjustments. Perhaps my own vision into the conflict is distorted by my having deliberately locked myself out of it; having ceased long ago to be a practising Catholic, and come to regard nationalism as degrading as it might be uplifting, limiting my territorial preferences to European union.

In the years preceding the Troubles, I saw and interpreted many things through my father's eyes. In recalling some of them I feel myself reasonably equipped to chronicle aspects of his life and explain the communal influences that picked him up and dropped him down, that loosed his tongue and made him hold it, that treated him to periods of fame, eclipsed by longer periods of obscurity. These influences persist, determining the conduct of other Ulstermen's lives as well. They may subside for a time, as a 'peace process' is spread on the table, gleaming damask and delft, but with no wholesome food in sight; or flare into renewed violence when a Semtex bomb brings down a building, or a stealthy gunman snuffs out a life. They belong to concatenated historical experiences which have imbued my fellow-countrymen – and women – with instincts that are as irrefragable as logic, as persevering as the weather and as dangerous as the terrible events we have been reading about ever since 1969.

Years ago, when my father periodically had to put up with intimidation because he was a Catholic, I could feel exasperation rising in me. But he would quickly remind me that Catholics too practised discrimination, even in the Republic of Ireland, where

Protestants were neither thick on the ground nor a threat to Catholics. 'We are all exactly the same', he said, 'in our willingness to follow the band, doing what our peers expect of us.'

In any case, he would also say, it is not necessarily a discordant act to celebrate communal differences, providing those differences are highlights on a broad cloth rather than bits scissored out of it. There then might follow a little lecture which went roughly as follows:

Where religious or moral sanctions are concerned, the great mass of Christian believers, whether Catholic or Protestant, professedly or implicitly adhered to the assumptions of the Middle Ages. They still assumed, on the whole, that received dogmas represented the secure conclusions of mankind. They might be wrong in these assumptions but were capable, nevertheless, of engaging one's sympathy by arguing otherwise. On the other hand, they seemed incapable – or less capable – of entertaining counter-argument, from whatever quarter. Because they had so much *in common*, Protestants and Catholics felt compelled to revile in one another the little unshared attributes.

Consequently, nits are picked with pickaxes; pin-pricks bleed like gouges; storms rage and fires blaze in chalices. Ancient misapprehensions are transmitted from generation to generation, and it seems impossible to launch newer, clearer, truer ideas about anything that relates to, or rises from, those misapprehensions. To invoke your version of the 'true faith' in protecting them is to sanctify you as defender and, when thought necessary, license you as aggressor.

My father realized fairly early on that the past, though important as an inspiration, didn't furnish him with reliable, permanent standards of conduct. These were better derived from contemporary, first-hand exploration of the extent to which his and the rest of society's abiding needs might be met. Of course, the past would inform that search, but it should never have an automatic lien on it. Having satisfied himself that Ireland's – and particularly Ulster's – malaise was only artificially religious, he believed Protestant and Catholic might be brought to a state of happy coexistence by a less mystical, and more scientific alchemy: socialism. He spent all but a few years of his adult life dreaming of discovering a formula – *secretum maximum* – that would bring loyalist and nationalist together beneath the socialist banner, marching out of the bogs of history and convention, religious bigotry sucking vainly at their heels. To my knowledge, he never came close to finding it. But the search yielded interesting lessons, just as a glance at his life may help to enlighten those who have tried and tried again to fathom the Ulster Troubles.

2

DEMOCRACY OF THE DEAD

By Christmas of 1935, construction work on St Anthony's church was completed, and I entered the world upon my parents' bed, in a street of small, red-brick terraced houses which had tiny front gardens with hedges of box, lilac and fuschia, and somewhat larger back ones with wooden fences and coarse grass that was capable of drawing blood from infant flesh. On sunny days, the shadow of the new church spire would crawl down Willowfield Gardens and finger Number 28.

I lived at that address for (I believe) four years before the 'curse of peace and goodwill' prised my family out of its uncertain niche in what was then – as now – a Protestant loyalist 'stronghold' or 'bastion' or 'ghetto', words frequently applied in print, aptly conveying the medieval flavour of the blood-heat therein. Often I have wondered how we, as Catholics, managed to survive even that short time, or why my parents had been prepared to risk life and limb – their children's as well as their own – in order to make a point. It was never going to work, this great idea my father seemed to have cherished. Charles McCrystal was largely self-taught. Like many who sip intellectual nourishment from their own spoon, he tended to remember every lesson he gave himself. He could recite large chunks of Shakespeare, the whole of Goldsmith's *Deserted Village*, the *Rubaiyat of Omar Khayyam* in its entirety, and Gray's *Elegy* nonstop. He had no Greek, but spoke knowledgeably of the fall of Troy and the adventures of Odysseus. Not only had he never been to China, he was painfully allergic to Chinese food (after a bowl of shark-fin soup, he awoke in the middle of the night with his tongue stuck to the roof of his mouth); yet he seemed to have a surprising amount of information about Ch'in Shih Huang Ti's successful effort to unify the seven Warring States ('He'd not find it so easy to unify *our* island, if he was alive').

Many of the things my father taught himself, he then imparted to others, including his three sons when they were prepared to listen. He often did so between puffs on a pipe that glowed and guttered with a jet-black, strong tobacco called Warhorse. This gave him a serene and professorial air, though he was so unselfconscious about it that no one, so far as I am aware, ever thought him a *poseur* (a word he was not slow, however, to apply to others). Having taught himself Gaelic, he became a Gaelic teacher. On learning to read Russian, he took his examinations and began teaching it to adults at Belfast's technical college. As a young man, he had taught himself economics and Esperanto, subsequently giving instruction in both, as well as in 'English and Article Writing', to classes organized by the National Council of Labour Colleges. He also taught himself (to read) German. He had books on philosophy and ancient history and five leather-bound volumes of *Goethes Werke*, printed in Leipzig, all of which he digested and, from time to time, ruminated over. But there was one thing he refused to learn, in spite of all the words he had read and heard on the subject. That is that, in the absence of a miracle (and he didn't believe in miracles), Protestants and Catholics are not destined to live harmoniously together in Northern Ireland.

As I write this, I have before me on my desk a charcoal head-and-shoulders profile of Charles McCrystal as the artist saw him in the year of my birth. The features are what some might choose to describe as 'poetic' (he did write poetry, with considerable skill and feeling, but not, I think, to great acclaim). Above a thin, straight nose, rises a prominent brow that finally buries itself in a shock of dark hair springing defiantly upwards, before reluctantly tipping backwards, as though in a strong wind. The visible eye that stares off the side of the page conveys both patience and expectancy. The mouth, delicately formed, is calm; the chin, firm but without aggression. A tartan scarf shows above the deep collar and wide lapels of an overcoat. Just below the lapel button-hole the artist has written the word 'Cathal', the Gaelic version of Charles. That name – pronounced 'Kaal' in Northern Ireland and 'Kaa-hill' south of the border with the Republic of Ireland – could spell trouble. It announced that he was of the Gaelic/nationalist persuasion; a 'taig', a Fenian, a Mick, a papist – someone capable of fomenting sedition and rebellion, if not actually doing it already, which, as a matter of fact, he was in a way – or had been endeavouring to.

Beside the charcoal sketch I have placed another image which had been among my father's effects when he died, aged 86, on 18 December 1991. It is a photograph of seven old geezers, posing with a young priest against the exterior wall of what might be either a church crypt or a public lavatory. My father stands at the back of the smiling group. Apart from him, there is none I recognize by name or countenance. Charles McCrystal looks frail, but cheerful. His white hair is wispy and unbarbered. Strong sunlight has squeezed his eyes almost shut. On the back of the photograph, there are words, in blue ballpoint, across the top left-hand corner. I recognize my father's shaky handwriting: 'Old IRA Belfast'. Well, well, I thought. A man whose entire life epitomized, for me, peace and humanity, had belonged to an organization that used bombs and bullets in a war against other humans. How could this be? Glancing at the picture again, I would guess he was in his mid-seventies when it was taken. By then, the *new* IRA, and the new Troubles were in their twelfth or thirteenth year.

I cannot recall ever having anything like a focused conversation with him about what his role had been in the 'Old IRA'. Even when he was an elderly widower, living alone and reminiscing with me during the brief annual holidays we took together (before fading sight and other infirmities made these memorable jaunts no longer possible), the subject received no serious or prolonged exploration between us. I am not sure that he would have wanted me to be privy to things which might compromise my career as a journalist.

Perhaps, if I am to be frank, it was I who avoided the confidences for that reason. It is very possible that my father sensed this distancing in me and consequently remained fairly reticent. An alternative possibility is that, because we did not see eye-to-eye on the most momentous aspect of all this – i.e., the use of terrorism as a valid instrument for upsetting a democratically assembled system, however incurably nasty it might appear – there was mutual circumspection, reducing the risk of an argument that might unnecessarily impair our summer jaunts. He may have regretted what he knew to be my views on the 'armed struggle' and the 'volunteers' conducting it. But equally, I think, he was finding it increasingly difficult to defend, even to himself, a relentless and merciless campaign of violence which had taken so many innocent lives and corrupted so many survivors. In his youth, I imagine, he had been seduced by the 'romanticism' of the Irish republican 'cause' – just as others have been seduced since then. It is not really difficult to understand that process, given the imagery that accompanied it. Ireland was a 'woman' defended by her 'sons' from the 'tyrant' (Britain). The word 'volunteer' had a more virtuous sound than 'warrior', just as 'the struggle' sounded more praiseworthy than 'terrorism'. Leaders of the 'Old IRA' included poets and teachers, people who loved children and worshipped God. They therefore reflected such sterling attributes as respectability, strength of character, learning, endurance, sacrifice and – when they died on hunger strike or at British hands – martyrdom. When my father was 'active' in the 'movement', the island of Ireland was in the throes of being redefined in a process fuelled by revolution as well as by diplomacy. The revolutionary sodality could see itself as midwife to the 'terrible beauty' Yeats recorded as being born. It was terrible, but was it not beautiful also? Worth the agony, the blood, the loss? When I close my eyes and try to imagine myself as my father, a teenager, in those redefining years of the 1920s, I can just about sense the heady powers that drew him into the republican movement. But when I have opened my eyes to what the modern IRA has wreaked on the country of my birth, on the country where I reside and work, on families, communities and democracy too, the imagery has lost all the allure that I fancied my father had perceived. Sometimes I persuaded myself that he had come to acknowledge that an Ireland stitched together by force would continue to bleed through its sutures for ever. He never actually conceded this in words that I can remember, and perhaps my surmise is entirely unfounded. But in the closing years of his life I sensed a certain disenchantment with the callous and self-destructive nature of modern, urban 'guerrilla' war, and even with the cache of traditions drawn on to sanction and sanctify it. Once, I threw Chesterton's words at him: 'Tradition means giving votes to the most obscure of all classes, our ancestors. It is the democracy of the dead.'

'I can't argue with that,' my father said. He admired Chesterton.

His discomfort was certainly nothing quite like the repulsion with which he came to regard the Soviet Union, following the brutal smashing of the Hungarian and Czech revolutions. It was more a pre-dawning acknowledgment that thugs sometimes run off with good causes before, inevitably, they run out of them. Nevertheless, despite the near-silence on the subject, I absorbed some hazy notion of his early involvement in clandestine republican activities.

He had been, I believe, a young IRA 'intelligence officer' in his teens. The duties of an intelligence officer would seem to have consisted of hiding guns when requested to do so. I have tried to imagine what the atmosphere in Belfast must have been like in his youth. My father was eleven in 1916, when two searing events surely dominated his existence. One was the Easter Uprising by republicans in Dublin and its knock-on effect on Belfast. The second was his father's heart attack which lost the family its only bread-winner. Four years later, after sectarian riots in Belfast and the partition of Ireland, the new Unionist-dominated parliament of Northern Ireland was established. In 1921, when my father was sixteen, the IRA and the British Army called a truce. But in the north, the Unionist authorities seemed bent on treating the Catholic/nationalist third of the population 'as if they were pariahs in the community', as my father's friend, Joe Devlin, then a Nationalist MP, put it.

The following year, when my grandfather was dying in a downstairs room of the family home near the docks area of the city, soldiers raided the house to search for arms. Had they been more insistent, it is likely that they would have found them, because my father had hidden some upstairs. But my grandfather, clearly ill, gave the soldiers a smile, both wan and idiotic, and jabbed a finger at the ceiling.

'Upstairs, you'll find all the guns you want.'

The troops gave my grandmother a nod of sympathy, and promptly left the house. She was angry with my father for placing the family in such jeopardy. She found the bag of guns and flung it into the water of Belfast Lough. Shortly afterwards, my grandfather died, aged fifty-four. I have no idea how many of my father's Catholic contemporaries knew of his clandestine republican activities. But I suspect that if they had got to Protestant ears, he quickly would have followed my grandfather to the grave.

I never got around to asking him why, on getting married, he had chosen to integrate himself among the Protestant working class of Belfast. He and my mother Mary, a farmer's daughter from County Antrim who was three years his senior, had moved to Willowfield after their marriage in 1932 (furnishing the entire house for £100). Perhaps it had something to do with his intelligence duties. One could argue that the existence of a Royal Ulster Constabulary barracks on a corner of our street made this unlikely; though one equally could argue otherwise. Nevertheless, I feel sure his design was somewhat grander than that, if no less quixotic. I do not think it was idealism as such, though there may have been traces of it among his motives, the chief one, I suspect, having been a stubborn trust that men of prejudice, once immersed in socialist principles, would identify thereafter only great virtues in each other, and be persuaded of the efficacy of unity, both in human and territorial terms.

In those days – more than thirty years before the most enduring Ulster Troubles broke out in 1969 – Belfast's tuberculosis death rate was the highest in the British Isles. The mortality rate for mothers had risen significantly since the First World War. The city's housing policy, in so far as it affected the poor, was nonexistent. Corruption on the city council (later to be called Belfast Corporation) seemed ineradicable. A world trade decline dealt Belfast's exports a crippling blow. One shipyard closed in 1934, and the other was greatly understretched. In the linen industry – a production line that had given Belfast the label 'Linenopolis' only a few decades earlier – more than 20,000 were out of work.

United in their misery and anger, the Belfast poor pushed their bigotry aside and marched together behind bands playing 'Yes, We Have No Bananas' to protest the Poor Law Guardians' refusal of adequate relief payments. It must have elated my father to see Protestant and Catholic working men and women, together, raging against a common foe – capitalist employers and their 'lickspittles' (a favourite epithet of his) in the Unionist government and in the the Orange and Masonic lodges. But his elation was short-lived. It required only a couple of political speeches, carefully laced with sectarian poison, to divide the protesters and set them at one another's throats again.

This had happened before. In 1907, for example, Protestant and Catholic dockers and carters conducted a joint-campaign for union recognition and higher wages. Three years later, the Home Rule argument boiled up yet again, causing that grassroots alliance to dissolve in bigotry. In anything of a constitutional nature, people were easily spurred to violence. The partition of Ireland in 1920 prompted the Troubles of 1920–22 in which 453 people died and 23,000 Catholics lost their homes.

It was no different in 1934. Sir Basil Brooke, then Northern Ireland's Minister of Agriculture, and for twenty subsequent years the Prime Minister of the government at Stormont, made a speech which left little manoeuvre for transcredal fraternity. 'Roman Catholics,' he announced, 'were out to destroy Ulster with all their might and power' and should not be given employment. These are notably unminced words for a politician, but then politicians in

Northern Ireland seldom affect delicacy. So, one day Catholics and Protestant workmen exhibited fraternal feelings towards one another; next day, they were hacking at one another's limbs. More than once it has occurred to me that the offering of comfort followed by its expedient withdrawal, the manifestation of tolerance yielding to a rush of enmity, were somehow the creations of a certain erratic intercommunal rhythm – the systole-diastole of a faulty heart – and that this was the way things are to be for ever.

It has been argued that Catholics, who form more than a third of Northern Ireland's population, had to some extent talked their way into second-class citizenship; expecting rejection from the majority, they made little or no effort to be accepted by the majority. This, I think, was partly true, though partly understandable. I once was told by an old Catholic dock worker that he often had to run a gauntlet of insults, kicks and punches just to get to the waterfront. He kept his nose clean, only to have it bloodied by bigoted dockers. 'It knocks the stuffing out of you,' he said. 'It's safer to stay at home sometimes.'

But my father was no 'fatalist' (another frequently used epithet of his), believing that, given time and the rapid spread of socialism, the Protestant working class would 'see beyond the brims of their bowler-hats', worn on Orange marches, and unite in the 'brotherhood of man'. When I was a teenager, he occasionally described winning over this Orangeman or that Freemason to his way of thinking; which might, I think, be roughly summed up as, Workers of the World Unite in Spiritual Independence!

'I'm sure I broadened his mind,' he would say about a conversation with a Protestant work colleague. 'He'd no idea of Karl Marx or Keir Hardie, of what James Connolly stood for. I told him a thing or two about how the wealthy landowners in this country had set worker against worker to keep the proletariat down. I opened his eyes, I can tell you. And when I'd done with him, he said to me: "Charlie, you're so smart you could be one of us Protestants." I really laughed at that and said, "Away-a-that!" And you know what his very next words were? He said: "I want you to know, Charlie, that if it ever comes to it, I won't be the one to shoot you." You see what can be achieved by reasoning with people!'

We were the only Catholic family in Willowfield Gardens. There must have been other Catholics in the wider neighbourhood; otherwise, there would have been no need for the new church or adjoining primary school, which my older brother, Colm, attended. But in our street, we were isolated and obvious 'Fenians'. When my mother first took Colm out in his pram, a neighbour, not yet aware of her religion, asked the baby's name.

'Colm,' my mother said.

'Call him what?'

'Just Colm.'

'Yes, but *what?*'

No self-respecting Protestant would give his sons the names we bore. 'Colm' is a Gaelic word meaning 'dove'. I was named Cahal Mary, the first word being a phonetic alternative to Cathal; the second, in honour of the Blessed Virgin – a custom once fashionable in the continent of Europe (e.g., Erich Maria Remarque, author of *All Quiet on the Western Front*) and much favoured also in Catholic Ireland (e.g., John Mary Lynch, the former Prime Minister, or *Taoiseach*, of the Irish Republic, or Joseph Mary Plunkett, the revolutionary poet executed in Dublin in 1916). My younger brother was called Brendan, after St Brendan, the Irish sailor-monk thought by some to have reached America before Columbus did.

I had a child's normal inquisitiveness. When Brendan was feeding at my mother's breast I asked: 'What's he drinking?' 'Milk,' she said. My next question was: 'Is there tea in the other one?' She shook her head laughingly, her dark-brown hair falling over her eyes as she bowed over my baby brother. Passing a fuschia hedge, I reached for a fluffy bumblebee to feel its softness, an early lesson that angry bees leave their stings behind. Determined to discover what Colm was experiencing and I was missing, I stumbled across a busy main road and, on hands and knees, climbed the steps of his school. But I cannot recall being desperately curious about the small parcels of faeces that were posted through our front door; or the rough stuff Colm endured from neighbours' children on his way to and from infant school; or the night visits to our house by black uniformed policemen from the station at the street corner. I did not remember feeling unusually threatened by the ransacking of the house in searches for sedition. My father told me years later that my screams could be heard all over Belfast during these rude visitations.

His words came back to me a couple of years ago, while I waited to interview the (now retired) Royal Ulster Constabulary's Chief Constable, Sir Hugh Annesley, at his east Belfast headquarters. I glanced at a display of uniforms in a glass case. They ranged, backwards in time, from today's holly green (with folded back lapels) to corvine black (high, stiff collar to keep chins up), the garb that graced Willowfield in my infancy. Seeing it again made me feel oddly uncomfortable, even after I had entered Annesley's room and been greeted by a perfectly nice Chief Constable engrossed with the task of reforming his force. I did not tell him what my father had related to me: that complaints about dog excrement being posted through our letter-box usually provoked a glare from an RUC sergeant, who would ram his chin into black serge and slap the revolver at his waist. Disinclined to look back on how his predecessors policed the province, he said: 'The future, not the past, matters.' Alas, for many in Northern Ireland, the future is the past, and vice versa.

As we talked, part of my mind lingered on the black uniform in the display case and the disagreeable experiences it symbolized. After the 1935 riots which had ushered me into the world, the National Council for Civil Liberties published a scathing indictment of Ulster's police. It condemned the RUC for its inaction against loyalist gunmen and found that the part-time force, the Special Constabulary (or 'B-Specials') was 'nothing but the organized army of the Unionist Party'. Among those who read the document was H. G. Wells. He urged others to do so, 'if you care for human freedom and dignity under the British flag'. Yet, even though the RUC has changed from being a nakedly sectarian force to one desperate to recruit Catholics, the British flag remains for many Catholics the big obstacle to the future, however their human freedom and dignity are massaged. The brick wall of religious sectarianism has been penetrated in many places since the British government got rid of Stormont and imposed direct rule on Northern Ireland in 1972. Institutionally, at least, bigoted practices have been banished by legislation. But one cannot banish it from the bloodstream so easily. Besides, the rubble of the broken wall is all around: holy relics with jagged edges, which are cluttering minds, slowing progress, harking back to things my father despised.

The people of Belfast, wrote the great Irish actor, Micheál MacLiammóir some years before the longest Troubles, 'are not by any means invariably harsh, pragmatical, cold, bigoted or rude . . . There are poets and painters who live in this ugly city that has for me a peculiar charm of its own. Perhaps it is the charm of disguise, for that is one of the first things you notice about it: it wears a mask. Everything possible is done to hide up the fact that you are in Ireland at all.'

He is quite right, I think. But I would not describe Belfast as 'ugly'. The city is rimmed with lovely hills which, if one thinks about it, convey an impression of a vast ring-fort, its two 'gateways' being the lough pointing eastwards towards Britain, and a southerly gap leading to Dublin. The hills have pretty names: Ben Madigan, Cave Hill, Black Mountain, Castlereagh Hills. One can almost hear ancient echoes bouncing off them down the years, forever trapped by the cliffs, escarpments and rising moorland, yet never diminishing in force, never escaping, like vapour, to the skies. My father, a great walker for his size (5ft 6in), knew these hills intimately, and strode them relentlessly. Some years ago when he and I were walking over Cave Hill, he paused and surveyed the panorama. 'It could challenge Athens or Naples,' he said (though he had been to neither). 'The hills make it look so secure, so invulnerable.' He took out his handkerchief and coughed some phlegm into it (catarrh was a lifelong bane). 'On the other hand, you could say they lock us in, restrict our horizon.' He cleared his chest again. 'We're like prisoners who don't want to see out,' is what I think he said.

His spoken observations tended towards the epigrammatic. He also was devoted to phrases such as 'It builds character', when one suffered hurt or disappointment, as well as snippets from his socialist lexicon ('A depraved man is a deprived man'), and his republican lexicon ('It's not loyalty to the Crown so much as loyalty to the half-crown'). I once heard him, however, patiently explaining to someone that 'loyalty' should not be confused with 'loyalism'. The former sentiment, he said, had been beautifully expressed by Samuel Butler thus:

> For loyalty is still the same,
> Whether it win or lose the game;
> True as the dial to the sun,
> Although it be not shined upon . . .

Loyalism, on the other hand, was less lyrically expressed in such Ulster chants as 'Up to our necks in Fenian blood', and 'We'll tighten up the rope, and we'll cut the auld Pope's throat', and in the batter-batter-boom-boom of the Orangemen's big Lambeg drums echoing in the darkened hills. These things seemed, more often than not, to give him some amusement; as though he was witnessing a piece of absurd theatre on which the curtain soon would fall and everybody would be able to go home. So, in Willowfield Gardens, he nodded at our glowering neighbours, went out of his way to include Protestants among his friends and to present himself to the citizenry of Belfast for what he was: a Christian who, like Emerson (one of the few Americans he admired), leant instinctively towards the idea of individual consciousness, as against historical creeds, bibles and churches; a devout Catholic who was not slow to stand up to priestly authority; a republican who sought a united Ireland that would do nothing to undermine Protestant security or loyalist culture; a Gaelic enthusiast who loved the English language; a haranguing socialist who (just) stopped short of joining the

Communist Party; a proletarian champion who wore plus-fours at golf and was addicted to chess; a persuasive public speaker who, nevertheless, would apply to Ireland Emerson's observation about the United States ('The curse of this country is eloquent men'); a devoted husband and parent who was (as I noticed on occasion) attractive to other women.

'Never lie. Never deceive. Never hide. Never cheat. Never take advantage. Never give up,' he would say to his sons.

I still do not know why we left Willowfield in 1939. It may have had something to do with the start of the Second World War. East Belfast supplied most of the ten thousand workers for the Belfast shipyards, few of whom were Catholics. The year before we did our flit, the total tonnage output was the largest for any shipyard in the United Kingdom. With the outbreak of war came rumours of spies and fears of sabotage. Any known republican living in east Belfast must have been an object of deep suspicion. At the same time, Charles McCrystal not only made no attempt to reduce his socialist-republican profile, he actually seemed anxious to expand it.

He was then chairman of the Gaelic League in Northern Ireland – an organization devoted to the revival of the Irish language and traditions. It was a fulfilling forum for him, not least because it attracted a number of intellectual Protestants. Even before my father was born, when the island remained united within the British union, wealthy Protestants with Ulster connections, such as Francis Joseph Bigger, George Sigerson, Sir Shane Leslie and Sir Roger Casement – names that rattled like ghostly chains around my childhood and teenage years – had been active in trying to preserve Ireland's Gaelic cultural heritage. Casement joined the Gaelic League in 1904. Among my father's cherished possessions was a photograph of Casement, taken some years before his execution for treason in 1916. According to handwriting on the back, it was given by a Miss McNeill 'to Mr & Mrs McCrystal [possibly my father's parents; equally possibly his uncle and aunt] in memory of her friend . . . a very good picture done in Germany'. My father refused to believe what most people now accept: that the infamous Black Diaries, published posthumously and showing Casement to have buggered his way around the world, were not British government forgeries. On him being sentenced to death in 1916 for trying to secure German aid for the 1916 republican uprising in Dublin against Britain, Casement's supporters sought a reprieve. In response, the government allowed the diaries to be circulated, creating a groundswell of revulsion against him. As a Gaelic Leaguer in 1939, my father's reliability as a British subject probably would not have rated much higher than had Casement's reputation in the earlier Great War. He all but shouted his affiliations from the rooftops.

I am puzzled, for example, by a grubby postcard, sent to him in that year, which has been franked twice across two green, halfpenny stamps. The message on the card is unremarkable: 'Dear Sir, Robin Flower, D. Litt., D. Litt. Celt., Deputy Keeper of M.S.S. British Museum is to lecture at Queen's University on next Thursday (16th) 8 o'c, under auspices of the Council for Protection of Science Scholarship on "Early Irish Poetry" in aid of refugees who have been evicted from their jobs in totalitarian universities on racial & political grounds. It is to be hoped that you & your friends will find it convenient to attend. M. Bulmer Hobson, Carnalea, Co. Down.' I now wonder if this was the same Bulmer Hobson who was one of the Irish Volunteer leaders involved, with Casement, Erskine Childers (author of *The Riddle of the Sands*) and other republicans, in running guns to Irish rebels in 1914. It would seem not unlikely.

The card is addressed to The President, Gaelic League *Coiste Ceanntair* [executive committee], *Ard Scoil* [high school], Divis Street, Belfast, which is where the League held its meetings and where my father taught his Irish language classes. My father clearly had picked up the postcard at Divis Street, along with his other official mail. But then he did a strange thing. He re-addressed the open postcard – his handwriting is unmistakably familiar – to Willowfield Gardens, as if to ensure that the postman would learn of his un-British pursuits and spread the unwelcome news among our neighbours. Whether or not it caused the excrement to be posted to us, hastening our departure from east Belfast, I no longer have any way of knowing. But it seems, in retrospect, to have been a risky bit of self-exposure, not without obvious dangers to his family. A lot of Northern Irish republicans were muttering that 'England's peril is Ireland's opportunity.' Hitler was imperilling England and her possessions in 1939. Any Fenian – even one who manifestly detested fascism – who was thought to be remotely willing to exploit that situation could end up with a bullet in his head, or a house burning around his ears. In the First World War, the crime for which the nationalist Roger Casement was hanged was one of colluding with the German enemy. And in the following year, 1917, almost the entire leadership of Sinn Féin was arrested, on suspicion of treasonable conspiracy with Germany. The atmosphere before, during and after the Second World War was no different.

Before that war had come to an end, I witnessed an example of what could happen in those sandbagged times, when the people of Belfast were still engaged in prising themselves from the wreckage caused by Nazi bombs (the shipyards were among Germany's priority targets). I recorded it, after my father had died, in a poem, 'After The Blitz'.

> We saw, my dad and I, a man
> Being kicked to death in Bridge Street
> (Or Blitz Square, as we called it then,
> The Luftwaffe having spared
> Only the granite *Northern Whig*,
> A Belfast newspaper). Passers-by
> Gave the hobnail boots a wide berth,
> Finding rival distractions:
> A fun fair, and a gospel tent,
> And a wee boy shouting 'Help!
> Help!' from a static-water tank.
> From the *Northern Whig* rushed no one
> To see what we were seeing:
> The swing and stamp of workmen's feet

'Mid cries of 'Fenian bastard!',
Which caused my dad to flinch and nudge
His son away from there. Next day,
In vain, he searched the paper,
Then glanced at me. 'Maybe he lived,'
He said, unconvincingly.

The memory has stayed with me as vividly as it has done with my
brother Colm who, on reading the lines I'd written, reminded me
that he, too, had been present. While I had no idea then that such
gang-beatings were common (which they were, inflicted by both
sides of the sectarian divide), a dreadful intimation that there was
something reprehensibly different about us in the eyes of others
began to enter my bones. And I was immeasurably thankful that
we had abandoned the house where I was born.

Shortly before the IRA's 1994 ceasefire, I returned to Willowfield
Gardens. It was as I remembered it: neat, small, tidy little front
gardens, varnished doors. The RUC station was still on the corner,
covered in steel mesh, its Union Jack flagpole somewhat diminished
by St Anthony's spire. I paused on the narrow pavement, glancing
up and down the quiet street, feeling self-conscious and intrusive,
fibrous memories knitting together as they drifted my way: my
father tapping me on the head with his newspaper as he arrived
home from work; my mother clearing wax from her ear with a
hairclip; stinging nettles at the back fence; the long, rough grass that
cut my fingers, the smell of floor polish from the linoleum in the
hall; the rattle of the letter-box and the quiet thud of something
falling to the floor.

At the end of the terrace is a short alleyway. I had ventured down
it only once, to commit my first offence against society. My fourth
birthday probably was behind me as I trotted at Colm's sandalled
heels down the alleyway to Billy's, a tiny, darkened shop that offered
sweets, cakes and dry groceries. Billy was small, thin and cockeyed.
His inturned eye watered furiously, as though it had been struck a
blow. His good eye was dim and appeared to be unfocused. It must

have been plain to any child that Billy was incapable of monitoring the whereabouts of all his goods at all times. Colm seemed to think him an easy target, and me a yielding accomplice. Before we went in, he whispered: 'Just two snowballs each,' referring to a moist, sugary confection coated in desiccated coconut and much in demand. We entered the gloom, studied briefly the half-blind sentinel, grabbed the snowballs and bolted, gulping down the sweet swag as we did so. But Billy's good eye was less dim than it looked, having marked us down as the papist children from 'the Gardens'. He complained to my mother. She looked for, and found, supporting evidence: two sticky mouths and chins and bits of desiccated coconut on our clothing. She was, I think, mortified by the thought of ensuing scandal. Waiting nervously through the rest of the afternoon, she must have wondered if the police would arrive before my father did. The police didn't come. Had they done so, the showdown could not have been worse than the one between my father and his sinning offspring. He began with Colm.

'Were you in Billy's shop today?'

'No.'

'Did you steal snowballs?'

'No.'

'You mustn't tell me lies. Did you take snowballs from Billy's shop?'

'No.'

'Well now, I *know* that's a lie. I know you were there . . . *stealing*. And I'm going to ask you just one more time. Did-You-Steal-Anything-From-That-Shop?'

'No.'

'Well, we'll see. Go and sit down.'

He turned to me as I studied my feet.

'Now, will you tell Daddy the truth? Were you in Billy's shop today?'

'No.'

'I said, the *truth*! Do you *hear*? Were you . . . ?'

'Colm made me do it . . .'

The betrayal of my brother ensured he got smacked, whereas I did not. I felt pretty good about that; exculpated, superior, virtuous. But we never entered Billy's again, even for a legitimate transaction.

I knocked on the door of Number 28 and, after some delay, a boy aged about eleven opened it. I smiled and said I once lived in his house, hoping to be allowed in. But the boy, ill-at-ease to put it mildly, said his parents were not at home. Later, I wrote to them from London, inquiring about the neighbourhood and asking if I might visit them on my next visit to Belfast. I received no reply. A few weeks later, however, I learned from a resident I managed to reach by phone that Willowfield Gardens now housed not a few members of St Anthony's congregation, all of whom lived in reasonable harmony with their Protestant neighbours. 'Some people keep themselves to themselves, but, please God, we've had no trouble in a good while,' she said. Within a year of that call riots again consumed east Belfast. Some Catholic families fled their homes, in the face of arson and gunfire. 'We're just huddled down,' she said when I phoned her again.

Some years ago, while idly turning the pages of Trevelyan's *History of England*, I came across a passage which my father had underlined:

The policy of colonization was favoured by government as the only means of permanently holding down the natives, who were growing more hostile every year ... Among the conquerors and exploiters of Ireland were Humphrey Gilbert, Walter Raleigh, Grenville of the *Revenge*, and the high-souled author of the *Faery Queen*. They saw in America and Ireland two new fields of equal importance and attraction, where private fortunes could be made, public service rendered to their royal mistress, and the cause of the true religion upheld against Pope and Spaniard. When Raleigh and Spenser were stone-blind to the realities of the Irish racial and religious problem under their eyes, it was not likely that the ordinary Englishman at home would comprehend it for centuries to come. And so, in the last years of Elizabeth's reign, Irish history, till then fluid, ran into the mould where it hardened for three hundred years.

In the margin, my father's pencil noted: 'In the last years of *this* Elizabeth's reign, the mould will crack.'

As I recall this little optimistic scrawl, my mind again harks back to 1798. It was called the 'Year of the French' because of support pledged, though inconsistently applied, by revolutionary France. Before the United Irishmen were brutally put down by vastly superior British forces, it must have seemed that the mould was about to crack. Two centuries later, however, it remains stubbornly intact. All that history demonstrates is that there are occasions when the mould can bend a little to accommodate, for brief periods, ideas and traditions that, basically, are alien to it – before rejection sets in once more, allowing the *forma* to regain normality. As I write, the bicentenary has yet to be celebrated, but, as in all great Irish anniversaries, strong emotions will surface among Irish people, north and south of the border. There is a propitious symmetry in the notion that the celebration might somehow coincide with a settlement of the Anglo-Irish 'problem'. Perhaps Queen Elizabeth's reign will promptly end at the conclusion of such a settlement, cracking the mould. Perhaps then pigs will fly.

3

CROCODILES AND ANTI-CHRISTS

Flying into Northern Ireland has always been a mildly confusing experience for visitors. When I lived in Belfast, the civil airport was called Nutt's Corner. Given the vagaries of the local people and the way they related to one another, this seemed appropriate; occasionally it was nicknamed 'Loonies' Bend'. Later the airport was transferred to Aldergrove, an RAF base, and Nutt's Corner became the site of a weekly car boot sale. Consequently, for many years, the first objects that unsuspecting arrivals would see on landing were camouflaged fighter planes and armed helicopters. These are still visible in a fenced-off section of the airport run by the military. Depending on weather or other aircraft movements, a plane from London Heathrow will lose altitude over County Down's Ards Peninsula, but just when you are braced for landing after the Irish Sea crossing, you find yourself over another body of water. This is Belfast Lough, a long, wide, salt-water fjord with two small towns – Whitehead and Groomsport – at its mouth (north and south of the estuary respectively), and with Belfast itself blocking its throat. The lough too is then left behind. Before you actually touch down, you will observe yet another sheet of water. This is Lough Neagh, the largest freshwater lake in the British Isles, and renowned among European restaurants as a major source of eels. Seventeen miles long and eleven miles broad, it is girt by no less than five of Northern Ireland's six counties: Antrim, Armagh, Derry, Down and Tyrone (Fermanagh has its own lake, Lough Erne).

When I was a boy, my father gave me a stone from Lough Neagh.

It looked like wood. 'It *is* wood,' he said, running his fingernail along its grain and fissures. 'It's petrified wood.' Lough Neagh's waters, he went on, had petrifying properties. I kept it for many years and last saw it in a drawer, on my return to London in 1970, after three years in America. By then, the latest Troubles were well under way, burning, bombing and shooting were a weekly occurrence, and relations between Protestants and Catholics were deteriorating at appalling speed. I hefted the heavy fossil, marvelling at how perfectly it epitomized Ulster attitudes, Ulster politics, Ulster culture. It preserved the past for ever. It yielded to no pressure other than the most brutal force. Other than that, it would never change. It was impervious.

My father had found it on the lough shore near Toome, a village on the southern side of the river Bann at the lough's northern outlet. The A6 road from Belfast crosses Toome Bridge into Co. Derry at this point, having wriggled through Randalstown in Co. Antrim. Immediately south of the section of road between Randalstown and Toome is flat, damp territory, about ten square miles in all, which touches the northern edge of the lough. There are small hamlets with names like Moneynick, Leitrim, Claremont, Cranfield, and Staffordstown. On a narrow road looping between Staffordstown and Cranfield there used to be a whitewashed cottage of unfathomable age. The Cranfield cottage was demolished perhaps half a century ago, but old sepia snapshots show a long, low homestead with a thatched roof, small windows and a doorway opening off a raised patio. A goat is tethered near a three-feet-high drystone wall with creepers spilling from its crevices. Sunshine lights the garden's long grass and tangled hawthorn hedge, and there is a slab of flat rock, used as a garden seat. The road skirting the property is surfaced with tar and gravel. Grassy banks and more hawthorn rise from it, all but obscuring the rough field beyond. In the cottage's open doorway, leaning against the whitewashed wall, an elderly woman wears wire-rimmed spectacles and a long, dark dress that drops below her speckled pinafore. Her right hand rests on a staff, or walking-stick. Her left is tucked behind her back. She smiles at the camera. She is my maternal grandmother, who died before I could know her, or she me.

Within that thatched cottage my mother, Mary McKeown, was born in 1902. None of the fading old photographs now in my possession (taken with my father's Brownie box camera, which I also retain) shows my mother's father, Patrick, so I assume that he was dead by then. A farmer of modest means, who probably rented, rather than owned, the land he tilled, he rode a donkey to the fields, to the market and to Mass. The animal accompanied him everywhere, and on all occasions. Consequently, my maternal grandfather was known in the locality as 'Paddy-ass'. My father, in his widowed twilight years, tried to identify for me the spot where this cottage had once stood. We drove fruitlessly up and down a road which time and toil had changed beyond his recognition.

'I think it was there,' he said. 'No, perhaps not. Try a bit further along . . .'

We never found the place. I do have a hazy recollection of having been there as a child; of eating blackberries, crab-apple jam and a slice of *fried* bread-and-currant pudding inside a cottage like the one in the photographs, and being eaten, in turn, outside it by midges that swarmed off Lough Neagh. But that's about all. Cranfield – original name, *Má Chreamhcaille*, meaning 'Plain of the wood of wild garlic' – had become Anglicized. We didn't bother to search for the Holy Well, once a venue for countless pilgrims, or the thirteenth-century ruined church. Nor, for that matter, did I succeed in discovering further lore about Grandpa 'Paddy-ass' or my grand-mother, whose maiden name had been McGee. I discovered little about my mother on reading her obituary, the headline on which referred to my father, rather than to his wife ('Well-known Gael Bereaved'). The item revealed only: 'Deceased was a native of Toomebridge district, being a niece of the late Mr. P. McGhee, a noted composer of sacred music.' I was approaching my eighth birthday when my mother, after a long and distressing illness, died of cancer. Even at that age, I think I knew instinctively not to probe memories that might distress my widowed father. Later, when he remarried, instinct again told me it might discomfit him to open a conversation about, and memories of, his first wife while he was married to his second. My concern probably was exaggerated, for on our annual jaunts, following my stepmother's death (cancer again), little items about my mother's character would crop up, without appearing to indispose him.

'Before we got married, your mammy wept bitter tears when she discovered she was three years older than me. Can you credit that? She thought I wouldn't want to marry her – for such a silly reason.' And: 'Your mammy was desperately shy.' And: 'If another man as much as looked sideways at her, she'd blush to the roots of her hair. That sort of thing mortified her.'

According to my father, she had another uncle, Willie McGhee, who went to America – 'to Hollywood, I believe. He was an actor, very handsome.' For many years my father had a red, black and chrome art-deco cigarette case and lighter combination sent by Uncle Willie, who also may have been responsible for my father's large accumulation of *Saturday Evening Post*s. But I think the migrant did not make a great success as an actor, and ended up selling pianos in New York instead. 'Your mammy was desperately fond of him,' my father said. 'Your mammy was a saint.'

As a Co. Antrim McKeown, she was a descendant of Scotsmen who settled in the Glens of Antrim, possibly as early as the thirteenth century, becoming very numerous, and blending easily with the native Irish. They joined in native rebellions against the impositions of English and Scottish settlement, which included dispossession. Many who abandoned their Catholicism and became Protestants in order to avoid this fate, changed their name from McKeown (or MacEoin, meaning son of Owen, an Irish variant of John) to Johnson. Those who did not take such a course would, on being driven from their hearths, have retained bitter memories of their humiliations, and having to live off their wits, not always legally. Their wits enabled them to evade the stewards of Lough Neagh in order to trap eels. They made poteen, an illicit, colourless spirit, efficacious in treating all kinds of ailments: fever, nausea, grief, melancholy and even hunger. These illicit goodies had to be handled cautiously. When my father was courting my mother, a friend of my mother's family presented him with a bucketful of eels.

'But I can't take the bucket on the bus,' my father said.

'Don't worry yourself, Charlie, we'll make a nice parcel of them.'

It has to be remembered that eels are kept alive until they are skinned and chopped up for the skillet. It has to be remembered, also, that they are wet, slippery creatures. For his bus journey from the Antrim countryside to Belfast, my father placed the brown-paper parcel on the luggage rack above his head. The paper became sodden, the eels wriggled out, dropped to the floor of the bus, curled around passengers' feet and caused hysteria.

'I could have pretended innocence,' my father said. 'The driver was glaring at me in the rear-view mirror. People were shouting and waving their fists. The eels were contraband. What did I do? I stood up and said to the other passengers: "Whoever did this doesn't know how to handle eels. Let me help." And I managed to grab a few of them one at a time and shoved them into a deep raincoat pocket and kept my hand on it until I got home. I can't resist an eel.'

On another visit to the country, he had walked in heavy rain ('got a bad wetting', as he put it) and took an unusually debilitating cold which made him feverish. His rustic friends told him not to worry and handed him a half-pint jug of clear liquid, his first confrontation with poteen. They urged him to drink all of it, which he did.

'And what do you know? I didn't wake up for two-and-a-half days, but when I did, I was lighter than air and walking with a powerful spring in my step.'

Another thing these Antrim people achieved by their wits was a network of rural semi-outlaws. Which brings me once more to the rebellion of 1798, in which Catholics and Presbyterians joined forces. People such as my mother's Catholic ancestors and their Protestant neighbours would have carried pitchforks, peat spades, scythes, reaping hooks and sharpened harrow-pins fixed on poles, in their successful breaching of the bridge of Toome, their capture of Randalstown and subdual of Ballymena. But with the United Irishmen forced to fall back, the bridge was used as a scaffold for the rebels, one of whom featured in a rousing song I learned at my primary school ('They come with vengeance in their eyes/ Too late, too late are they./ For Roddy McCorley goes to die/ On the bridge of Toome today'). The failed rebellion and the hangings that followed were, I know, in the minds of the civil rights marchers when their procession crossed the bridge of Toome in 1969 on its way from Belfast to Derry. Further along the route, at Burntullet Bridge, the civil rights group was attacked by screaming loyalists, wielding bricks, bottles, iron bars and cudgels studded with nails. In Northern Ireland bridges do not always join communities; they often merely serve to split them.

Yet even before the IRA's 1994 ceasefire, Toome and Randalstown had managed an uneasy coexistence. While Randalstown accentuates its British planter background by painting kerbstones red, white and blue on the Orange Twelfth of July, and Toome flies the Irish tricolour all year round, good neighbourliness is also given room.

In the 1980s, my father and I went to Randalstown to visit a Catholic widow – a family friend of many decades – who had a hip problem, and found it painful to walk great distances. She mentioned her immediate neighbour, a deeply committed loyalist. 'There's nothing he won't do for me,' she said. 'If there's anything in the house that needs mending, or anything heavy that needs carrying, he'll do it without being asked. I couldn't have a more considerate neighbour. What do you think of that?'

I thought well of it. It reminded me of Ireland's eighteenth-century Protestant middle class which often was inclined to concede to others that liberty of conscience they sought to secure for themselves. Their stand alongside the long-persecuted indigenous (Catholic) Irish, which figured so strongly in my father's thoughts and deeds, might well have finally ended the historic struggle between England and Ireland. That it did not is due, in part, to the machinations of the Irish aristocracy. Largely foreign in origin, the aristocracy sabotaged the united stand.

There is an extended note in the first chapter of a battered volume, *Insurrection of 1798*, that had been on my father's shelves. Written by a Redemptorist priest, the Rev. Patrick F. Kavanagh, and published in 1916 – the year of a more successful uprising – it acknowledges: 'The Protestants of the middle class have ever proved themselves the sincerest friends of their persecuted fellow-countrymen of another creed, while the aristocracy, with the lower rabble, their clients and dependants, have been their most relentless enemies.' When the United Irish Society was started in 1791 by a Belfast merchant, Samuel Neilson, and a Dublin barrister, Theobald Wolfe Tone, it had three propositions: that 'English influence' endangered Irish liberty; that parliamentary reform was required to counter that influence; that such a reform should include Irishmen of all religious denominations. Tone, a Dublin coachmaker's son, was a Protestant who had published a pamphlet, *An Argument on Behalf of the Catholics of Ireland*. North and south of the country, his name is honoured today, in ballads, banners, bars and bands. Two centuries ago, the government, responding to cries of alarm from the Irish aristocracy, arrested society members, suspended habeas corpus, sent large numbers of troop reinforcements to Ireland, and encouraged the formation (in 1795) of the Orange Society. This last bit was a brainwave of sectarian triumph. To become an Orangeman one had to speak the following words:

In the awful presence of God, I . . . do solemnly swear that I will, to the utmost of my power, support the King and the present government, and do further swear that I will use my utmost exertion to exterminate all the Catholics of the Kingdom of Ireland.

The government's response was successful, driving the United Irishmen into an insurrection whose defeat provided all that the British Prime Minister (William Pitt) required for promoting a formal union between Britain and Ireland. It was a crucial victory for sectarianism, for what is today called 'the Orange card'. Despite my father's belief that a way would be found to bring Protestants and Catholics together, he never had any illusions about the 'Orange card's' capability of again reducing the 'lower rabble' (a phrase he, of course, would never have used) to a state of 'unconscious cerebration'.

The trouble is, some would argue, that the 'Orange card' tends to be produced annually, anyway – in the July–August 'marching season' – thus guaranteeing perpetual manifestations of prejudice. 'It must be admitted,' the distinguished Irish actor Micheál Mac-Liammóir acutely observed, 'that few districts in the civilized world have any annual festival to compare with Ulster's Twelfth of July, when the most beautiful lilies, of a colour that matches the name of the ancestral home of King William of Orange, are plucked from Protestant gardens to be worn on Protestant breasts, where the beating of the heart rises to the same pitch of ecstasy (though not of volume) as the beating of a thousand drums, beaten and beaten from early morning until late into the night with bare fists and palms as well as sticks until . . . Ulster manhood is appeased. Sashes and banners of the same fiery orange hue are everywhere in this all-male rhapsody of fever and fervour, sashes and medals and badges worn by boys of eight and men of eighty: bowler-hats, black suits, stiff collars and dark ties are de rigueur; the streets are impassable and uncrossable, sometimes for hours together, and the poor papists remain – if they are wise – indoors and wait . . . How long, O Lord, how long?'

MacLiammóir, who died nine years into the Troubles, aged seventy-nine, was an excellent, if unusual, witness. He was born in Cork, divided his childhood and youth between London and Madrid, learned Irish at a Gaelic League class at Ludgate Circus and returned to Ireland as a successful painter with strong theatrical ambitions. He wrote prose, plays and poetry in Irish and English. Among his great admirers was my late, greatly loved cousin, Fionu-alla O'Shannon, herself a compelling actor on stage and television, who worked with MacLiammóir in the 1950s – 'the kindest and most considerate of mentors and friends, who provided me with one of the greatest, most fondly remembered experiences of my life', she said. Another admirer was my father, who shared the great actor's passion for Gaelic and who went to his stage performances in Dublin and, more rarely, in Belfast. My father knew that MacLiammóir was homosexual, but I'm not sure what impact this made on his appreciation of the artist and his works. It was a subject not much discussed *en famille* in Northern Ireland. I know that he regarded homosexuality as irrelevant to a person's status and achievements, but I'm less certain of how he saw it from a moral standpoint. My brother Brendan mentioned to me once that he had detected 'a touch of homophobia' in my father's outlook. If that is right, then perhaps one should not be too surprised, given the sexual repression generally to which Irish – and particularly Northern Irish – Catholics were subjected in my father's day, as indeed in my own. When I was a teenager, there was a Belfast hairdresser who called himself (I think) Anton. He had wavy, blond hair and rode a woman's bicycle. When he cycled to and from his salon in the centre of the city, passers-by called after him: 'Fruit! Fruit!', or 'Hey Pansy, how about a perm!', or 'Would you bend for a friend?', or 'Short backsides – sorry, back-and-sides!' Anton reduced the menace by blowing kisses at his tormentors. But I don't think he reduced the ingrained prejudice.

Another widespread prejudice, throughout Ireland, was anti-Semitism. It had been very marked at the beginning of the century when many Lithuanian and Latvian Jews, fleeing from pogroms, landed in Ireland and, abandoning original plans to continue to New York, settled there. From impecunious beginnings, they prospered, until certain Catholic priests resurrected ancient anti-Semitic hatreds among their congregations. 'They murdered Christ!' the priests cried from the pulpit. The settlers were again uprooted from some Irish towns. At one time I suspected that my father had 'a touch' of anti-Semitism. He had used a phrase, 'the Jew', in conversation, and I'd asked him why he had not said 'Jews' instead, since 'the Jew' suggested a stereotype. He was deeply wounded.

'Surely you know me better than that, Cahal óg!' he protested –
using my childhood name; 'óg' (rhymes with 'rogue') means 'young'
or 'junior'. A long, bitter argument ensued. He was astonished that
I should think him capable of prejudice. I did my best to mollify
him. But I thought later that he did protest too much. Recalling
this, I try not to be reminded of the indignation with which people
of prejudice – Orange-hued or green-hued – deny their bias. Yet,
at the same time, I have to give the full weight to my father's
prolonged and principled struggle against such human weaknesses.
And, unlike MacLiammóir, he did not say, 'How long, O Lord,
how long?', but 'How soon, O Lord, how soon?'

Nevertheless, the answer would appear to be 'Very long', rather
than 'Very soon'. The 'Orange card' is a passport to Britishness, if
not to the God Whom MacLiammóir was addressing so passionately.
Orangemen will never give it up. No one should require them to
do so. But the triumphal ya-boo, yobbo flourishing of the card does
raise temperatures and does, occasionally, create mayhem. Shouldn't
they therefore keep it in their pockets, only taking it out at night,
in the privacy of their bedrooms after they have said their prayers?
'You must be jokin', son,' an Orangeman journalist once told me.
'Sure, if we don't wave it nobody'll know we have it. What's the
point in that?'

It is hard for me to convey properly how a young Catholic
bystander feels when surrounded by hunch-shouldered Orange
marchers assembling for a rally. In the late 1950s, some years before
I left Belfast, I was sent to write a feature article about one such
rally. Trudging alongside the marching Orangemen, I felt terribly
exposed. I hunched my own shoulders and froze my face in an attempt
to look like a typical Ulster stalwart, unprepared to surrender an inch
of his cherished land or culture. In the field where we eventually
gathered I took out my notebook with some trepidation. A few eyes
turned my way with curiosity. I edged towards a couple of Protestant
reporters of my slight acquaintance, greeting them heartily as though
they were long-lost cousins. I announced in a voice loud with
approval: 'Great turn-out isn't it?' My colleagues stared at me as

though I had lost my senses. I later analysed my behaviour. I concluded that what I had done was to wave an Orange card which was neither in my possession nor my entitlement. Unable to shake off the childhood memory of the man kicked to death in Bridge Street, I was doing what many Catholics did, certainly in those days: avoiding trouble by camouflaging their identity. It was, I recognize now, a kind of paranoia. My father laughed when I told him about it.

The 'Green card' is also waved when judged expedient, I reminded him.

He banged the bowl of his pipe against the heel of his shoe and reached for his Warhorse tobacco. 'Of course it is. And the reason is basically the same. When support for a cause threatens to erode, you re-demonize the opposing side. It's so primitive it's laughable. Every symbol, or metaphor for a symbol, is hoisted.' He lit up, puffing and puffing away until I started to believe that his train of thought had become entangled with the smoke rising from his head. He cleared his throat. 'Those who want wars would like them to be holy ones,' he said. 'It's amazing how people can believe that "our tender loving Father in heaven" will look down and approve of their bitterness and their butchery. Yes, of course, you find it on both sides. People talk about nationalist *piety*. That's the right word, for I've seen grown men slabbering like babies over the mere mention of Cathleen Ní Houlihan, or the Flight of the Wild Geese, or "A little drop of Thy Holiness, O King of the Graces . . . and guard me from my enemy". It's the right word for the wrong sentiment. Who was it wrote, "Ah yet, when all is thought and said./ The heart still overrules the head"? Eh?'

From Toome, the A6 flies like an arrow through flat, monotonous countryside to Castledawson, a rural loyalist 'stronghold' and home of Northern Ireland's last Prime Minister (1969–71), Sir Robin Chichester-Clark, later Lord Moyola, naming himself after the stream running through his estate. Here you pick up the A54 to the busy town of Magherafelt, then take a lumpy minor road to the village of Desertmartin. This is where my father's forebears lived, themselves also descended from Scotsmen who are said to have arrived in the north of Ireland in the seventeenth century, probably from Aberdeenshire. 'McCrystal', or 'McChrystal', means 'son of Christopher' in both Irish and Scottish Gaelic. My father's stentorian delivery of lines by an ancient Irish poet – *Gile na gile do chonnarc ar slighe i n-uaigneas;/ Criostal an chriostail a guirm-ruisc rinn-uaine* – used to puzzle me until I concluded that this was a joking reference to our name ('The brightest of the bright met me on my path so lonely;/ The Crystal of all Crystals was her flashing dark-blue eyes').

As a twenty-year-old he had worked for the University Press in Aberdeen. He liked the granite of that city and of the people living there. He was introduced to a Scottish priest, also called McCrystal, who taught scholastic philosophy at Blaris College, a Catholic seminary in the city. 'Ah, but his family were originally Irish,' my father explained to me. I sometimes suspected that he was reluctant to acknowledge the Scottishness in his background, lest that should in some way diminish what he felt to be the totality of his Irishness – though, for the life of me, I couldn't see how it should matter. Two months before my father died, an old friend of his, now living in Portsmouth, wrote to me to say he believed we might be descended from Sir Henry Cristall, an *English* knight sent to Ireland by Richard II to instruct four Irish kings in English customs. During seven earlier years in captivity among the Irish, Sir Henry was married to the daughter of his captor and became fluent in Gaelic. 'Were I a betting man,' my father's friend wrote, 'I'd put my money on old Henry being your early Irish progenitor, and not some cute little Christopher out of Caledonia.' I don't know whether my father would have been amused or appalled by such a suggestion.

From the Belfast hills you can see the slopes of the Mull of Kintyre. In many regions of Northern Ireland, speech patterns are distinctly Scottish: 'Och', and 'Aye', and 'Auld', and 'Houl' yer wheesht or I'll be pushin' hame!' (Be quiet or I'll go home!). The Glens of Antrim are thronged with the direct descendants of Catholic Scots bearing such names as McDonald , McSparran and McGregor, and speaking with an almost-Dumfriesian burr. But my father was impatient with those who described themselves as 'Ulster Scots'.

'Have you noticed,' he once asked me, 'that the Unionist people rely on negativism to sustain them? They shout, "No surrender!" and "Not an inch!" In claiming to be Ulster Scots, they're making another negative point. They're as Irish as I am, but can't bear to be thought so. It's a perverse kind of racism. If more than three centuries of Irish life don't make a people Irish, I'd like to know what does.'

The Desertmartin 'sons of Christopher' lived not in the village itself, which lies, most of it, in a dip in the road, but in the scrubby, boggy, slabby heights overlooking it: the 1,600ft mountain called Slieve Gallion. There are McCrystals in its foothills today, in a place called Tirgan, a corruption of *Tír Gann*, meaning 'poor land'. I believe an ancestor of my father left this region in the 1850s, for Belfast. Recently, I went to Tirgan for the first time. It was a bright day, allowing a breathtaking view of Lough Neagh. Straight ahead, some ten miles away, I could make out the Staffordstown bulge at the lough's head, where, seventy years earlier, Charles McCrystal courted Mary McKeown, and posed for pictures with her mother and her older sister, Ginny.

Desertmartin is an Anglicized version of Gaelic words that mean 'Martin's hermitage', implying a history of religious devotion. Today, the village announces its religious preferences with a great flutter of Union Jacks and by painting its kerbstones red, white and blue, as in Randalstown. Many years ago, before his health began to fail, my father and my brother Colm drove there to try to unearth some family history. They went into a pub somewhere in the area of Desertmartin and ordered Power's whiskey, my father's favourite tipple, distilled in the Irish Republic, but usually available in Northern Ireland. The pub's customers ceased talking. Faces stiffened.

'What?' the barman said.

'Two glasses of Power's, no ice, just water,' my father said. The barman glanced at his other customers, most of whom were looking on sullenly. He turned back to the new arrivals and rapped the bar with a forefinger, as though banging a drum.

'Ye'll get no such whiskey in this house,' he said. 'Thon's a republican whiskey ye're askin' me for. We don't sell that sort of whiskey. And I'll tell ye somethin' more into the bargain. We don't serve them who's askin' for it.'

So they swallowed their chagrin and left, walking dry-mouthed to the Catholic church and its cemetery. I recently followed in their footsteps, avoiding the pub, to confirm what they had found. The graves are on the north side of the church. Three of the tombstones were particularly interesting. One lay flat, the other two being erect. All were covered in the lichen of ages under which I could make out the the name 'McCrystal', occurring twelve times.

I always have a slight *frisson* on seeing the name, given its rarity, even when spelt with an 'h', as in 'McChrystal's original and genuine snuff', manufactured in Leicestershire. A somewhat more powerful pulse disturbed my equanimity in 1982 when the name occurred in a book. It was called *Cal*, a beautifully crafted novel by Bernard MacLaverty, also born in Belfast. The narrative is a fairly contemporary one, based on the latest Troubles, in which the eponymous hero carries out various tasks for the IRA. I was alarmed to find in it a string of 'coincidences' which has dumbfounded all to whose attention I have brought them, not excluding Mr MacLaverty himself, and his British and American publishers, Jonathan Cape and George Braziller respectively. The fictitious Cal is not only given the surname McCrystal; he is born 'Cahal', as was I. Since the only other Cahal – or Cathal for that matter – who has used the shortened version I chose for myself is my eldest son, this seemed particularly odd. But what follows is even more so.

The fictitious Cal lives in a Belfast street in which the McCrystals are the only Catholics, and are, consequently, intimidated by their neighbours. His mother dies when he is eight. He has a brother called Brendan, not to mention an aunt called Molly – in real life, the name of my father's only sister, now dead. Further, it emerges that the fictional Cal, at the age of eleven, has a secret crush on one of the young choristers in his parish church, who is given the name

Moira Erskine. I was surprised to read this too, since a real-life Moira Erskine had enslaved me at eleven with her dulcet tones and dimpled beauty in my local church.

When I traced the author of *Cal* by phone to his home, then on the Isle of Islay, he professed to know nothing about me or my family. He assured me that these were coincidences 'written entirely without any malice'. After later editions changed the main character's surname to the less uncommon 'McCluskey', my father mentioned to me that the MacLaverty family had lived round the corner from him in Atlantic Avenue, in the north Belfast parish of Newington. 'His daddy once asked me if I could help find him a job,' my father said. According to one of my father's oldest and closest friends, who lived a few streets away from the MacLavertys, 'young Bernard used to come to my house as a wee boy to play with my children. I'm amazed he never heard of the McCrystals.' It is a great mystery, is it not? When the book was published, my father wrote to me: 'It doesn't make sense. Our entire family seems to have been researched in order to create a novel!' Later still, my brother Brendan wrote to me: 'About MacLaverty, he knew me quite well. Indeed I was in his house many times.' It turns out that one of Brendan's closest boyhood chums was a cousin of MacLaverty, and that they frequently played a table-soccer game called Subbuteo in the MacLaverty home. All of which has deepened my perplexity. I bear him no ill-will, and I never threatened him or his publishers with a law suit (though I have no doubt that I could have done, with the likelihood of success). But I remain puzzled as to why a man who writes so sensitively and revealingly should have been so unwise in the course he adopted and so unforthcoming in his explanation of it.

Trying to make sense of such curiosities was not much more difficult that trying to decipher the names on the three Desertmartin tombstones. On doing so, I realized that however spartan life must have been in the poor mountain land, the living of it was at least prolonged. I managed to spot three nineteenth-century centenarian McCrystals among them, one of whom, Thomas, died in 1835, aged 114. Several were well into their nineties. 'Potatoes-and-buttermilk, a pipe of tobacco and a jar of whiskey – that's the proven formula,' my father liked to say. Why our McCrystals moved from Desertmartin, for lives that may have been better but shorter, I have been unable to find out. But my great-grandfather may well have been the one to abandon Slieve Gallion for Belfast, marrying a woman from Rostrevor in Co. Down, and producing three sons, James, Michael and Patrick. He prospered in business, giving his three boys a fine education. But all three had a greater attachment to the jar of whiskey than to potatoes-and-buttermilk. Michael died, in alcoholic penury in Liverpool, where he had been, I think, a stevedore. James was my grandfather, an upwardly mobile printer who believed that only half-educated Irishmen were interested in the Gaelic language. Patrick also was a heavy boozer but was 'rescued' by Marion, the woman he married, and had a successful law practice in Mullingar, in the Irish midlands.

With or without alcohol, clan longevity probably would have eluded James, my paternal grandfather. He was corpulent, with a moonlike face and slightly protruding, insolent eyes (according to a photograph). He liked to tempt fate. An amateur actor and Shakespeare addict, he had a habit, indulged outdoors as well as in, of bursting into Shakespearean soliloquys, as his mood took him. One evening, waiting for a horse-drawn tramcar, in Belfast's city centre, his mood took him into *Henry VI* (Part One). Sweeping his cloak dramatically about his corpulence, he boomed:

> 'Lord regent, I do greet your excellence
> With letters of commission from the king . . .'

A black serge uniform passed by, then stopped. In Belfast, policemen are called 'peelers', after Sir Robert Peel, who organized London's nineteenth-century police force. The 'peeler' turned and looked at James McCrystal in spate.

'. . . For know, my lords, the states of Christendom,
Mov'd with remorse of these outrageous broils, . . .'

The 'peeler', a country bumpkin, glared, his face reddening at being
thus mocked, as my grandfather stretched out passionate arms.

'. . . Have earnestly implor'd a general peace . . .'

The baton came down on his head with enough force to knock
him out. He soothed the indignity with whiskey as he later described
what had happened to his adoring wife ('He could do no wrong in
the mother's eyes,' my father said. 'She worshipped the ground he
walked on').

The blow didn't kill him. Nor did drink. His premature death
in 1922 was said to have been brought on by 'heart strain', a result
of over-zealous cross-country running. It was disastrous for his
family – a widow, four sons and a daughter. They moved to a
smaller house. The eldest boy, also James, joined the merchant navy.
Four years before my grandfather's death, but when he was more
or less confined to bed, my father was withdrawn from school. He
had won a scholarship to St Malachy's College (which I myself was
to attend) but was forced to abandon it, in order to work as a
grocer's delivery boy for two shillings a week, and later as an
apprentice bacon-slicer (until his death he bore the scar from a deep
cut he accidentally inflicted on himself). That should have been
that. But it wasn't.

As a young teenager he became a printing apprentice in the firm
which had employed my grandfather James. He attended evening
classes, read voraciously, became actively political. I suspect that by
the time he had left his Star of the Sea national (primary) school he
had absorbed as much as he might have done by staying on. Among
his surviving schoolbooks is a red, clothback copy of *Fallons New
School Reader (Advanced Book)*, a significant milestone in his intellectual development. Among its disintegrating pages are well-thumbed
extracts from Goldsmith, Shakespeare, Dickens, Sir Walter Scott,

and short poems with marks against certain lines that he was to quote throughout his life, among them Cowper's 'Cruelty to Animals'. How often, on him catching me about to pull the wings off flies, or stamp on a beetle, had I been reproached by those lines of chastisement!

> I would not enter on my list of friends
> (Tho' graced with polish'd manners and fine sense,
> Yet wanting sensibility) the man
> Who needlessly sets foot upon a worm.
> An inadvertent step may crush the snail
> That crawls at evening in the public path;
> But he that has humanity, forewarn'd,
> Will step aside, and let the reptile live.'

I have never been able to reconcile those sentiments with a contrasting acceptance of murdering for 'a cause'. Not that my father ever killed anybody; he was incapable of committing such an atrocity himself. But to have been in the IRA, whether it was the 'old' one or the 'new' one, entailed making some personal decision which sanctioned killing by others. For that is what the IRA was, and is: a killing machine, and it seems to me irrelevant whether, as a member of it, you hide a gun or pull its trigger. To 'let the reptile live' but exterminate a particular human being must surely imply that you regard your victim as 'lower than a snake's belly', to recall a phrase from my childhood. IRA or Sinn Féin spokespersons have a remarkable talent for crying over the graves of their innocent victims ('Yes, terrible, but war's like that') as well as of their 'martyrs'. It is as though crocodile tears might dilute the blood that has been shed; take the red out and transform it into something other than murderous flux. There are many crocodiles in Ulster. And we can joke about them.

Belfast Joke: A man goes into a bar on the Shankill Road, leading a crocodile on a chain. 'Hey, barman! Do ye serve Roman Catholics?' 'Yeah, OK.' 'Good, will ye please serve one to my crocodile?' Har-har.

In my father's primary school reading book there is a poem entitled 'The Loss of the Birkenhead'. His childish hand has substituted 'Irish' for 'English' in the line, 'Our English hearts beat true – we would not stir . . .' He was absorbing, from an early age, the kind of words and thoughts and prejudices which place Catholics in a recognizable – and hence self-isolating – box. It began with the alphabet. Belfast Catholics used to say 'Ah-b-c', whereas Protestants said, 'Ay-b-c'. Catholics aspirated 'h'; Protestants didn't. It ended with them throwing petrol bombs at one another.

I think my father was my grandmother's favourite son. Virtually untutored herself, the former Mary Doyle from Randalstown was as impressed with 'our Charlie's' seemingly boundless knowledge as she had been with her late husband's dramatic effusions. Frequently she made my father feel that he was indispensable to her. Within a year of him going to Aberdeen, she prevailed upon him to return, lest she die pining for him. Shortly after he rejoined her (she did not expire for another quarter of a century), my father went to public-speaking classes and was selected by the Independent Labour Party as a candidate in upcoming elections for the parliament at Stormont. It is far from certain that he would have won; but had he done so, he would, at twenty-two, have been as young as William Pitt when he was elected for Appleby in 1781. In the event, my father withdrew from the fray when my grandmother 'went down on her bended knees and begged me, with tears streaming down her face, not to bring shame on the family'. Why so?

'The mother didn't like the idea of me being a socialist, though she could put up with it. What she couldn't bear was the idea of me being a socialist in *public*. Remember, the Russian Revolution had stoked the fires of hell. The [Catholic] Church – especially in Ireland – was on a witch-hunt for communists among the faithful. Being a socialist was the same as being a communist. I think Keir Hardie, who'd founded the ILP, had just died, one of the greatest men who'd ever lived. As far as the [Catholic] hierarchy was concerned he was anathema. As for those who had fallen in behind him, well, there was talk of excommunication in the air. So the mother pleaded, and I obeyed. And she made me promise not to become a communist – and I kept that promise too.'

My grandmother's prejudices were widespread among Catholics, rural and urban. They were narrowly dogmatic and unyieldingly bigoted. Her church was one source of this. Priests at Mass spoke from the pulpit about '*non*-Catholics' – rather than about Presbyterians, Methodists, Church of Ireland members – as though to underline an assertion that if you were not a Catholic you were nothing at all. They and the greater part of their flocks believed wholeheartedly in the existence of weeping statues and other miracles. They pointed to the dark cruciform shape on every donkey's back and explained: 'They have that because Jesus rode a donkey.' Consequently, they also believed that if you passed an infant under a donkey's belly, it would be cured of colic. Catholics swallowed whole the Church's insistence on censoring 'evil' books – i.e., those seen to address things sexual, iconoclastic, or otherwise detrimental to 'traditional Catholic Irish values' (casualties included Aldous Huxley's *Point Counter Point*, Bertrand Russell's *Marriage and Morals*, Seán O' Faoláin's *Bird Alone*, and anything at all by James Joyce). On hearing an Irish bishop intone, *'Penes quos potestas sit sacorum bibliorum, editiones et versiones adprobare vel permittere ex iis liquet, quae supra statuta sunt'*, they would bow their heads obediently and pretend to know what was going on. And they thoroughly approved of the Irish Cardinal MacRory's claim, in 1931, that the Protestant Church of Ireland was 'not even part of the Church of Christ'.

Much of that craven, helpless, thoughtless allegiance has now gone. But the traces remain perplexingly strong, even in the cities and towns where rock music from high-street shops easily wins against peals from the belfry. I know Catholic men and women of my own generation who believe with all their hearts that Adam and Eve were actual people, that the snake in the Garden of Eden was your actual Lucifer, and that it's somehow shameful not to be able to correctly tick off the vestments a priest wears at Mass –

amice, alb, cincture, maniple, stole, chasuble. They rub great clefts in holy statues at church entrances, as though they were Aladdin's lamps, pray to certain saints for worldly favours and spend the best part of their lives making themselves ready for heaven, which to them is an actual, defined place whither they will go, with the help of prayer and the sacraments, and be reunited with the already departed.

It is against that sort of thing that one has to measure the vapourings of such contemporary Ulster Protestant clerics as the Rev. Ian Paisley, especially when he is roaring on about the Pope being the 'harlot of Rome', the 'anti-Christ', or simply 'Old Red Socks'. When one encounters, as one has encountered in the not very distant past, maledictions against Protestants – and even discrimination against them in employment practices, especially when parish priests have had a say in it – one begins to understand not only the mindset of Ulster nationalism, but the self-serving vindication Ulster Unionism manages to extract from it. The real maladies of my native province have been not merely economic or historical, though these of course are omnipresent; they have been – and still are – moral and political.

Conflicting ambitions and inveterate feuds keep Ulster in a perpetual fret and fever of uneasiness even when the guns are silent. Not until the door of my father's century began to close, and the strain of nearly three decades of terrorism had produced a natural exhaustion, did anyone think that anodyne was required. My fellow-countrymen, for the most part, desire to live quietly and reap a little material prosperity after all the sacrifices they have endured. They want, understandably enough, a democracy which is underpinned by nationality. But they are split over how the democracy should be engineered, and at odds over the hue of their nationality. Even in the euphoria that followed the IRA's 1994 ceasefire and the beginning of a 'peace process', the abruptness of the change produced an accumulation of freshly smarting wrongs and grievances. The removal of old sources of irritation has been followed by the introduction of new poisons of, as yet, untested formidability. The problem of religious persecution has been greatly reduced, but the recollection of it keeps communities apart, and provides fuel for an 'armed struggle', even during a temporary cessation of hostilities. Heartfelt cries for peace in Northern Ireland cannot totally obscure problems of prejudice, or prevent them becoming more intractable and more complex. In periods of 'non-conflict' difficult questions arise. Are clemency and justice to prevail over the spirit of revenge? Is the régime which follows the Troubles to be made as tolerable as may be to those who will claim to suffer under it? How shall one prevent the rôles of persecutor and persecuted from being reversed? The road ahead is not sunlit.

'One of the enduring folk memories of the Ulster-British people is the fear of massacre – the fear that the people may cease to be, at least culturally,' said David Trimble in a Northern Ireland lecture in 1989, six years before being elected leader of the Unionist Party. Until Mr Trimble was seventeen, he received no formal education about Ulster or Irish history, learning only from what his grand-mother told him and from 'reading Orange banners and the gossip of children'.

My father was too feeble then to have made any comment on Trimble's fear of cultural death, but I'm sure he would have understood. But he would have expected Trimble to understand, assuming he was an honourable man, the same sentiment from a nationalist who might substitute 'Irish people' for 'Ulster-British people'. He had, in any case, suspicions about the way 'culture' was used by both sides as though it was the holy grail. This is, at first, surprising, when one considers his enthusiasm for the theatre, poetry, song and so on. But Charles McCrystal's curious ambivalence about 'culture' is at least comprehensible in a poem by him, published in the late 1920s.

> I sought for things sublime
> And looked about;
> My cultured taste enabled me
> To seek them out,

To comprehend the stars
And analyse
The beauty and the magnitude
Of heaven's eyes;

To think of space and time
And marvel still
That man could not appreciate
Creation's will.
I contemplated thus,
And heaved a sigh –
'Alas, that men should live in vain,
And crudely die!'

Yet I could understand
How twittering birds,
Poetic in their warblings,
Supply my words.
To me the babbling brook
Expresses song,
In which I join in harmony
The whole day long.

The shimmering lake on which
The dancing ray
Of sun-reflected light
Makes merry play,
The fluttering leaves which speak
Of Autumn time –
Ah! these are the things I seek,
These thoughts sublime.

God! What is that I see? –
A hungry mob.
Torn by bitter anguish,

The women sob;
The skeleton face of a child,
Its death-like eyes
Seeking, it knows not where,
A paradise.

They were the scenes I saw;
My cultured mind
Had dwelt on abstract nature –
And I was blind!

Curse the culture which brings
A mental peace,
Indifferent to the masses' cry
For their release.
Such is my task in future;
Let me subscribe,
In smashing the weapon I harbour'd –
Society's bribe.

Society's bribe was 'Culture', the title of the poem. But my father
neither smashed nor discarded it. In fact, the range of his cultural
activities expanded. Having abandoned parliamentary aspirations,
he concentrated on building and supporting a family. This meant
operating a monotype machine at W. & G. Baird, a printing company which published the *Belfast Telegraph* . The company was run,
and generally staffed, by Freemasons and Orangemen. Masonic
lodges abounded in Ulster in those days (probably still do) and it
was generally assumed that if you were a Mason you were also an
Orangeman (and vice versa). W. & G. Baird was in Union Street,
a dreary, narrow place facing the back door of the *Telegraph*. For
many decades, Baird's employed no Catholics. I believe my father
may have been the first one to be given work there. I don't know
why he was allowed to breach an old tradition. His expertise in
the print industry was fairly widely acknowledged, but, even so,

expertise was not necessarily the path to advancement when sectarianism laid down the rules. I suspect he had one or two close Protestant friends employed there who may have spoken up for him. Nevertheless, at Baird's he stuck out like a sore thumb.

Most Ulster people take their holidays on or around the Twelfth of July, a day as glorious to Orangemen as the Twelfth of August is to shooters on the grouse moors. The month before 'the Twelfth' is spent in a flurry of preparations – piling wood for bonfires, dry-cleaning banners and collarettes, painting kerbstones and gables, teaching children how to chant Orange ditties, stocking up on alcohol, and generally getting into the right mood to celebrate the Protestant King William of Orange's 1690 rout of the Catholic King James at the Battle of the Boyne – a river that runs through the Irish town of Drogheda. The month after it is spent recovering from the excesses that accompany the holiday. A day or so in advance of 'the Twelfth', Charles McCrystal would arrive for work to find that his colleagues had taken considerable pains to bedeck his desk, his chair, his monotype machine, his hat-peg, his overhead light, with red-white-and-blue bunting, Union flags and, occasionally, pictures of the reigning monarch. This ceremony happened every year. His response was always the same. He would survey the decorations, turn to his watching colleagues, murmur, 'Well, thank you', and then remove every scrap from his immediate work area, saying nothing more, refusing to be intimidated, commencing his tasks for the day, feeling their eyes boring into the back of his head, daring him to show anger.

'Never anger made good guard for itself,' he would tell his sons, quoting the Bard.

He referred to such incidents at home, but I cannot recall him making a big fuss about them.

'But Daddy, why don't you *do* something?' I exclaimed.

'*Do* something? Look at me! I am not harmed. I am not embarrassed. I've lost no pay. I'm about to sit down to my tea. Patches have not appeared on my clothes, or holes in my shoes. It promises to be sunny tomorrow. I feel great. My conscience is clear and my dignity unblemished. What do you want me to do?' He waited for my answer and, seeing that I had none, he beamed at me, then leaned over his chair and turned on the wireless.

Often he seemed amused, in a rueful kind of way, or distracted by other things, some of them melancholy. There had been a great deal of grief in his life, particularly over the demise of his father. In 1924, his two cousins – the only sons of his Uncle Patrick – died in Mullingar within months of each other. One, aged twenty-one, fell from his horse while riding in the woods; the other, eighteen, succumbed to tuberculosis. But his anguish over those tragedies was almost nothing compared with his suffering, about twelve years later, when his own younger brother, Pat, committed suicide.

My Uncle Pat, who died in his early twenties before I was born, was also a poet, though his themes were less ideological and more historical/romantic than those which characterize my father's poetry. Uncle Pat wrote of Irish battles and Irish martyrdom 'for the Cause' (That night around the camp-fire's glow/ The chieftain cherished pride/ In every Mac and every O'/ Who for the cause had died). He had had a fall which damaged his eyesight. As he gradually went blind, he became increasingly depressed. His handwriting wavered. He began a novel, but failed to finish the opening chapter. My grandmother's anxiety is recorded in the message she wrote in big capital letters at the top of a half-filled page: 'Pat Avick be smileing' [sic] – 'avick' being phonetical Gaelic for 'O, son!' In the years that followed, my father found it hard to talk about his lost brother.

Less grievous distractions quickly cropped up. There was the war and the Blitz, followed by weekend schools in Co. Donegal and elsewhere, organized by the National Council of Labour Colleges. My father was appointed editor of a Gaelic-language newspaper, An t-Ultach ('The Ulsterman'), subsidized by the Dublin government (retaining, at the same time, his printing job at W. & G. Baird). He travelled the country, examining students in Gaelic, presiding at meetings of the Gaelic League, taking up a new subject, hypnotism. His hypnotist's manual, which I secretly digested as a teenager, in the vain hope of mesmerizing girls into imprudence, is full of paragraphs which intoxicated me, if nobody else.

The many methods of producing the hypnotic state contained herein are in our opinion the cream of hypnotism which we unselfishly reveal to you, every method is given in detail so that nothing is left to the imagination.

Powerful glances have been known to halt people in their tracks. We all know the power of the Snake with its uncanny rhythmic sway and its beady penetrating eyes, of how its prey becomes so fascinated that it is actually rooted to the spot on which it stands.

These and many other novelties were to distract him in the years following our abandonment of Willowfield Gardens and flight to north Belfast where I suspect he was regarded as a bit of an enigma: a brainy chap who identified with those chiefly reliant on brawn; a chap whose small, slender hands should have been turning the key of portals grander and loftier than the fake-grained varnished door of a modest terraced house.

Charles McCrystal was a quiet man with a long, sloping forehead rising above pale eyes. Like the majority of men in our new – more denominationally balanced – north Belfast neighbourhood at that time, he spoke quietly, walked purposefully and seldom dallied for gossip. To our new neighbours, he was a dignified, undemonstrative figure whose wife was shy, had fine skin and appeared to be in delicate health. Few of them, I think, appreciated the intellectual muscle behind the mild manner, or the uses to which it was being, and would be, put.

4

THAT'S THE WAY FOR BILLY AND ME

In my childhood, schools were strictly segregated on sectarian lines. They are less so in today's Northern Ireland – one of the positive ripples in a pool murkily negative. One of my nephews boarded with a Protestant college in Coleraine (a 'Protestant town'). His sister attended an academy in Belfast which, in my youth, was the preserve of Protestants and Jews. Another nephew received part of his education at a school founded with a formal commitment to integration. Every child learning the alphabet now chants '*Ay*-B-C', rather than '*Ah*-B-C'. Yet the framework for estrangement remains very much in place, its creators and custodians being, generally speaking, clerics and politicians. They underpin their influence on a community with well-tested instruments designed to cleave it, especially the younger members of it. They may do so consciously or unconsciously, but they do it, nevertheless, with relentless commitment to those suspicious of change. My own three sons avoided the divisions, having been removed from Belfast before they were old enough to begin their education there. But I did not.

My recollection of early schooling has, in part, misted over. There are a great many things – pre-school things – that still occasionally come to mind. Some, as I have already indicated, are associated with Willowfield: my father's clenched face on hearing the declaration of World War II from our wet-battery wireless; his burying a coconut shell in the tiny front garden and promising a palm tree; my tearful mother being banished to the kitchen by Dr MacSorley while he probed me for the cause of 'stoppage of the bowel', suspecting a tapeworm. The faint, though not unpleasant, rubbery-uric scent of the undersheet that accompanied me on my transition from cot to bed has stayed with me. I remember an incident before that transfer took place. My cot was brought into my parents' bedroom, probably because I was sick (as a child, I believe I did not always enjoy rude health). During the night, I was aware of a commotion in my parents' bed. I heard sounds that alarmed me: moans and movements of baffling urgency. I was too scared to cry. When they both peered into my cot next morning, smiling and consoling, I put the night's commotion behind me. But, years later, by which time the significance of that bedroom incident had dawned on me, I marvelled at how indistinguishable can be the sounds of pain and pleasure. I remember also the comforting smell of chewed rusks, and the comforting taste of Gibbs toothpaste, a whole block of which I ate, believing it to be a minty confection. But what I cannot retrieve is the full, authentic pulse of early childhood. Perhaps this is due to the upheavals that befell our family at that time: the flit and flurry before the war, and the fury of the Blitz during it.

There are images, too, that I suspect are more reassuring than realistic: summers alchemized by time and distance, events embellished by nostalgia, and all the other delusions that may be heaved up by the recollective effort. But I can focus, without much difficulty at all, on my primary school in Newington, in north Belfast. Its grimy red bricks rise against the downward slope of Newington Avenue; the black roller-blinds drawn down its windows to conform with the wartime blackout; the chant of our arithmetic tables, and the barks of the teachers we gleefully demonized; the (mostly) scrubbed faces of boys and girls (also sedulously segregated). In such a focal remembrance do I begin to find appropriate tints for sharpening the sepia.

I was a thin, pale, nervous child. One of my (thankfully short-lasting) nicknames was 'Ghostie'; another (at a prep boarding school I was to attend), 'Sheep'. As a shy four-year-old, I trudged into the

Holy Family school for the first time on my 'fallen arches' (flat feet), too young to be much upset by events beyond the neighbourhood: not least among them, the war in Europe. Not many Belfast people were well off then, and it was not uncommon to see small schoolboys wearing their sister's hand-me-down skirts, pinned in the middle to provide a slim, pathetic illusion of trousers.

I thought of this dreadful poverty – it diminished Catholic and Protestant lives alike – a few years ago on revisiting the docks area of the city. Pile-drivers snorted and thudded, drowning the cries of seabirds which drifted and dawdled over the quays of the Lagan river's lower reaches. When I was a child, the snorts and thuds were on behalf of Britain, hugely reliant on Belfast's shipbuilding capacity. Now, as I stared into the river, the clangour behind me was for Belfast itself, a recreative surge in the midst of mayhem by terrorist gangs. One memory swirled in the water below me. It was, I think, just before the outbreak of war, when I had my first encounter with this waterway. Belfast's skyline was soon to change under German bombardment, but in general the city looked as it would continue to look until I abandoned it in my twenties, before a very different kind of war altered the skyline further. The Grand Central Hotel dominated Royal Avenue, the main thoroughfare; the fruit and vegetable markets occupying much of Oxford Street bustled; the Gaumont and Imperial picture houses competed for audiences, and oysters were to be washed down with porter and stout at Mooney's in Cornmarket. All these landmarks have disappeared, or shrunk, or otherwise changed shape in the past quarter-century, their sites currently occupied by smart red brick, totemic atria and other modern delights. A stroll on Royal Avenue, Donegall Place, High Street and Great Victoria Street revealed a shopper's Belfast that was unfamiliar to me: miracles of glazing that reflected the sky; bright-red brick façades, free of the grime of ages; broad pavements with fresh tiles; ornate doors that breathed exotic essences into the street air each time they swung open. Yet beneath that grand exterior I felt little had changed. Chatting to wee, hard men in bars and youths with dead-fish eyes on street corners, I quickly formed the impression that Belfast's modernity is not much more than skin-deep, and that the pulse of sectarian hatred beats as enduringly as ever.

Physically, spiritually – and very visibly – the river was Belfast's great artery in my childhood. Thousands of workers streamed across it daily, on foot and bicycle, to serve what was still the biggest shipyard in the world. The quays heaved with passenger ships whose destinations included Liverpool, Heysham, the Isle of Man and Glasgow. And even though the depression of the 1930s had taken its toll, the city retained a muscularity and resourcefulness that enabled it to survive the 1941 Blitz and to ride out the worst that terrorism could inflict since 1969.

My father loved the river as passionately as he loved Belfast's hills. As a boy, I often joined him for Sunday walks along the old barge towpath above Shaw's Bridge. We would stroll for (it seemed) hours past the dark-green swirl where old men fished for carp and bream, and into low meadows where young men pandered to their girlfriends. When my brothers and I showed signs of fatigue, my father would urge us on with lines from the Scottish poet, James Hogg:

> Where the pools are bright and deep
> Where the gray trout lies asleep,
> Up the river and o'er the lea
> That's the way for Billy and me.

I wondered: Who's Billy? Most people named Billy were Protestants. Orangemen were known as 'Billy-boys', after their hero, King William.

On one of our walks, my father gestured to a spot on the riverbank where a close friend of his – a Protestant who had married an Irish-Italian Catholic – had committed suicide by chaining himself to his bicycle and pedalling into posteriority. I cannot be sure why he did this, though there was talk about intimidation at work, on the grounds that he had 'married a papist'. I never learned what happened to his widow, but eventually their only child left the country and never returned.

As the pile-drivers drilled foundations behind me for the 'new Belfast', a chilly breeze off the water dispersed my effluvial reverie. I looked around and was immediately struck by a Lagan peculiarity: passers-by seemed not to give the river much attention, even though it was in the process of being spanned by an eight-lane motorway, a new railway bridge and a weir – all part of the current regeneration. On neither of the major mid-town bridges do people even glance at the water below, as they do in Dublin, London and Paris. It is almost as though citizens, convinced that the artery has been sympathectomized, are equally sure that it cannot be restored, and that, unlike Updike's East River in New York, the Lagan will never achieve the status of 'a river grander than its shores'. As a brochure of the rejuvenating Laganside Corporation observes: 'For too long . . . Belfast has turned its back to the river.' One may find symbolism there. Rivers flow outwards; Ulster's thoughts flow inwards. As I discovered at quite an early age.

Much of what I absorbed in those early Newington years was coloured by my older brother's confidences. Under masses of black curls, Colm's eyes were grey-blue pools of innocence set widely apart. But it was more than his looks that gave him credibility. Nearly two years my senior, he was my pipeline to and from a wide, unknown world to which my access otherwise was restricted. Having gained experience in two schools – St Anthony's and the Holy Family – he was expert in the peculiarities of schoolteachers. His perspicacity stretched to other institutions, among them the Church itself, making him extraordinarily well informed on all sorts of things. He revealed to me the secret of his first Confession: 'A trap door opened . . . A U-Boat . . . the Germans grabbed me . . .' His confidences, generally imparted in the bed we shared, were really a series of early warnings about what life held in store for me. Often they were more alarming than the wail of the air-raid siren on the roof of the nearby RUC barracks on Antrim Road (in those days, it was hard not to live in the vicinity of policemen). On the eve of my first day at school, for example, he warned me about Miss Cleary, from whose class he had just been elevated. Miss Cleary, he said, punished her charges by striking them on the hand with a blazing stick. If you cried, she laughed, 'Heh-heh-heh!' One boy's arm was burnt right off. 'Now don't you go wetting the bed,' Colm yawned, too late.

In my turn, I tried something similar with my younger brother, Brendan. But it never seemed to work very well. Brendan had been born a sceptic. He believed nothing until he saw it – or, better still, ate it. The most terrifyingly plausible concoctions, relayed to him with rolling eyes and earnest diction, could not penetrate his sang-froid or impede his relentless chomping to the pips of an apple. He did not believe in nonsense from anyone; when offered it, he rejected it and wandered off on his own, often glum, pursuit of truth – or, more often than not, food. When I tried to bully him, he would not yield. When I mocked him, his eyes glowed under long, dark lashes, but did not fill up. The way to his heart lay not in expressions of brotherly love (not that we were much given to them), but in sweets, chocolate, plum puddings, apple tart, jam roll, ice cream, marshmallows and soda pop.

It was the Blitz of 1941 that chased us from our first north Belfast home in Baltic Avenue. The street had a pub, the Hole in the Wall, and – directly opposite, almost hidden from view by an air-raid shelter – an off-licence, Baltic Wine Stores, which dispensed whiskey in whatever receptacle the customer cared to produce. Beyond these modest Bacchic temples lay the Waterworks, across Antrim Road. The Waterworks provided much of Belfast with drinking water, but the Luftwaffe, knowing from their intelligence maps that they were bombing the *Wasserwerk*, and not the *Schiffswerft* of Harland & Wolff or the *Flugzeugwerk* of Short & Harland, let fly anyway on the buildings near by. Houses across the the street from us were destroyed. When I drove down Baltic Avenue not long ago, the bombed site had been reoccupied by an electricity substation. A steel-mesh cage protected The Hole in the Wall from para-military ground attack. The Waterworks, partially filled in, was no longer a reservoir, but a park where old gentlemen took their ease.

Bits of memory flew at me like shrapnel: air-raid sirens, the growl of planes and the detonation of their cargoes; searchlights silvering a barrage balloon in the turbulent night sky; my father's flashlight finding Brendan's potty as we cowered beneath the stairs; a frantic banging on the front door and soldiers escorting us to the air-raid shelter. On the way there, Colm, clutched in the arms of a fire warden, pointed excitedly to an unexploded incendiary bomb beneath a waiting ambulance. In the shelter's fetid and fearful air, neighbours said rosaries aloud, over and over again, numbing the mind for the operation on the soul. To address the stomach, slices of dry soda-bread were passed around, though I cannot imagine anyone feeling hunger at such a time. In the yellow glow of candlelight, I was aware of my mother nursing an imperturbable Brendan and Colm's face all tightened up, despite the praise being heaped upon him for spotting the fire-bomb. I cannot remember if I was scared or exhilarated. Perhaps I was in shock. But in monitoring others I was, it seems reasonable to assume, seeking evidence – from flickering facial expressions, vocal cadences and nervous responses – that all was not as bad as it seemed. Mrs Keaney, whose husband owned Baltic Wine Stores, produced a whiskey bottle containing (to my father's profound disappointment) Holy Water, which she sprinkled over us all; a final ablution to prepare us, perhaps, for the blast heavenwards. When the siren confirmed the 'All Clear', I stood beside Colm, our day clothes over our pyjamas, both of us shivering in the acrid night, queuing for the bus that would remove us from the street for ever.

The bus took us to Randalstown, a neat little linen-bleaching town 22 miles away, not far from where my father had courted my mother. I remember nothing of the journey, only a jostling confusion that marked its beginning and a somnambulant discipline blurring its end. I awoke in daylight on a spare mattress on the dining-room floor of a spacious, red-brick bungalow, owned by the Storey family on Station Road. In a kitchen where water was drawn by a hand-operated pump, Mrs Storey's enamelled ladle moved deftly from pot to bowls. She was a sturdy countrywoman with a son and five grown-up daughters, some of them close to my parents' age. 'Eat them porridge,' Mrs Storey said, before handing us over to the comforting embraces of her daughters. We were lucky evacuees. We were together. We were with friends of my parents. Our mother was on familiar territory. Our father could, without unbearable effort, travel up from Belfast at least a couple of times a week, or as often as his work and associated duties as a fire warden permitted. It seemed at the time, and seems now in retrospect, to have been a long evacuation period filled with unusual contentment. That summer *was* golden: a cocker-spaniel called Sport tumbling with us on the lawn; steam trains chuffing past the rear, vegetable garden; rides in a wooden, dung-scented wheelbarrow; piggyback adventures over fields and down country lanes, shimmering and abuzz with insects.

On the River Main, which flows into Lough Neagh in a shallow, frothy-brown torrent, Randalstown used to be called Mainwater. It received its present name when it was constituted a borough by charter of Charles II. The majority of its population is Protestant (obvious enough, as I've said, from the painted kerbstones). They must have, to say the least, mixed feelings about their royal charterer, since, in his dying hours, he received absolution from a Catholic priest, although he had not previously avowed his attachment to that religion. Such things stick in memory, as does the insurrection of 1798. They get handed down, like old chests and relics, from generation to generation; and if they look like being forgotten or mislaid, the ritual reminders come into play to remedy the lapse. But I do not recall having experienced any of this in my wartime refuge. As an evacuee, my days and nights were largely friction-free. I attended the local school, carrying to and from the little schoolhouse my Mickey Mouse gas mask in a cardboard box. Three or four benches ahead of me, a little girl asked the teacher – a lovely, sweet-smelling young woman called Miss Deakin – what 'fuck' meant. Miss Deakin gasped and seemed to be about to swoon. She staggered down the narrow aisle, clapped her hand over the little girl's mouth and dragged her from the classroom. I was not curious enough to either discover her fate or to seek the answer to her apparently ill-judged question. There was a brief rumour, I think, that it was a word used by soldiers. Having used it, they were destined for hell, via the battlefield or elsewhere. Once a week, we each also carried a sod of turf for the school fire: in building up fuel reserves for the succeeding winter, we were experiencing, perhaps, our first definite conception of civic obligation. At weekends throughout that summer there were trips to Lough Neagh, rides on the bar of my father's bicycle, excursions to farmers' fields to help with the hay. We picked blackberries for jam and crab-apples for jelly, and ate eels caught by poachers in Lough Neagh. In Randalstown, I smelled, for the last time, the stench of flax in retting ponds, and heard, for the last time, the noise of the corncrake across shimmering land. We drank daily from a well of affection that seemed bottomless.

And suddenly it was over.

The house we came back to in Belfast was in Ponsonby Avenue, three streets away from Baltic Avenue and one street away from Holy Family School. Among our neighbours were salesmen, teachers, a carpenter, a post office official, a fruit-market wholesaler, a journalist, a sausage-skin salesman, an insurance salesman, a newsagent/confectioner. It was, by and large, a fairly quiet street in which every householder seemed to be gainfully employed. Some years after we moved there, a widow down the street, a Mrs Magowan, was battered to death by the man she hired to paint her house. He was set free, it was murmured, because he was a Protestant and his victim was a Catholic. Other than that, the neighbourhood generated no misconduct, waste, unnecessary drudgery, unnecessary quarrels, or the spectre of new wars. The art of living fairly comfortably and harmoniously seemed achievable. Children old enough to play on the street did so without fear of being molested or run over. They were in bed by eight, or at the latest nine. Discipline was tight.

When he brought us to Ponsonby Avenue towards the end of 1941, my father was not unlike other daddies. He administered punishment with the 'taws', a leather strap with 'fingers', applied to the legs. He also administered candy apples, boiled sugar sweets known as yellow man and Buntings lumps, a delicious dried seaweed, dark red in colour and encrusted with sea-salt, which was called dulse in Northern Ireland and dilsk in southern Ireland. He was a fine story-teller. In the evening when he was available and on Sunday mornings when we would climb into his bed, he produced from his imagination (or perhaps from his own memories of child-hood) epics which involved heroic battles with giant spiders ('See that scar on my hand? That's where it bit me'), and brandy smugglers who guarded their hoard at the Gobbins caves on the Antrim shore of Belfast Lough and who despatched intruders by 'the death of a thousand slices – see that scar there?' He gave us raw whiskey for toothache and diluted it for colds. Coal-tar soap was applied to skin ailments, such as hives and scabies; Harrison's Pomade to the scalp (we once or twice had an epidemic of nits), Sloane's Liniment and Wintergreen to strained muscles, boracic solutions to infected eyes and – every spring, without fail – sulphur-and-treacle to the intes-tines, said to be as efficacious for the blood as Senna tea was for the bowel. Castor-oil was for emergencies, such as one I created on finding an uninflated balloon in a secluded area called The Glen.

My father's face froze when I told him.

'What colour was it?

'White'.

'Did you pick it up?'

'Yeah'.

'Don't say "yeah". It's *yes!*'

'Yes.'

'Did you put it in your mouth?'

'Yes, I blew it up, and . . .'

He was out of his chair in a flash, diving through the kitchen into the scullery, pulling out drawers, upsetting shelves, saying nothing. He returned with the Castor-oil and a tablespoon. 'Open your mouth! Open your mouth, I say!' I gagged, cried, pleaded, but the wretched stuff went down. He made me gargle with something else. Later, when I was thoroughly purged, he explained: 'German planes drop things: toys that explode when children pick them up, poisoned balloons, all kinds of things.' It would have been too complicated for him to go into the origins and perils of such unGermanic-sounding weapons as discarded 'French letters'.

I cannot say that my childhood was ruled by a heavy hand. My father had a naturally sunny nature, and an exuberance which frequently prompted him to perform a vigorous tap dance on the kitchen lino. Being virtually tone-deaf never stopped him from bursting into songs popular at the time. 'Yabba-dabba-dabba, said the monkey to the chimp . . . Then one day a big baboon married them, and very soon/ They all went away on their yippa-dippa honeymoon'. Though not given to such displays herself, my mother almost always was amused by them in her lively husband. She was a gentle, contemplative creature, and it is quite possible that my father's performances were designed to lift her from her occasional reveries. I cannot recall having witnessed any disagreements between them, though once I detected a kind of tension which may have followed an argument. Certainly, my mother blushed furiously when my father broke a silence by humming a song that contained the words, 'to make a scolding woman hold her tongue, tongue, tongue'. He could convulse her with laughter too. I was about six when our gaslight was replaced by 'electric-light' and our big black range, with its ovens and hotplates, gave way to a modern coal fire. My parents then decided to redecorate the downstairs rooms, an extremely messy enterprise in the hands of those untrained to do it. Soon, the place was a shambles: paint spattered everywhere, wallpaper askew. My mother began to look worried. Suddenly, my father grabbed her around the waist and, waving his paintbrush at everything in sight, whirled her through the debris, singing: 'Oh, when father was painting the parlour, you couldn't see mother for paint . . .'

Yet exuberance was not allowed to compromise decorum. In our house indelicate subjects got little airing. We said 'B-T-M' for 'bottom', and 'Och-och' for defecation. The bluest word in my father's vocabulary – in front of his children, at least – was 'damnable'. He believed in strong self-discipline and tested his own with cold baths, winter and summer ('It builds character'). He delighted in the fact that Brendan and I, in our teens, would swim daily in the less than fragrant waters of Belfast Lough well into November.

Our swimming expeditions were to a spot on the lough's north shore between Whitehouse and Whiteabbey. It is a loyalist area, though it has a Catholic church, the Star of the Sea. My father swam there as a boy and was beaten up twice by local boys because of his religion. He was attacked a third time by a 'big bruiser of a man' who 'came at me with a stick as I left the water and headed for my pile of clothes'. Giving this sinister figure the slip, he managed to recover his clothes, except for one of his boots, and ran all the way home half-dressed. Ever since hearing that story, I had some reservations about going there. But for Brendan and me it was an easy twenty-minute bicycle ride to an uncrowded seafront, so we risked the journey when we knew the tide was in, and were bothered by no one.

The area took on much greater notoriety in 1952, however, when I was seventeen. In November of that year, Patricia Curran, the only daughter of a High Court judge, Sir Lancelot Curran, was found murdered in the grounds of the family home in Whiteabbey. Such were the sensitivities of the province that this case caused an unexpected stir of sectarian rumours. The Currans were Protestant. Sir Lancelot, a former Attorney General of Northern Ireland, would later become a Lord Justice of Appeal in Belfast. They lived in a large house, The Glen, at the end of a dark driveway curving upwards beneath the branches of trees. Patricia's horribly mutilated body was found by her brother, Desmond, and a police officer. The Ulster police believed that the identity of the murderer was known by someone in the vicinity. They called in Scotland Yard. Fleet Street's top crime correspondents also arrived in force. By and by, a Scottish Leading Aircraft Man, Iain Hay Gordon, based at a Royal Air Force station in nearby Edenmore, was arrested and charged with the murder.

It then emerged that Gordon was a friend of Desmond Curran. They had first met in a church. As their friendship developed, Gordon was invited on a number of occasions to The Glen for dinner. There he met Desmond's family, including Patricia. After strenuously denying the crime, Gordon was put under intensive interrogation lasting three days and confessed that he had kissed Patricia in the grounds of The Glen, got carried away and lost control, stabbing her with his service knife. Found guilty but insane (evidence was given that he was schizophrenic), he was sent to a high-security mental hospital in Antrim. Shortly afterwards, still grief-stricken over the loss of his much-loved sister, Desmond Curran became a Roman Catholic. He went to live in South Africa where, four decades later, he told a television documentary team that he had forgiven Iain Hay Gordon. Predictably, I suppose, the fact of his entering the Catholic Church was, in the eyes of die-hard Ulster people, only slightly less controversial than the circumstances of his sister's death. Catholics expressed a belief that their Church was the best choice for easing the pain of bereavement; Protestants smarted over the conversion of one whose family belonged to the Protestant-Unionist Establishment. But some of the evidence in the murder case also gave pause for concentrated thought. It turned out that the thick-bladed service knife which Gordon claimed to have used for the murder and then thrown into the sea was not the murder weapon; it was a thin stiletto. Secondly, although Gordon said he had killed Patricia in the grounds of the house, heavy bloodstains were found over a large area of the floor of the girl's bedroom, stains too deep and widespread to have been caused in, say, a domestic accident. Finally, in 1959, only six years after being incarcerated, Gordon was released and allowed to return to his home in Clackmannanshire. To this day, many people old enough to recall the case, and the campaign to free Gordon, believe that his confession was forced out of him and his conviction based on a lie around which members of the Northern Ireland Establishment closed ranks. To this day, he denies having murdered Patricia Curran.

In our house, the taws were used to address lies. When we

hid them and lied about their whereabouts, we risked a sharper alternative, a rod from the front hedge. 'I will take anything but a lie; lying earns a flogging,' he said when I had denied scrumping from an orchard beside the Waterworks. My brothers and I put him to the test by scrumping some more, bringing home the apples and telling him they were stolen. He bit into one and chewed for a long time, his eyes squinting at the fruit. Then he put the apple down. 'It's not ripe,' was all he said – in a tone less than censorious. If we handed him a sweet, juicy one, he would bite into it, chew appreciatively and pronounce: 'Only the best *for* the best!'

Yet there were certain deceits which he did tolerate, particularly if they were designated as 'jokes'. One of these involved himself and some friends when they were at a weekend summer school run by the National Council of Labour Colleges. Among the friends was a young university professor called O'Neill, who had what my father described as 'a baby face' and prematurely thinning hair. Professor O'Neill was worried that his babyishness would be accentuated by baldness. So, having consulted in secret, his companions told him of a sure-fire cure that was all the rage in America and the Far East. All the professor had to do, they said, was soak a bowl of raisins in olive oil during the day, rub them thoroughly into his hair at night and retire to bed with a towel around his head. The process had to be repeated for two weeks. 'Within a couple of months he was as bald as a billiard ball, ha-ha-ha!' my father said.

I heard him recalling the 'joke' for the benefit of one of his closest friends, Alfie Beringer, a German from the Black Forest who used to visit us in Ponsonby Avenue. Alfie didn't see the joke at all. Although he was fond of my father and admired his principles, he eyed him severely over his rimless glasses and thought the joke to have been not very principled. My father loved Alfie for his sharp intellect, which was mitigated by an acute shyness. 'Alfie's a great oddity,' my father frequently said with much affection. He loved 'oddities', in whom Belfast abounded in the 1940s and 1950s. 'Johnny-look-up-at-the-moon' walked the city for miles on a clear night, his head tilted upwards, bumping into trees, lamp posts and hedges and nearly getting himself killed crossing roads. 'The Lady in Green' was a middle-aged eccentric who dressed entirely in that colour: green shoes, stockings, skirt, blouse, coat, scarf, hat, feather. 'Corky' was a one-legged woman who dressed elegantly, took pains with her makeup and emerged from her house on Antrim Road to scream obscenities at passing buses. Shopkeepers tended to be 'oddities'. One of our local newsagents kept his ice cream in the outside lavatory. A local grocer repeated every order ten times ('Pound of sugar, pound of sugar, pound of sugar . . .'). A sweet shop a few doors from 'Corky's' house was nicknamed 'Dirty Jimmy's', due more to the state of his fingernails than to the state of his mind.

Alfie Beringer was 'odd' in a quieter way. His family were wealthy Catholics who owned jeweller's shops, one of which was in Belfast's North Street. He lived in Whitehead, a bracing resort sixteen miles along the north shore of Belfast Lough, with two sisters who appeared to bully him. 'Every time I've gone to visit him there,' my father said. 'the sisters have forced him out into the garden to smoke his cigar amid the spinach beds. Did you ever hear the like of it?' But Alfie never objected or showed resentment. He had close-cropped white hair, a thin, pink face and a long neck. He travelled by train daily to Belfast and cycled from the station to his work at the shipyard where he was a senior draughtsman. Although he was well aware of my father's political enthusiasms, I don't think they discussed these at any length. On the few occasions I sat in on their conversations, they were into Kirkegaard, Pascal, Leibnitz, Schiller, Goethe and stuff well above my head, and, I would guess, above the heads of everyone else in Ponsonby Avenue.

If Ponsonby Avenue wasn't exactly intellectual it was, at least, 'respectable'. When I was a boy, it was fairly evenly mixed, with Catholics having a slight majority. In Belfast as a whole, Catholics tended to be considerably less well off than Protestants. They had larger families. They had trouble getting jobs, because the job market was controlled mainly by Protestants. The major employers – engineers, ropeworks, shipyards – operated 'no-Catholic' or token-Catholic policies (I guess Alfie Beringer's German name distracted attention from his Catholicism). If you came across some-one doing menial work, the chances were that he or she was a Catholic. When Catholics did find employment, they often found it hard, or even impossible, to earn promotion. In the slums of Catholic west Belfast, these disadvantages bore down heavily on the community whose horizon, generally speaking, was unyieldingly bleak. But a few Catholic (or predominantly Catholic) neighbour-hoods were much less enmired. Like my own neighbourhood, they were not overtly 'nationalist' or 'republican' – to use the epithets by which Catholics usually were categorized, then damned. Those inhabiting them were, as often as not, in jobs. Consequently, they tended to keep their mouths shut and their lace curtains carefully drawn. The fact that they were even better-off materially than slum-dwelling Protestants enhanced their feeling of respectability. Other than churchgoing, I don't think there was a great deal of social mixing. Neighbours did not visit each other's houses, unless they were blood relatives. In what was, after all, quite a short street there were people I never got to know. There was a family called Honey, in which there were three sisters, who lived two doors from us. They were seldom seen outdoors. I desperately wanted to get to know the youngest sister, who was about my age, and pale and pretty and mysteriously compelling. But without being in the slightest impolite to me, she kept her winsome distance as I lurked bashfully on the street side of her front hedge, too tongue-tied to speak. So I was obliged to construct dreamy scenarios featuring alternative neighbourhood beauties: Protestant girls named Milli-cent and Freda, and Catholic girls called Eithne and Ursula. But such fancies could quickly be dispersed by realities.

Ponsonby Avenue had the misfortune to be connected – by a long, crooked, walled alley – to a neighbourhood known and feared as 'Tiger Bay'. The people of Tiger Bay were largely poor (poorer, certainly, than most of the families in my own neighbourhood), and almost exclusively Protestant. They celebrated Orange Day – 12 July – with a massive bonfire on which the more frenzied among them burned their own furniture, the better to consume the Pope's effigy. On occasion, Tiger Bay children would run up the connecting alley to hurl stones and epithets at children they suspected (sometimes wrongly) of being Catholic. Just as often, Catholic children would retaliate with – or even initiate – a skirmish. But that did not make Tiger Bay off-limits to us. It was, we children learned, a 'ghetto', whatever that meant. But we gladly patronized its fish-and-chip shop, opposite the alley entrance. As a child I had no hesitation in venturing through the place, on errands for my mother. These short excursions often meant queuing at a Tiger Bay vegetable shop and listening to the latest gossip. Once it went like this:

'Ach, Mrs – , how're ye doin'? Is that wee Sammy with ye?'

'Aye, 'tis indeed, and he's a wee heart-scald – aren't ye, Sammy?'

'Naw he's not, how old are ye, Sammy?'

'He's two. And wait 'til ye hear this; his daddy learned him. Say "Fuck the Pope", Sammy. For the nice lady here. Go on, say it! "Fuck . . . the . . . Pope". Ach, he's shy.'

'Ach, he's a great wee chile, and comin' on great!'

It was quite light-hearted, really. I joined nervously in the laughter of the queue, without feeling threatened. What I felt was wonderment over a parent encouraging her child to utter that forbidden 'soldiers' word' and to boast about it, loudly, in public. But that is what a large part our intercommunal tension amounted to in the so-called 'good years' after the war when food rationing played with people's priorities: a harsh word here, a sectarian slogan there; or, infrequently, one group of boys armed with washing-line poles tilting at another group of boys armed with homemade catapults, shouting 'Charge!' and 'Proddie pigs!' and 'Dirty Fenians!' and – more damningly – 'College boys!' The Tiger Bay boys had a marvellous chant which was meant to offend supporters of Éamon de Valéra, the Dublin leader.

> De Valéry had a canary
> Up the leg of his drawers.
> When he was sleepin', we were peepin'
> Up the leg of his drawers.

We tried frantically to compose a retort insulting to Winston Churchill. Unable to find a word that even vaguely rhymed with 'Churchill', we gave up.

These juvenile altercations were no worse than the collisions I read about in my *William* books. It was a matter of 'Them' and 'Us', a frictive response to perceived social differences, rather than crude sectarianism, even though the former was quite often dressed up as the latter. One of the poorest of Tiger Bay's families was in fact Catholic. The children walked up the alleyway daily to attend Holy Family School in Newington. They went to Mass on Sundays. But they were never attacked within their 'ghetto' for being Catholics, and never, as far as I know, intimidated into leaving it (though they have long since done so). Indeed, one of the highlights of *our* year was to join the Tiger Bay revellers on bonfire night and throw scraps of timber on to the roaring flames consuming our Pope. While we had our mock fights, and even our more realistic, though fairly harmless, ones, in the adult world, religious discrimination was such a daily occurrence that both sides had become almost conditioned to expecting it. But it was not hard to see what was fuelling it. On his fairly frequent trips across the Irish border, my father picked up bits of news that annoyed him profoundly: evidence of anti-Semitism in high places, renewed emigration and an increasingly assertive Catholic Church's interference in state affairs – particularly when it sniffed socialist ideas in the air. And just try to imagine the impact on Ulster Protestants when the Irish coalition government at the time sent a comforting message to the Pope that they 'reposed at the feet of your Holiness the assurance of our filial loyalty and of our devotion to your August Person, as well as our firm resolve to be guided in our work by the teaching of Christ and to strive for the attainment of a social order in Ireland based on Christian principles.'

'That should go down well on Sandy Row,' my father said sarcastically, referring to a notoriously aggressive loyalist street in Belfast. He was totally convinced that Protestant attitudes in the North were, to a great degree, bolstered by Catholic attitudes in the South. 'If the Church would keep its neb [nose] out of politics down there, we might have a chance up here,' he said. But by and large, the lid stayed on sectarian extremism in the post-war years.

The Troubles changed all that. Of course bigotry never lay far beneath the surface in Northern Ireland at the best of times. One accepted discrimination, or tried to duck it, or occasionally challenged it head-on. But it was not consistently white-knuckled, even on Orange Day. The critical powers of my fellow Ulster folk are no less admirable than those of any other people. But their criticism was narrowly targeted, and thus, when it manifested itself, it tended to do so in violent spurts rather than in a broad flow. Ardent emphasis was constantly placed upon the difference between Protestantism and Catholicism by stalwarts of both – so much so that the close intellectual resemblance of the two systems, their identity in nine parts out of ten, sometimes escaped us. Ulster Protestants and Ulster Catholics shared a patristic outlook on the world. They had similar historical perspectives. Their notions of the origin of man, of the Bible, of heaven and hell, demons and angels, were all more or less identical. He who would be saved must accept the doctrine of the triune God and must be ever on his guard against the whisperings of reason. The Pope, as I've said, did get in the way of a greater confluence of Protestants and Catholics, but that problem was dealt with by one side, symbolically at least, by burning him annually in effigy and declaring 'No Pope here!' on the gable walls of mean urban streets and on little roads to nowhere out in the countryside.

The most venomous reactions were prompted by questions of territory and nationality. So when the IRA launched its terrorist campaign against the police, the Army, businessmen and those who happened to find themselves in the wrong place at the wrong time, the two communities were set at each other's throats as never before. Tiger Bay, like other rundown Protestant areas, was presented with a firmly defined target which it concluded was sustained by a republican – that is to say, Catholic – armoury. Consequently, barbed-wire was placed on the high walls of the alleyway to impede incendiary raids by one neighbourhood on the other. But other missiles were lobbed over this barbed barricade, smashing windows and breaking bones. Guns were fired. Violent death ensued. Adults took over what had been, for us, nothing more sinister than a big playground fight. And although my elderly father continued to live there, the feeling of security that the Newington neighbourhood had imparted to me quickly trickled away like blood on a butcher's slab. Ponsonby Avenue was joined at the top end by Newington Avenue, a dog-legged street that bent downwards to the school, and at the bottom by Atlantic Avenue. There never was much outside intrusion to interrupt our games of hide-and-seek, hop-scotch and kick-the-tin. Milk, coal and herring were delivered in horse-drawn vehicles. The dead were removed in extravagant horse-drawn hearses. Unlike the streets adjoining it, Ponsonby had a smooth, concrete surface. On a windy day, one could, with the help of an open umbrella, reach great speeds on roller-skates without much fear of traffic collisions. But although the street was fun, the 'wastey' was even better.

The 'wastey' was an area of waste ground that had supported a dozen or so tall and rather elegant houses of Duncairn Gardens, a thoroughfare whose lower end was much less salubrious than its upper end. The Luftwaffe chose to flatten the houses at the upper end, creating for us a rubble-strewn football pitch, a dusty cycle track, an assortment of half-bricks, cobblestones, scorched timbers and lead piping ideal for the construction of schoolboy lairs. The lead piping even fetched good scrapyard prices. In winter the 'wastey' offered snow for igloos and snow-fights. In summer, it was a hard-baked park on our back doorstep. Some of the children I played with then I never was to know as adults: 'Mucker' McDaid who joined the American Army, Brendan Cassidy who went to Brussels, 'Spud' Murphy who emigrated to Canada and died in middle-age, Billy Dunbar, a pale, tense lad with twitchy elbows, who died young.

From these and others I imbibed certain ideas: that when passing a dead dog or cat one must make the sign of the Cross and say,

'One, two, three, no fever in our house!'; that to deny your religion when challenged by 'Proddies' (Protestants) was to lose your soul; that the worst possible 'Proddies' were those who had 'turned' – i.e., abandoned Catholicism for Protestantism. I have no idea how many had made such a conversion down the years. The only evidence for it is often the oddly 'Catholic' surnames these Protestants continue to bear. The leader of a notoriously brutal gang, the Shankill Butchers, for example was called Murphy (the IRA shot him dead in 1982). From my odd encounter with Protestant children beyond my neighbourhood, I heard, though could not bring myself to believe, that Catholic priests 'did things' to Catholic nuns, thus filling up the orphanages; that Protestants lived temperate lives, whereas Catholics drank to excess and 'bred like rabbits'.

It is remarkable how ignorant prejudices have stuck to this day. A Dublin Jesuit friend of mine, Edward O'Donnell, spent much of his youth in Northern Ireland. In the late 1970s, when working as a human relations consultant in the Irish Republic, he wrote a book, *Northern Irish Stereotypes*, which reads like a replay of my own childhood discussions and confrontations. The 'real' stereotype that Protestants had of Roman Catholics, his researches showed, 'is that they are ordinary enough people, but Irish-nationalist-republican. They are seen as brainwashed by priests, having too many children, and as being superstitious and bitter'. Roman Catholics, on the other hand, thought Protestants were 'in control of the country and are determined to remain in control, even at the cost of bitter murder. This is because they are seen to be loyal Orangemen; ordinary, British people.' Father O'Donnell found that Catholics tended to use four words to describe themselves: 'long-suffering', 'deprived', 'insecure', and 'unfortunate'. Protestants tended to use words such as 'power-holder', 'loyalist', 'hard-working', 'British' about themselves. In his conclusions, O'Donnell acknowledges that communication *is occurring* across the 'sectarian divide' in Northern Ireland. But, he adds, depressingly: '. . . it would seem to follow that since the bitterness is persisting the way these findings indicate, the communication is also involved in perpetuating the situation'.

In other words, the bile of bigotry so manifest in the year of my birth and in subsequent wartime years churns on undiminished.

When Ian Paisley, Ulster's turbulent Protestant preacher and hell-fire politician, was a gawky, relatively unknown bachelor-cleric, Catholic bigotry was much in evidence in Ireland. In the north, Bishop Farren of Derry warned Catholics: 'If you allow your children to be contaminated by those who are not of the fold, then you can expect nothing but disaster.' I was an uneasy member of the fold then, though no longer a child and coping with Protestant 'contaminants' without disastrous results.

Another of the fold was Maura Lyons, a Belfast working-class girl of fifteen. She ignored the warning. Eldest of a family of five from the Catholic Falls Road, she was a stitcher for the Star Clothing Company where, in 1956, visiting gospellers caused her to doubt her Catholicism. She contacted a minister of the Free Presbyterian Church who, in turn, introduced her to Paisley. Paisley was about to marry Eileen Cassells, an east Belfast shopkeeper's daughter who has always called him 'Honeybunch', and he invited Maura to the wedding. The encounter – and its bizarre sequel – made Paisley a household name. While 'Honeybunch' was on his honeymoon, Maura Lyons joined his church and told her parents of her conversion. Her father beat her and called in three Catholic priests who 'seemed determined to force me into convent life', she said later. She escaped by jumping from a bedroom window. Free Presbyterians smuggled her into Scotland – a criminal offence, since she was a minor. Irish newspapers, north and south, went wild. The Royal Ulster Constabulary searched for the girl, and found a wall of silence. I remember the fret into which Belfast got itself over this 'religious drama'. The names Ian Paisley and Maura Lyons were on all tongues. Trolley-bus queues hummed with the controversy. Drunk men on Falls Road swore vengeance for what they claimed was a kidnapping. Drunk men on Shankill Road waved in triumph about a Fenian girl 'coming to Jesus'. The police were criticized for not probing zealously enough, and for probing too hard. Reporters spent days and nights dogging Free Presbyterians. One of them, from the now defunct *Daily Herald*, told me he had climbed over Paisley's garden wall, only to have Paisley's dog 'bite the arse out of my trousers'. Would he sue? 'Nah, in the mood the country's in, a jury would take the word of a Free Presbyterian dog against a journalist's.' He promply submitted an expenses claim to his newspaper.

Two months after Maura Lyons disappeared, Paisley publicly played a tape-recording of her describing her conversion. He was laconic with the truth: the tape, he said, had been found among milk bottles on his doorstep. He also showed his talent for playing the beleaguered hero. 'If I knew where the girl was I would not take her to the police,' he said. 'Very well, I am commiting an offence. I will do time for it. I would be proud to do time for Protestant liberty.' Eighteen months later, the Belfast High Court noted that 'Mr Paisley was in touch with the girl when *prima facie* she was abducted'. Then, on the order of the court, Maura Lyons was returned to her parents – and, it soon emerged, to 'the fold'.

Most Ulster Protestants were embarrassed by the 'Maura Lyons affair'. But it helped launch Ian Paisley into the political firmament (where he has flashed and thundered as though the end were nigh). Politics, as much as religion, has made 'the Big Man' a persevering force among his voters and votaries. Years later, his daughter, Rhonda, then Deputy Mayor of Belfast, told me: 'There are some kids who kiss his picture every night, though he is against all idolatry.' And there is no doubt that he *is* idolized. If ever there was a case of unconscious cerebration it is the response of the average Paisleyite to the leader and to his perceived enemies. 'Many people follow him blindly but don't stop to think', said a Protestant local councillor who has observed the Paisley phenomenon down the years. Members of Paisley's congregation once beat up a *Sunday Times* journalist, David Holden, for taking notes of a sermon. Holden, an Arabist, was in Northern Ireland, seeking – and finding in abundance – similarities with conflicts in the Middle East, his special 'beat' (having survived Belfast, he was murdered in Cairo while on assignment in 1977).

It is said that humour, in its highest form, is the sign of a mind at peace with itself, for which the contrasts and contradictions of life have ceased to jar (though have not ceased to be). Paisleyites tend to be humourless. Paisley himself, however, sees a joke when he makes one. He would acknowledge the humour in the Pharisee earnestly rinsing, rubbing and polishing the *outside* of his cup, forgetful of the fact that he drank from the inside. But he's no rib-tickler. The man who has exerted such a bleak influence on Northern Irish politics was born in 1926 in a largely Catholic neighbourhood of Armagh. His father, James Kyle Paisley, was a Baptist pastor and drapery store assistant who had served in the Ulster Volunteer Force during the 1912–13 Home Rule crisis. His mother, Isabella Turnbull, was a railwayman's daughter from Stirling in Scotland, who had been converted to 'born-again' Christianity in Edinburgh when she was – like Maura Lyons – fifteen. Later, when the family moved to Ballymena in County Antrim, the boy and his elder brother Harold were ordered to keep to themselves and to the Bible.

In his teens, Ian Paisley rose at 3 a.m. to pray. Harold joined the Royal Ulster Constabulary and became a Plymouth Brethren fundamentalist. Ian went to technical college, worked on a farm and preached religious sermons from a 'tin hut' mission hall, and was ordained into what became the Free Presbyterian Church. An elderly cleric who 'laid hands' on Paisley at his 1945 ordination prayed: 'Lord, give this young man a tongue like an old cow.' The Lord obliged. Paisley, since then, has rasped across continents: via a 'hot gospel' university in South Carolina which awarded him an 'honorary doctorate' and the forums of Europe where, from his seat as a Euro-MP, he attacks ecumenism and popery. In his size eleven shoes he has tramped the globe, delivering envenomed diatribes, cajoling, ridiculing, mimicking, letting off the artillery of his talent at all prepared to listen. One of the most striking things about Paisley is that he was organizing mass protest demonstrations in Northern Ireland well before such events became fashionable vehicles for the civil rights movement. He was also prepared to confront the law long before he came to castigate the IRA for doing so. Breaches of the law became inevitable as a result of Paisley's attachment not only to pugnacious fundamentalism but to the wilder fringes of Unionism. In the mid-fifties, he would play on loyalist paranoia with such statements as: 'The dark sinister shadow of our neighbouring Roman Catholic state, where religious liberty is slowly but surely being taken away, lies across our province. The demands and aims of the Church of Rome are growing, and as our Protestantism declines with the blight of modernistic apostasy, the ascendancy of that Church is becoming more and more marked in our Ulster life.'

At the same time, he attended the inaugural meeting of, and subsequently joined, a group calling itself Ulster Protestant Action, which has since been described as 'a potentially armed expression of extreme loyalism', though he was not actually involved in paramilitary activity. (It disintegrated in 1966 after the murder of a Catholic by loyalist paramilitaries.) One of his biographers, Clifford Smyth, finds it 'hard to resist the conclusion' that Paisley was aware of the existence of a revamped Ulster Volunteer Force, which was then 'in all probability involved in the procurement of weapons'. Clifford himself is an interesting study, not least because of his book, *Rome – Our Enemy*, whose cover shows the Pope's fingers dripping blood on the map of Ulster. The second paragraph of this strange volume, which Smyth concedes was 'written in haste' in 1974, says: 'The fact is that the Church of Rome is behind the present unrest, the murders and the bombings. It is the Church of Rome which educated the gunmen, it is the Church of Rome which orchestrated the campaign of violence and political action against the Protestants of Ulster. It is the Church of Rome which seeks their extirpation. The strategy used is not new; ingredients are found in the Spain of the 30's, in the Anschluss of Austria, in the Munich fiasco.' When I showed the above passage to my father on one of my visits to Belfast, he laughed so hard that he took a fit of coughing which I thought would be the end of him. Clearing his catarrh into a handkerchief, he said: 'There's no dividing line between sanity and insanity, but I think Mr Smyth should see a doctor.'

I have no idea if Smyth and Paisley see eye to eye in all things.

But their intemperate words on religion are similar. They do harm to the case they have espoused. They use cudgels to crack nuts. They seem capable of reaching for anything with which to keep the bonfire going. In 1966, Paisley caused a riot by marching on the General Assembly of Irish Presbyterianism, claiming it to be less than true-blue. He was jailed for a short term. Across the land he led his ranting tribes, disturbing the peace and achieving a kind of martyrdom when hauled before the courts.

As a young reporter, I first observed 'the old cow's tongue' scouring orthodox Unionism. Arrested for deafening the residents of Donaghadee, a breezy, mainly Protestant resort in County Down, with his loudspeakers, Paisley appeared before a special court, held in the room of a local hotel. The hotel owner happened to be a Catholic. He confided in me that a Catholic priest had celebrated Mass in the same room earlier in the morning. I sidled up to Paisley before the court convened.

'Mr Paisley,' I whispered, 'are you bothered by the fact that you are about to respond to your summons on the very spot where the act of transubstantiation was celebrated by a priest of the Roman persuasion this very day?'

The 'Big Man's' eyes bulged. He turned for confirmation to a court official who shrugged. Another journalist confirmed what I had said. I waited for the explosion, but just then, the magistrate arrived and the court went into session. The charge of (I think) disturbing the peace was dismissed on a technicality. Paisley boomed: 'Thank God for the victory.' He was – is – more than a preacher in whom prejudices of a darker age than normally found in Ulster have found refuge. Like many Ulster people, he did not – does not – accept the conditional when the absolute will do. He absolutely wanted to be the spiritual *and* temporal leader of Ulster Unionism. He was soldier/priest, politician/priest, pulpit/priest. Like Luther before him, he gave psychical explanations of physical events. One day, in the midst of a great storm, Luther said: ' 'Tis the devil who does this; the winds are nothing else but good or bad spirits. Hark! how the devil is puffing and blowing!' Likewise, Paisley blamed threats to the rock of Ulster Protestantism on 'the Harlot of Rome'.

In 1530, Luther wrote: 'When I try to work, my head becomes filled with all sorts of whizzing, buzzing, thundering noises, and if I did not leave off on the instant I should faint away.' Had Luther been writing in the late twentieth century, he would have identified the noises as coming from Ian Paisley: torrent lava from a volcano's mouth. The Unionist establishment feared and loathed Paisley almost as much as it feared and loathed the growing assertiveness among Catholic nationalists. Paisley divided Unionists in much the same way as Colonel Gadaffi divided Arabs. He was too extreme for one wing; not extreme enough for another. In the 1960s, 'moderate' Unionism saw little alternative to concessions to the nationalist community. Anticipating them, Paisley thundered on about 'treachery', making life impossible for the moderate Unionists and forcing nationalists to press ahead more firmly for their civil rights. In 1966, Terence O'Neill, the reformist Prime Minister of Northern Ireland, responded to Paisley with a blast which might easily have been reserved for IRA terrorism a few years later. 'To those of us who remember the thirties,' O'Neill declared, 'the pattern is horribly familiar. The contempt for established authority; the crude and unthinking intolerance; the emphasis upon monster processions and rallies; the appeal to a perverted form of patriotism – each and every one of these things has its parallel in the rise of the Nazis to power.'

Well, O'Neill's dead, and Paisley lives. O'Neill's successors are gone, yet Paisley continues to lord it over his own turbulence. It was Paisley who contributed to Belfast's Divis Street riots in 1964 – a precursor to the Troubles – by threatening to remove an Irish tricolour from a west Belfast Catholic ghetto. He claims not to hate Catholics individually 'as people'. Some Catholics in his North Antrim constituency agree. In 1992, when nationalist parents fought a proposal to close a primary school on the grounds that it had only ten pupils, it was Paisley who petitioned on their behalf. On the other hand, he often has an odd way of showing it. Hearing that an Italian ice cream parlour had opened on Belfast's Shankill Road, he addressed a local meeting. 'You people of the Shankill Road, what's wrong with you? Number 425 Shankill Road – do you know who lives there? Pope's men, that's who! Forte's ice cream shop! Italian papists on the Shankill Road!' And God help the Catholic priest who dared to cross his path. One who objected to Paisley's use of a town hall for anti-Catholic meetings provoked a typical afflatus. 'Priest Murphy, speak for your own bloodthirsty, persecuting, intolerant, blaspheming, politico-religious papacy, but do not dare to pretend to be the spokesman of free Ulster men . . . Go back to your priestly intolerance, back to your blasphemous Masses, back to your beads, holy water, holy smoke and stinks and remember . . . we know your Church to be the mother of harlots and the abomination of the earth.'

My father chuckled when he read this too. I'm not entirely certain how he regarded Paisley. In a way, he thought Paisley was Irish republicanism's best weapon, discrediting Unionism through his excesses in the way Gaddafi discredited pan-Arabism through his. But he also admired Paisley's affection for the working class and his contempt for the Establishment (in all its forms).

'If he hadn't been a religious tub-thumper, he'd have been a great socialist,' my father said. 'When religion becomes the ally of mastering force, you better look out.' He quoted, regretfully, some lines, the origin of which he had – uncharacteristically – forgotten.

> Never let man be bold enough to say,
> Thus and no farther let thy passions stray;
> The first crime past compels us on to more,
> And guilt proves fate which was but choice before.

There were elements in Paisley which I detected in my father: an answer for everything, a relentlessness in debate, and an inclination to cock a snook at authority. I suppose Ulster people generally do tend to have these attributes, and perhaps my father had them in no greater degree than most. For a while in the Second World War years, he sported a small, dark moustache that gave him, despite his

slight build, a dismaying resemblance to Adolf Hitler. I'm pretty
sure this was a deliberate affectation, a challenge to authority to
inspect his Identity Card. He also had a particularly jaunty gait,
partly a consequence of a bad leg injury in boyhood, or rather the
clumsy surgery with which it was repaired (leaving one limb slightly
shorter than the other), and partly a compensation for having flat
feet, a condition I inherited from him. But the Hitler moustache
was, I think, an indicator of his temperament; a certain contrariness
which, if not exactly iconoclastic, caused him at times to reject
conformity – except in his children ('Walk straight! Chin up!
Shoulders back! Chest out!').

It was widely assumed in the neighbourhood that my father was
well off. I don't know how this impression gained currency. We
did not have a telephone until the war was over. There was no
motorcar at the front door until even later. We did not eat out with
any great regularity. Several times a year, on Sundays, he would take
us downtown to the Continental Café (a modest Belfast equivalent to
the Lyon's Corner House in London), next door to a shop that sold
holy statues, pictures, medals and rosaries. These outings ceased
when he caught me prising used American GI chewing-gum from
the underside of a café table, with the intention of giving it hours
of happy, additional mastication (gum was gold in those days; Belfast
boys greeted every passing US uniform with the eager cry, 'Got
any gum, chum?'). Perhaps the fact that my father had not one, but
two fountain pens in his lapel pocket created the illusion of mild
prosperity; or that he wore Donegal-tweed plus-fours at golf; or
that we always went away for summer holidays. The impression
certainly existed before the time arrived for my brothers and me to
be sent off to prep boarding school in Dundalk, causing him a
considerable financial burden. But it was an impression I also shared
at the time.

'How much does your da earn?' my classmate Brendan Hyland
asked one day, between a group rendering of 'Roddy McCorley'
(the rebel hanged on Toome Bridge) and the six-times tables. I
opted for a ball-park figure. 'Ten pounds a week,' I said, glancing

at him for his reaction. Brendan, who later became a successful chemist and irresistible raconteur, was the son of two doctors who must have been, in my view, millionaires.

'Whew!' he said, clearly impressed.

On the back of this guesswork of mine, this stab in the financial dark, I therefore felt quite secure, overlooking the fact that my trousers were patched, that chicken dinners were infrequent, and that powdered eggs and margarine were major items in our diet. There was a thing called, honestly enough, a 'mock hamburger', highly recommended by the Ministry of Food's advice centre in North Street, not far from where my father worked. It contained twice as many potatoes as minced meat, herbs, oatmeal, chopped leek and Worcester sauce. The advice centre also offered recipes for 'mock suet pudding' (two varieties) and ('For Holidays at Home') a bread, fat, egg and jam mixture called 'Poor Knight's Fritters'. But I don't believe we ever turned up our noses at a treacle sandwich or, if treacle was scarce, a sugar sandwich. Occasionally we had Lough Neagh eels and wild rabbit, but the latter tended to go 'off' very quickly unless cooked within a day of its delivery by friends from the country. In our scullery once, I saw a skinned rabbit on which fat maggots seethed. A great many years passed before I could face rabbit stew.

Holy Family parish imposed (if that is the word) a certain decorum on its parishioners. I have no doubt at all that the imposition was broadly accepted because of the need to 'set an example' to those of our neighbours whom successive parish priests described – rather dismissively, I thought – as 'non-Catholics'. Unorthodox behaviour, such as rolling home drunk, thumping your wife or losing control of your children, was to run the risk of 'giving scandal'. To associate with a Protestant of the opposite sex was to 'enter the occasion of sin'. Entering a Protestant church, for any reason at all, was to commit sin. At the bottom of Newington Avenue, the two Rodgers sisters wore their school uniforms unfashionably short, the hem of the frock being at least two inches above the knee, as opposed to the normal two inches below the calf. How we sniggered at the indecency of it! But one morning, on entering school, their head teacher, having become aware of our sniggers, forced the sisters to pin newspapers to their hems. How we guffawed at the absurdity of it!

As a child I had little truck with girls. I had no sisters. My Aunt Molly's brood included five girls, but they were either too young or too familiar to be of much use to me. Before my mother died, the only other women in my life were her sister Ginny; a lodger called Mary McEvoy, from County Tyrone, who later ran a pharmacy; a Mrs Madden who was a cousin of my mother and whom we loved for her apple tarts; other cousins called O'Kane (also apple tart experts), and the beloved Storey sisters who helped take care of my brothers and me when we were wartime evacuees in Randalstown. Direct encounters with females of my own age were rare and generally, for me, acutely embarrassing. Girls, for much of my childhood, caused me to blush, even the Honey girl two doors down, who probably was equally shy. I longed – not, I hope, too obsessively – to solve the mystery that their garments hid from me. Could they know my thoughts? I blushed as they skipped by.

There was an epileptic girl whom I learned to avoid, after she pursued me a few times demanding kisses. Another girl named Bernadette was said, by her female cronies, to have a crush on me. But until I was ten or eleven, I kept my distance (physically, at least) from what my father called 'wee scaldies'. 'Stick to your books, and don't let the wee scaldies turn your head,' he'd say. I should have listened. I was eleven, I think, when a very pretty Protestant girl, Freda Matchett, from the Limestone Road, allowed me to kiss her twice (once on each cheek) as payment for lending my chemistry set to her brother. My head was thoroughly turned. I mooned outside her house for hours, neglecting my school homework. I was glum at home and dreamy at school. My voice and my heart were breaking simultaneously. 'Didn't I tell you', my father said, 'what the wee scaldies would do!' I thought of her recently, the day after a Protestant mob surged up the Limestone Road to burn Catholics out of their homes.

The death of my mother detonated my security as powerfully as had the Blitz. I was not, at first, quite old enough to take in the deeper significance and implications of this loss. As I recall, my immediate reaction, on being told the news by my grandmother, early one November morning, was that my mother had played a rotten trick, dying within a few weeks of two crucial events: my ninth birthday and Christmas.

I have an early photograph of her, smoke-damaged from a fire in my older brother's house. She is sitting, straight and formal on a stool in Abernethy's Studios in High Street. She is wearing a 'flapper' dress fastened on one shoulder by a bow. Her eyes are large and widely spaced; her hair thick, dark and parted on the left. She looks young, in her late teens, or early twenties, certainly before she was married. It is a postcard photo, and her image must have pleased her. On the back of the postcard she has written to my father: 'Best wishes from The Original'.

She had been ill for some time, and at one point returned home from the Mater Hospital. I cannot recall how long she stayed before being rehospitalized, or indeed much else about her visit. I do have a memory of her being, in that interval, unusually loving and reassuring, but not saying very much. I have managed to preserve a mental picture of her then, sitting on the arm of a sofa in our parlour, her pale face bowed towards me, her eyes searching mine in a way that stopped my chatter. My brothers and I were not to know that that was the last time we would see her alive.

In the few days after her death, I took comfort from not having to attend school and from the heroic feeling of being in the vanguard of grief at her funeral. It wasn't really until weeks afterwards, when I found my father alone in the front parlour, weeping silently over some photographs, that the first genuine lances of lamentation pierced my heart. With the blackout lifted and the Germans on the run throughout Europe, my own world still contrived to become a bleaker place.

5

GREEN AMONG REDS

Holy Family school played a large part in our childhood evolution. It imprinted upon us definite conceptions of religious and, to a less measured – or measurable – extent, patriotic duty. This allegiance was directed at what was then the Irish Free State, rather than the Northern Ireland statelet which, under one-eyed Westminster supervision, organized our lives and elbowed us into or out of the future. Nevertheless, our years at the school helped us, more than we could have imagined then, to adjust to the spirit and character of the polity, however unedifying the polity was to turn out to be. There was a lot of cohesion in our lives then, compared with the disintegration that was to occur later.

The most formidable civilizing influences were, of course, the Holy Family teachers. The headmaster, Arthur Donnelly was called 'Oul' Nick', a sobriquet, we noted gleefully, that was also reserved for Satan. The outside corners of his eyebrows sometimes stuck up like horns, and he had a disgustingly effective way of quelling subversion, silencing disruption or punishing inattention. The duster he used for wiping the blackboard clean contained, apart from chalk-dust, large deposits of spit, the better to achieve erasure. This soggy object was his weapon. Squeak in class, and you got it up the face. His aim was unerring. In the twinkling of an eye, he could hit a boy at the back of the class with this missile. The stench from at least a month's saliva (flavoured by dark pipe-tobacco and tooth-rot) would linger for an hour, chastening one for a week or more. That said, 'Oul' Nick' was a kindly man. In the icy winter of 1941–42, my mother trudged through snowdrifts to save us making the short but awesome journey home for lunch (or dinner, as it was called then – and probably still is). Mr Donnelly, I clearly recall, was extremely solicitous, helping my mother with the hot soup and sandwiches she had brought into the school for us. I suspect he knew that she was ailing. He shed tears behind his horn-rimmed glasses at her funeral.

His deputy was Mr Cush, a sartorially neat teacher who achieved the feat of making me understand algebra. He too had impressive eccentricities, the most severe of which was directed against his own son, also in my class at one point. What he did was to 'make an example' of his son, a spirited boy desperate (I consider in retrospect), for perfectly understandable reasons, to be seen to identify with his peers rather than with his parent. Cush Jr. was never praised for his classroom triumphs, but he was excessively chastised for his minor failures. 'Come here, boy!' the daddy would say in response to a mild omission by the son, and we immediately knew the latter was about to be 'made an example of'. The deputy principal would grasp his erring offspring by the collar and slam his head, again and again, against the blackboard in an explosion of rage and chalk-dust. 'Sit down, boy!' he then would say quietly.

Almost all of us liked Mr McCaughan, one of the younger teachers, who came from mid-Antrim. He had country ways: a ploughman's stride, rounded shoulders, hooped neck, fresh complexion and a hog-caller voice. He was famous among Newington residents for this bark, which rose with his blood pressure into an apoplectic howl. But his actual bite was mild. There was something of the overgrown boy in him. When he taught us to sing 'Roddy McCorley', he was beside himself with enthusiasm. 'They came with vengeance in their eyes,' he howled in his rather good baritone, his eyes flashing vengefully, his cane whistling past our ears as he conducted his young choir. His favourite song, which he insisted upon us singing with near-demented fervour, was 'God save Ireland, cried the hero; God save Ireland cried them all!' We came close to incontinence in our mirth, by simply watching his expression as he roared to make the windows rattle. I think he sometimes saw us as his pals, and he therefore took it badly when a large boy, nicknamed 'Buckie', hurled an inkwell at Mr McCaughan's head, drawing blood.

'What'd you do that for, Buckie?' we asked him in the playground lavatory afterwards, as we pinched the ends of our foreskins, ballooning them with trapped urine, then releasing it in great high squirts that often reached the top of the lavatory wall, and occasionally went over it.

'Ach, he deserved it. He was going to start picking on me again,' Buckie said.

The man who taught me best of all was 'Bob' McCreeve, a burly, no-nonsense teacher with a deep gravelly voice. It had been rumoured – not only by my brother Colm – that Mr McCreeve had sewn pennies into his punishment strap. Probably because I always had a desire to please him, I never once felt the weight of it. But it creaked ominously when he wagged it casually in the air above our heads as we practised our copperplate writing, recited 'The Boy Stood on the Burning Deck', or drank our Welfare State milk from half-pint bottles with cardboard tops. He never got excited, or lost his temper, or over-indulged us with his praise. He was one of those rare instructors whose combined exudations of force and warmth commanded, and was granted, instant respect. When my mother died, he didn't say a word. He simply gave my shoulder a gentle squeeze when passing my desk one morning a week or so after her burial.

During my mother's prolonged spell in hospital, some rather serious people came to stay for short periods. I knew, though I can't recall precisely how I knew, that they were republican activists. Most of the dialogues between them and my father were in Gaelic, of which I then had little understanding. One or two had just been released from Crumlin Road jail where they had been held in the 1940s, either because they had committed subversion or because they might do so, while Britain was at war with Germany. Ponsonby Avenue was their first stop after leaving prison and before returning to their families. One of them was not Irish at all, but Welsh. His

name was Terence Hood, though he preferred to be known as
Tarlach Húd (and indeed wrote under that name for Irish periodicals,
including *An t-Ultach*, the paper my father edited). He was not in
the IRA but was, like a number of Celts from 'across the water'
sympathetic to the IRA's cause. He was a big guffawing man with
jet-black curly hair. I liked him, both for himself and because, in my
mother's absence, he seemed to be pleasantly distracting company for
my father, whether in playing chess or conversing in Gaelic, which
the Welshman spoke with great fluency. One of his triumphs was
to teach me to say '*Llanfairpwllgwyngyllgogerychwyrndrobwllantysiliogo-
gogoch*', a Welsh mouthful meaning 'St Mary's Church in the hollow
of white hazel near a rapid whirlpool and the Church of St Tysilio
near the red cave.' I cannot remember how long Tarlach Húd
stayed with us. But I do know that he left our house for the last
time, wearing a new suit with a flower in the button-hole, on the
morning he married a pretty Irish woman. While they were on
honeymoon, sweet-toothed Brendan, who had already outwitted
the bridegroom at chess, tracked down the remains of the wedding-
cake to a biscuit tin. To this day, my brother is haunted (though I
think that is not quite the right word) by the thought that the cake
he secretly polished off 'may have been set aside to celebrate a
possible product of the marriage'.

After our mother's death, Colm and I had night terrors. His took
the form of fierce shouts and sleepwalking. Mine included strange
delusions, among them a conviction that the haloed Madonna
shimmering above my bed in moonlight from the window, was the
true, living face of my mother. I have no recollection of the
symptoms that may have been visible in Brendan. He probably
went, as my father would have said, 'into his shell'. Or perhaps he
did not quite understand what was going on. On the evening my
mother's body was brought home, to be displayed in her coffin in
the front parlour, Bobby Storey, my father's Randalstown friend,
who was a schoolteacher, addressed Brendan with all the gentleness
that his gruff nature could muster.

'Will you miss your mammy, Brendan?'

'No.'

'Ach, and why not?'

'She'll be coming back.'

Most of the people who were there to pay their respects, turned their heads away. Cheeks trembled. Bobby Storey murmured to my father: 'Ach, he's too young to realize . . .'

The sight of my mother's corpse did not disturb me unduly, even when I was lifted up to enable me to kiss her marble-cold forehead and wonder at the blanched and rigid lips that had once kissed my cuts and bruises and said, 'Come here, Cahal óg!' It was not my first dead body. Three or four years earlier, we had been on holiday in the wilds of Donegal. An old woman known to my father had died, and we made a quick, respectful visit. She was stretched out on her bed under the thatch, not much more than skin and bone in her burial clothes. A rosary was twisted around her yellow, gnarled fingers. Cotton-wool protruded mysteriously from her ears and nostrils. But what excited me most were the pennies on her eyes (to keep them closed, I later learned). I made a greedy grab for these coins. Mild consternation followed and I was escorted from the room. But it never put me off viewing corpses. And although my hand's contact with my mother's cold, rigidly entwined fingers told me that things were bad, I quickly revived in the exhilarating blur of tobacco smoke, whiskey fumes, wood varnish, and the whiff of lavender and rose water given off by gently keening women. It wasn't like the great wakes I have been to in Donegal, where a definite party spirit prevails and mourners sing songs, not all of them dirges. But my mother's wake, or what I have retained of it, was an agreeably social affair where reminiscence would thread its way around the room, now moistening cheeks, then bubbling over in mirth, stitching us all together into an easy, appreciative relationship with the dead woman as the candles beside her coffin burned down, converting their molten tears to coagulum.

The funeral went to Milltown cemetery at the top of Falls Road, which always has been Belfast's main coffin route (the Protestant dead had their own cemetery on the same road, but opposite

Milltown). I was familiar with the landmarks on the way: a flour mill, a textile factory, a public baths, a hospital, various churches; symbols of sustenance, protection, healing and purification that one hopes to enjoy as one progresses from ontogenesis to oblivion. If you stood today on the roof of one of the Royal Victoria Hospital buildings, you would have a fine view of the hospital's 80-acre site and of the city beyond, ringed by those dark, blue-green hills. One could imagine oneself to be at the bleeding hub of two concentricities: an outer territory where citizens are prone to hate and attack one another; and an inner one where professional rectitude is applied to restoring the damage. And you would find it hard not to despair of man's inability to learn from his injuries. As H. L. Mencken once observed, 'The aim of medicine is surely not to make men virtuous; it is to safeguard and rescue them from the consequences of their vices.' But even the medical excellence practised within the bleeding hub is no safeguard.

The report of the funeral was in the *Irish News*, short and rather formal.

The funeral of Mrs Mary McCrystal, wife of Mr Cathal McCrystal, of 53 Ponsonby Avenue, Belfast, the well-known Gaelic scholar took place from the Holy Family Church to Milltown Cemetery on Saturday.

A lady of charming disposition, she was held in the highest esteem, and her passing at an early age has caused deep sorrow among a wide circle of friends. Sympathy with her husband and three little boys will be extended by all.

Gaelic League bodies in the city and from other parts of the North were represented, particularly those associated with the Feis Bheal Feirsde [Belfast Gaelic festival], and also the medical and teaching professions.

I know now, though I did not in those early Ponsonby Avenue years, that my father had been preoccupied with my mother's illness, with the stresses imposed by the blackout and with the losses of those whose remains he had been obliged to identify at O'Kane's in Donegall Street. One entire family, the Flynns – longtime friends

– was wiped out by a direct hit on their house in Lincoln Avenue. Many bombed citizens were completely unidentifiable. 'It was all guesswork,' he said later. 'There were pieces of bodies stuck to the [overhead] tram wires. There were fingers in the gutter, bits of arms and legs and brains all over the place. You couldn't work out who they belonged to.' He also had his myriad commitments: his job, his columns for the *Irish News*, his Gaelic League meetings in Belfast and Dublin (where he rubbed shoulders, off and on, with Sean T. O'Kelley, a pioneer in the Gaelic League – and in the early Sinn Féin – who was to become first President of the Irish Republic in 1945). In 1943, the year before my mother died, he was deeply immersed in organizing the League's fiftieth anniversary, as well as mourning the death of Winifred Carney, a former solicitor's clerk from Bangor, who went on to organize the atrociously treated Irish millworkers in 1912 and 1913, becoming a friend and colleague of James Connolly, the Irish labour leader and insurgent. It was she who typed the 1916 Easter Proclamation for Connolly and Pearse, and was interned in Dublin's Mountjoy Prison for her part in the Rising. Returning to Belfast, she married George McBride, a Protestant handbag manufacturer who, in his widowhood, was to visit us often in Ponsonby Avenue for years afterwards.

My father continued to churn out articles for a Dublin socialist magazine in which he would bemoan (among other things) a tendency among some socialists to lose their fire on achieving office, municipal and otherwise.

The only way to accelerate progress [towards 'decent legislation'] is simply to observe the fact that we are Socialists, which means that we have no interest in hobnobbing flunkyism while men seek work, machines lie idle and the vitality of the world is going to waste.

He was also a chess addict in those years. Occasionally, he would arrive home with champion chess players to challenge Brendan who, inscrutable as ever, was checkmating the world at six, to my father's evident delight.

I have never considered Charles McCrystal to have been other than a devoted and responsible father. But he was a man who relied shamelessly on women to perform the tasks that otherwise would have impinged on his extramural activities. His wife dead, he did his best for us, I'm sure. He tried to divert us with pet mice and freshly hatched chickens. The mice, housed in a cardboard box placed over the outside lavatory, chewed their way through and dropped, one by one, into a watery grave. Cats ate the chickens. One cat was quite mad and attacked my irate father, who, for once closing his eyes to Cowper, promptly despatched it with a hurling-stick (the Irish equivalent to a hockey-stick). We got a small dog, a fluffy black-and-white Donegal collie. It was stolen. We got another, a fox terrier. It went madder than the cat. Neighbours helped whenever they could. In time, the weight of mourning slid slowly from us, and we took advantage of the reduction in parental supervision.

We risked drowning by skating on the frozen surface of a static water tank on a smaller 'wastey' across Duncairn Gardens. We raided the orchards of the houses beside the Waterworks, sold lead, buying bagfuls of broken biscuits with the proceeds. We exchanged empty jam-jars for cinema seats in the Lyceum ('the Lykey'), the Capitol ('the Cappy') and the Duncairn ('the Dunky'). Before trams were replaced by trolley-buses, we placed pennies on the line to be squashed, knowing that it did not invalidate their worth. Having learned to play a few 'Moore's Melodies', I stopped attending piano lessons (who would supervise my practising at home?). With sullen reluctance, we went to Irish dance lessons at a house in Eia Street, a quarter of a mile away, but were withdrawn after Colm put a hatchet through a sofa, accidentally-on-purpose. In summer, we clung to the backs of moving lorries. In winter, we turned part of Atlantic Avenue into an ice-rink, causing the elderly to fall down and bus drivers to rage. Looking back, I recognize that we McCrystal brothers were beginning to develop a certain reputation.

My father must have noticed, for he began to employ live-in servants. We didn't call them servants. We called them housekeepers.

They were not a great success. The first was from County Cavan, just south of the Irish border. Her name was Eileen and she came to us highly recommended by my Uncle Frank Slevin, Aunt Molly's husband. She could not have been more than eighteen. Eileen, I believe, gave less of herself to us than to American GIs stationed in Belfast. She was said to be 'flighty'. But she was good enough to provide me with my first sexual arousal. When she had performed her domestic chores, she would tuck us into bed and kiss us good-night. There were two or three occasions when, in warmer mood, she lay down beside me, pressed my head against her skinny chest and sang into my ear:

> Put your arms around me, honey, hold me tight.
> Huddle up and cuddle up with all your might . . .

She smelt of soapflakes and flour and essences too mysterious for me to define. On witnessing my excitement, Eileen would laugh, jump up and leave the room, singing on her way downstairs and out the front door, to pick up the latest tune from her latest American date. She left Ponsonby Avenue hurriedly, taking with her some of our family stores of tea and sugar. She had been huddled up and cuddled up once too mightily, and got herself pregnant.

Our second housekeeper was more devoted to booze. I think her name was Florence. She was in her early forties, with long black hair and a mournful expression – 'a face as long as a Lurgan spade', my Aunt Molly said. I vividly recall us returning from the two-week summer holiday to find the poor woman in bed, blue in the face and semi-comatose. There was an empty bottle of methylated spirits by her bedside. My father couldn't wake her. Each time he shouted, 'Are you all right?' her eyes would open briefly, roll upwards and close again. Again our stores were depleted; Florence had pawned the family linen and other valuables. She was followed by the most extraordinarily terrifying woman I ever have known. Her name was Murphy, and there was something seriously wrong with her mind. She was, I suppose, in her fifties (my poor father seemed, without much supporting evidence, to have seized hold of the notion that the older they were the steadier they were). She had bad ankles and a worse temperament. A spinster, she nevertheless preferred to be addressed as 'Mrs Murphy'. As with a number of unpartnered Catholic women – and indeed men – in Northern Ireland, she derived pleasure from undermining the sense of security of children placed temporarily in her care. I do not know why this should be, or how common it is, or if it is a recognized syndrome. I can only suppose cruelty does play a part in love, that by causing a child to doubt a bond with one person, you can enhance your own relationship with him, as a more reliable source of love and affection. Probably it is an unconscious act. Those who do it tend to scoff at the parental indignation, claiming a harmless joke. Murphy, though, was no joke. One afternoon, arriving home from school, we were told to wash our faces, polish our shoes and put on our Sunday-best clothes. She pointed to a large Gladstone bag. 'I've packed what else you'll need. You're going to an orphanage,' she said briskly and matter-of-factly. We set up a great howl. We wanted our father . . . She had no *right* . . . We weren't *going* with her.

'Your daddy already knows,' she said savagely. 'Hurry up and get ready. We've a bus to catch.'

We scrubbed and sobbed. It couldn't be true. She twisted an ear. 'Hurry up,' she insisted. We must have made a sorry picture stumbling beside her down Ponsonby Avenue, tears tripping us. People stared. A neighbour hurried across the street.

'Mrs Murphy, what's wrong with those children?' she asked.

Murphy shuffled past her, shrugging resignedly. 'They're an ungrateful lot, and me taking them on a picnic and all.' Which turned out to be true: the Gladstone bag contained sandwiches and a flask of tea.

It was Murphy who made our second dog mad by banging its head against the backyard wall. The yard was her favourite theatre of war. On winter nights, when the notion seized her, she would force the three of us to strip naked and wash from a bucket outside the kitchen window. I can only assume the object of such cruelty was to preserve our upstairs bathroom from splashed floors and wet towels, and preserve herself from having to clear up afterwards. One frosty dusk, Mr Donnelly the dentist, whose surgery on Duncairn Gardens overlooked our yard, happened to glance out and saw us shivering in the buff. Appalled, he alerted my father when he arrived home, and the wretched woman was sent packing. My warmest memory of her is of her hopping around a room, her face contorted with pain, after Brendan lifted a broomstick and walloped the witch on the ankles with it. There was nothing for it but to send us to boarding school.

Nevertheless, Ponsonby Avenue continued to be my home until I got married in 1958. I have always felt an allegiance to it, even long after I had moved away and sank new roots. It was from there my mother's remains were removed to Milltown Cemetery. And it was to Ponsonby Avenue that my stepmother came to live more than two years later.

The street is predominantly Catholic now; one of the many unwelcome and unwholesome effects of the Troubles being that mixed neighbourhoods no longer exist in certain parts of the city. My father preferred it when it was more evenly integrated; when Protestants and Catholics said 'Good morning' to one another on Sunday mornings, on their way to their separate places of worship. Not very many years ago, just before he too left the Ponsonby Avenue house for the last time, he talked about how the Newington neighbourhood had been an example to the rest of Belfast. 'Do you remember the Unionist candidate coming into the street at election time to address us from the back of a lorry? All the same old rant about King and country and loyalty, and his rival being a servant of Rome. Bob [a Protestant neighbour] gave me such an ashamed look that I felt sorry for him.' Later, he said: 'I often think what a remarkable thing it is that Newington [school] produced so many boys who went on to make names for themselves.' And indeed many did do well: Denis McAlindon, a brilliant scholar and linguist who joined the British Diplomatic Service; Vincent Hanna, the journalist and broadcaster (and lawyer); Frank Greene, for years the nation's weather man; Bernard MacLaverty and – from the northern edge of the parish – Brian Moore, another award-winning novelist, now living in California. Many of my school chums became doctors, dentists, pharmacists, teachers, hi-tech printers, priests, lawyers, businessmen – all now well-versed in the ways of the wider world. Recalling my father's remark, I wonder if, for all his unshakeable socialism, my father wasn't expressing pride in the fact that 'Newington' had consigned so many to the bourgeoisie. Within a few streets from us, two Protestant lads grew up, unaware of the even greater fame that would engulf them: Kenneth Branagh, the actor, and James Galway, the flautist.

Charles McCrystal remained 'working-class'. He used to underline this by signing most of his Dublin magazine articles 'Plebeian'. Such was his intellect and energy, he could have become almost anything he wished – other than a mathematician or a musician. He never made the claim, as some do, that his religion impeded his preferment, even though I knew that it undoubtedly had done so. What held him back? One might answer: history's enclosure – a surrender to the ghetto mentality. But that might not be right. The 'ghetto mentality' is something he continually railed against. Yet the break-free opportunities he was offered – Aberdeen, Dublin, the Gold Coast – were grasped tentatively or not at all. He was all for change and experimentation, yet I have often wondered if he was avoiding fresh environments in which his deeply held beliefs and commitments might run the risk of being diluted or weakened by distractions alien to his quiet mission in life, however imprecisely that may be defined.

In the mid-1970s, when I was in Ireland on a magazine assignment, I picked him up and we went for one of our favourite hikes up Cave Hill, the dramatic escarpment overlooking most of Belfast. We ascended via a limestone gully called the Sheep's Path, where he paused and, looking along the gully, said: 'I wonder where the water went.' After the war, Colm and Brendan and I frequently accompanied my father on walks here. Water tumbled over the limestone pebbles into little pools the size of fruit-bowls. Cupping his hand, my father would drink, and pronounce it 'cool, clear, unadulterated, crystalline water'. We always responded with the same joke: '*Mc*Crystaline water!' But now the spring – and the joke – had dried up.

I went back with him to Ponsonby Avenue, where he rummaged in his bookshelves and handed me a slim volume entitled *Why You Should Be A Socialist*, by John Strachey. It was published by Victor Gollancz Ltd., in the year my mother died, and in the short interval between the death of the British humorist Heath Robinson and the lifting of the British wartime blackout. It asked: 'Who rules in any given community? The answer is, those people rule who own the industries and land of the country. This is a fundamental political truth. It is only on the basis of this truth that one can talk sense about politics.'

My father took the book from me, flipped over some pages and said, 'There!', as he handed it back to me. This is what I read:

Imagine a country in which a certain group of men owned the entire water supply. Would not this group of 'water-supply-owners' rule that country? Could not a child tell you that so long as they managed to hold on to the water supply, they could dictate to the rest of the people? It might be that the rest of the people had the right to elect their rulers. But the owners of the water supply would say, 'If you do not elect us, we will cut off the water.' Therefore the people's right to elect whom they pleased to rule them would be, in practice, almost worthless.

Strachey was hypothesizing about a situation – the privatization of the country's water resources – that seemed, at the time of writing, so extreme a prospect as to defy the imagination. It was, for the then Labour Movement, and for many outside it, a prospect capable of contemplation only as an absurdity of Heath Robinson proportions, in much the same way that we today might ridicule the idea of privatized air.

I closed Strachey and was about to return it to the shelves. But he stopped me. 'Keep it,' he said. 'It'll remind you of the good socialist you were, before London corrupted you. Regard it as a souvenir!' His words prompted me to recall aloud my teenage years, travelling to loyalist east Belfast to view the Soviet film *Battleship Potëmkin* in a little darkened hall rented by the Communist Party; and reading the *Daily Worker* and being so enraged by the 'exploitation of the masses' that I was in a mood to commit murder. My father nodded and smiled. 'Oh well, when you're young you want to kill all round you. When you get older you wouldn't hurt a fly. That's life, eh?' He started to stuff his pipe with the Balkan Sobranie I had brought him. The tremor in his hand quietened as he put a match to the bowl. 'Mark my words,' he said. 'They'll privatize water yet. You think I'm joking? There'll always be men who'll enrich themselves on the elements of nature. Water's next.'

He sounded uncharacteristically downcast; like a man whose mission in life had been frustrated. Of course he was getting on a bit by then. He was no longer in demand. The days when he could hypnotize a classroom of Celtic Studies students at Queen's University – through the medium of Gaelic – had long gone. His friends were dead, or not far from being so. Russia was a disgrace; China not worth talking about. I think he knew a united Ireland would not occur in his lifetime.

Charles McCrystal was not a communist, though he patronized the party's bookshop near the city centre. He took the *Daily Worker* and, less frequently, the magazine *Soviet Weekly*. He was chairman of the Northern Ireland–Soviet Friendship Society, which many believed to be a cover for subversive acts. He had, I suppose, one of the strongest senses of what was fair and unfair of any person I have known. Once, after I had started attending St Malachy's College, on Antrim Road, we had a house visit from the parish priest (or 'administrator', as he was called). His reverence was alarmed to find the *Soviet Weekly* on a table directly beneath an illuminated picture of the Sacred Heart. He expressed alarm. My father held up a hand and said, very softly: 'Please leave, Father. Do come again, but remember to mind your own business.' His reverence quickly took his leave of us.

My father was irritated, though not surprised. The Catholic clergy had been on the warpath against socialism long before the Russian Revolution. Once when I was a young teenager and passionately attached to the idea of socialist revolution, he handed me a book which he thought I should read, even though, like him, I would probably disagree with the sentiments expressed in it. The book, *Socialism and the Workingman*, was written by a Catholic priest and published in Dublin and Belfast in 1911. It warns of a 'dangerous feeling of discontent' among the masses in Ireland, and 'a smouldering fire of dissatisfaction' being fanned into flame by 'social agitators'. It points to 'a duty to put an end to the controversy by defining what Catholics ought to think'. And it quotes the words of Leo XIII, 'the Workingman's Pope', on the need to preserve the Christian spirit 'against the contagion of Socialism'. No wonder my grandmother had knelt before my father and begged him not to stand as a socialist parliamentary candidate. I think it was a year after this minor confrontation with the parish priest that I first delved into James Joyce.

'Start with *Portrait of the Artist as a Young Man*,' my father had urged.

Dante broke in angrily:

– If we are a priest-ridden race we ought to be proud of it! They are the apple of God's eye. *Touch them not*, says Christ, *for they are the apple of My eye.*

– And can we not love our country then? asked Mr Casey. Are we not to follow the man [Charles Stewart Parnell] that was born to lead us?

– A traitor to his country! replied Dante. A traitor, an adulterer! The priests were right to abandon him. The priests were always the true friends of Ireland.

– Were they faith? said Mr Casey.

. . . Dante bent across the table and cried to Mr Casey:

– Right! Right! They were always right! God and Morality and religion come first.

Mrs Dedalus, seeing her excitement, said to her:

– Mrs Riordan, don't excite yourself answering them.

– God and religion before everything! Dante cried. God and religion before the world.

Religion has been disturbing the peace of Ireland for a long time, I remember thinking to myself.

The minor confrontation with the visiting priest had a more ominous sequel. In 1955, when I had not long left college, my father joined an all-Ireland 'cultural delegation' to Moscow and other Soviet cities. In retrospect, it seems an insignificant matter. And, for a short time even then, it appeared to cause little concern. The Belfast newspapers had reports that carried no hint of the row that would ensue. The *Irish News* account was unremarkable, typically referring to 'Northern Ireland' as the 'Six Counties'.

A party of six Irishmen – two from the Six Counties and the others from the Republic – who travelled to Heysham last night on their way to Russia as guests of the Soviet Government, were joined at the steamer shed by a seventh man who declared that he was travelling to Russia in a 'personal capacity'.

The man, who gave his name as Robert McKinstry, architect, of Rugby Road, Belfast, was not on the original list of six invited by the Irish–Soviet Friendship Society to spend a month in Russia.

The two Belfastmen in the party, which leaves London by air today, are Mr John Boyd, writer and broadcaster, and Mr Cathal McCrystal, a leading figure in the Irish language movement.

The other members of the party are Mr James Plunkett Kelly, the dramatist; Mr Anthony Cronin, associate editor of 'The Bell'; Mr Liam MacGabhann, Dublin journalist, and Mr Sean de Burca, sculptor.

The party plan to visit Asiatic and Caucasian areas in Russia.

Mr McCrystal said he would write an account of his visit for several Gaelic publications. He intended to study the cultural background of the minority groups in the Soviet.

It did not take very long for the scandalized Catholic bishops to stir things up. My father's argument, that cultural exchanges (with however unattractive a power) were a thoroughly good thing and that nobody should stick his/her head in the sand, did not prevail among all his peers, or many priests of his acquaintance. His promise, in the course of an interview with the *Belfast Telegraph*, to write an objective account of the trip for several Gaelic publications, was ill-received. His 'cultural' friends were scandalized. The bishop of Down and Connor, who also happened to be a slum landlord, harangued him from the pulpit of St Patrick's in Donegall Street, a church my father occasionally visited. Priests crossed the street – and, I like to imagine, themselves – rather than greet the tainted delegate to Moscow.

Some of the stories published on his return suggested that my father was either naive about Soviet Communism or somewhat disingenuous in his response to it. I cannot say. Perhaps he was both, or perhaps neither. In the annals of the Cold War, 1955 does not stand out, the most memorable events of the year behind the Iron Curtain being the formation of the Warsaw Pact and the explosion of a Soviet, one-megaton hydrogen bomb. The crushing of the Hungarian revolution was still one year off.

ARMS AND THE POLICE

A member of an Irish delegation visiting the Soviet Union said on Moscow radio last night that he was 'disappointed' to find Moscow policemen carrying guns.

The delegate, Mr Charles McCrystal, is a member of the Irish party which has been visiting Russia. In his recorded talk he said: 'Coming as I do from Northern Ireland, where the fact that policemen carry revolvers is criticized, I was disappointed to find that Moscow policemen also carry guns.

'I expressed myself forcibly on this aspect of Soviet security, pointing out that as the emphasis of the U.S.S.R. is on peace, therefore all displays of this nature should be abandoned.'

He was definitely of the opinion that the Soviet people were pursuing peace with an 'almost fanatical zeal'. [British news item]

The Hungarian revolution and the brutal Soviet response to it was not quite a manifestation of the Russian people's 'almost fanatical zeal' for peace. Reading the above item today, the phrase has a ridiculous ring to it, dropping as it did from my father's lips. For one thing, the Soviet people's 'zeal' was for staying alive and out of Siberia. For another, it was not in my father's nature to espouse fanaticism about anything. I suspect he may have had to slip in the bit about the Soviet zeal for peace as a trade-off for his observations about armed policemen. And it seems fairly obvious he was using the armed police in Moscow as a stick with which to beat the armed police in Belfast. Such are the intricacies of the propaganda game. He returned to the subject on returning home to face journalists' questions. These do not seem to have been either particularly probing or overtly offensive. The fairest treatment he received in the press was from the Protestant (and Unionist-aligned) *Belfast Telegraph*.

POLICE CARRY GUNS SO HE PROTESTED
GAELIC LEAGUER IS BACK FROM MOSCOW

Mr Cathal McCrystal, chairman of the Ulster branch of the Gaelic League, who returned to Belfast today after his controversial visit to Russia, said he was disappointed to find that Moscow police carried revolvers and he immediately lodged a protest with the authorities.

He was told that it was a Russian tradition for the police to carry a revolver which, it was believed, acted as a greater threat to burglars and other criminals than a baton.

Mr McCrystal then asked if he could have a copy of the crime figures for the city, and was told that none was published as 'the people are not interested in statistics of that nature'.

Mr McCrystal's overall impression of the visit was that Russia was so vast and life so varied – 'like a kaleidoscope', was his description – that it would take him at least three weeks at home to 'digest' it all.

He was impressed by the friendliness of its people, by the easy relationships that exist between executives and workers, and by the great strides that have been made in equipping industry with modern machinery.

He told a 'Belfast Telegraph' reporter that all the people he met during the trip were contented with the present form of government.

Nowhere, he said, had he found evidence of any serious interference with religion and pointed out that no fewer than 100 orthodox churches were functioning in Moscow and its suburbs.

'Religion is not progressing, but it is holding its own,' commented Mr McCrystal.

Of the Russian women, Mr McCrystal said: 'They are worked very hard.'

All day, he said, women were engaged shovelling snow off the streets of Moscow. In the offices of 'Pravda', the Communist Party newspaper, the compositors and 50 per cent. of the journalists are women.

Mr McCrystal interested himself mainly in the language and culture of the people. He found that in states like Georgia the people used mainly their own language, took part in their own folk dances and played their own games and regarded the Russian language, dances and games as only secondary.

What did he miss most of all? – people whistling. In Russia, explained Mr McCrystal, whistling was considered to be a sign of bad public manners, while linking arms by couples was also frowned upon.

While there Mr McCrystal was invited to write an article giving a pen picture of Belfast for a geographical journal, and another explaining the structure of the Gaelic League and the technique used to revive the Irish language. For each of these he was paid the equivalent of £20.

Referring to the criticism that had been made of his visit by members of the Gaelic League, Mr McCrystal said he expected the next meeting of the Ulster branch of the league to be a stormy one, but 'the prospect does not bother me'.

But I think the actual occasion – his forced resignation from the League branch he had chaired for more than twenty years – did bother him. He was banned from writing for the *Irish News* ever again. But he either maintained a straight face or smiled at everyone, and continued to read his prayers – quite ostentatiously – at Sunday Mass, from a black Missal published in the language of the steppes and the Godless. Coming across it recently, I noticed it was actually published by the Pontifical Russian College in Rome. Within its leaves were a card imprinted with the Sistine Madonna, and an old leaflet containing a Gaelic 'prayer for Holy Year', published in Belfast in 1950.

Eventually, James Plunkett Kelly – the Dublin novelist James Plunkett – wrote *The Circus Animals*, an amusing, fictionalized account of the Soviet trip. But the controversy was less amusing at the time. The affair was heavily publicized, my father being quoted in British newspapers as saying : 'Friends have ceased speaking to me,' and 'Other friends just pass me by in the street.' I don't think he was terribly surprised at being criticized for making the trip across the Cold War tundra, but he was taken aback by the critics' vindictiveness. 'Gift-Bearing Muscovites', declared the *Irish News*, in one of several digs at its former columnist. 'Went to Russia – now he's shunned', announced the *News of the World*. However, none of our neighbours shunned him, or betrayed by look or gesture that they were scandalized. They observed, I would guess, a man who had been attacked by powerful forces and had not been reduced by the experience.

I asked him at the time why he wasn't furious about his treatment. He chuckled into his pipe-stem and gave me a look that was both amused and disbelieving. 'Did I never tell you about the man with two brains? Sure?'

Then followed the story of the death of Conor MacNessa, king of Ulster two millennia ago. It was MacNessa's custom in battle to cut off the head of an opposing chieftain, open the skull, extract the brain, cover it in lime, roll it into a ball and dry-shrink it. He had quite a few of these trophies. One of them – the brain of a Leinster king – was stolen and MacNessa went after the thief. But the latter, using a sling, shot the brain-ball at the Ulster king's head, where it lodged in his skull. His physicians cautioned against removing it and MacNessa recovered. 'Avoid violent exercise and, above all, don't excite yourself,' the physicians said – or words to that effect. But on learning from a druid that an innocent man called Jesus Christ was at that very time being persecuted in far-off Jerusalem, the king flew into a rage at such unfairness. Such was his fury that the brain-ball popped out of his skull, followed closely by the brain of MacNessa himself. 'That was the end of him,' my father said. 'If only he'd controlled his fiery Ulster temper!'

So my father kept his head, beamed at everyone, and earned the sympathy of an impressively large number of Protestant friends, most of them socialists. He had brought the Catholic hierarchy to a point of incandescence, but had not disgraced his family (his mother was dead by then); he had been treated unfairly, yet was at ease with his conscience; he was admired by many working-class Catholics and well regarded by members of the Protestant community. To some extent, at least, his mission – to have a number of Catholics and a number of Protestants to think as one – seemed to be on course. Not that my father would have put it that way. Although he had great faith in his convictions, he had no exaggerated view of his ability to imbue others with them. Once or twice in my presence, he quoted what Goethe had written in the twilight of his life.

> The masters' works when I behold,
> I see achievements manifold.
> But when my own work I review,
> I see what I have failed to do.

6

LES ENFANTS PERDUS

Rising today above the Sheep's Path, the newish housing estates, the woods, whins and scree, is Cave Hill's highest point; a steep outcrop which, over the two centuries since the Napoleonic Wars, has been referred to as 'Napoleon's Nose'. The caves are the nostrils, deep, dark and dank. For as long as anyone can remember, generations of children have climbed into these orifices and shouted things that came most readily to them. Depending on whether the shouters were of the Protestant-loyalist persuasion or the Catholic-republican variety, the words echoed were generally either 'Fuck the Pope!' or 'Up the rebels!' – infantile war whoops that did little more than reverberate within the emperor's stony sinuses. They neither offended His Holiness nor gave succour to the 'rebels', who were in any case well out of earshot.

'Napoleon's Nose' is as good a place as any from which to sniff the Ulster air. I last went there, alone, in 1996 when the slopes of the mountain were frost-firm. The natural light was failing by the time I reached the big lower cave and turned to face a city again huddling in the uncertainty of the 'peace process', following the IRA's bombing of Canary Wharf in London. Office windows gleamed far below. The communities along both shores of Belfast's long sea-lough were glowing in the dusk. Noise from road traffic grumbled upwards from the M2 motorway. Noise from arriving or departing aircraft tumbled down from low cloud above my head. With the deserted caves at my back, I contemplated my father's particular associations with the mountain.

In 1948, I was twelve years old, and my father was again immersed in controversy. As chairman of the Wolfe Tone Commemoration Committee, he was looking for a suitable place in which to hold a *ceilidh* – a kind of Celtic 'knees-up' – in celebration of the 150th anniversary of the United Irishmen's rebellion. The search gave him the opportunity he had been dreaming of. Because he had striven for much of his life towards a brotherhood of Catholics and Protestants (preferably under an all-Irish roof, rather than a British one), and because 1798 had briefly epitomized this ideal, he applied to Belfast Corporation for permission to stage the *ceilidh* in the Ulster Hall, a downtown venue regarded as one of Belfast's Unionist citadels. It was like presenting a red rag to a bull – except that the rag was green. The application was at first granted, and then, after invitation cards had been printed, suddenly withdrawn, following a specially called meeting of the Unionist-controlled estates committee.

Looking back, it's not really hard to see why. Belfast was flooded with pro-nationalist propaganda: elegies to Wolfe Tone and long-dead hunger-strikers, such as Terence MacSwiney, a former Mayor of Cork. A 'Wolfe Tone Commemoration' booklet had a garish front cover, depicting an Irish soldier standing on the British union flag and hoisting the Irish tricolour. It devoted a full page to MacSwiney's poem, 'A Call to Arms', and carried articles that encouraged youth to 'march down freedom's road'. It also contained a rather revealing article by my father, entitled 'Fenianism', the name of a nineteenth-century nationalist movement seeking the establishment of an independent Irish republic – a name derived from *Fianna*, a band of Irish warriors of the second and third centuries AD, proving (if proof be needed) how long tags and symbols survive in Ireland. The article said:

My earliest association with the word 'Fenianism' was when seven years of age and on my way home from school. I was stopped by a group of boys who demanded to know if I were a Fenian. I took to my heels and escaped without answering, for I knew that the word 'Fenian' was synonymous with 'Catholic'. And thus it has ever been. In spite of what

Protestant patriots have contributed to free our country from foreign domination, the enemy has succeeded in making 'Sinn Féiner', 'Rebel' and 'Fenian' terms of contempt, to be associated with one section of the community in order to alienate it from the other. These tactics not only succeeded in separating still further Catholics from Protestants, but actually caused a breach between Catholics themselves. The fiction of a Rebel as an uncouth, irresponsible person was fostered to such an extent that so-called respectable Catholics were ashamed to be identified with the various movements for freedom. Some of these people eventually took the stage to become prime actors in the national drama – after peeping furtively from the wings to see how successful the play was going to be.

The sectarian bullying he referred to in this personal account continues. As a boy, I was instructed by catechists and others that such encounters gave one very few options: either 'deny your religion' and survive physically, or assert it and be damned spiritually. The meaning of this was clear enough. It was far better to suffer, even die, for your faith than to denounce it as a matter of temporary expediency. It is the theme of martyrdom-and-Salvation, and it translated effortlessly into the 'armed struggle' for a united Ireland, justifying suicidal attacks on 'the enemy', hunger-strikes to the death, and, by stretching a point here and there, murder.

'Would it', I asked a priest in my primary school, 'be all right to tell a Protestant gang that you're a Protestant while saying under your breath, "like bricks" or "only joking, God"?' He stared at me meditatively. 'It would not,' he said.

My father took a more pragmatic view. 'Self-sacrifice may be fine if the motive is to avoid betraying somebody. In this case, you're not betraying God because he knows what's really going on.' I found this advice perfectly satisfactory.

In 1948, tens of thousands from the Irish Republic travelled north to join the jamboree celebrating the United Irishmen of 1798. Emotion-filled rallies were held in various parts of Belfast. The city authorities had the jitters. Even though neither the Royal Ulster Constabulary nor the Stormont Ministry of Home Affairs voiced an objection to a commemorative *ceilidh*, the Corporation refused to lift the ban claiming it feared a breach of the peace. The Commemoration Committee sued.

ULSTER HALL WRIT MOVE
If the Court holds that there has been any breach of contract the alternative question of damages may arise. The writ was issued in the names of Mr Cathal McCrystal, Chairman of the Commemoration Committee, and others . . . [1948 news report]

Against many expectations, it won. In granting an injunction against the Corporation, the Lord Chief Justice said he was satisfied that a spirit of tolerance and commonsense would prevail among all citizens. 'It must and will be recognized,' he said, 'that in a free country such as ours, those who observe the law are entitled to have their legal rights recognized and protected by the law as administered in the King's courts . . . I have such belief in the citizens of Belfast that I have no doubt whatever that my confidence will not be misplaced.'

My father, I cannot help thinking, ought to have been happy with this outcome. It rubbed some municipal noses in their own bigotry, opened a Unionist Establishment citadel to Irish nationalist revelry, and showed that the Northern Ireland judiciary was capable of fairness. But he made no effort to reduce the acerbity of the many speeches he delivered to large audiences after the High Court victory and the successful *ceilidh*. Some of them seemed to sail close to the wind.

UNITY OF IRELAND
Mr Cathal McCrystal, chairman of the Belfast '98 Commemoration Committee, welcoming the gathering, said that the next time they came together it would be to take control of Belfast and to celebrate the unity of Ireland. Referring to the injunction secured against Belfast Corporation in connection with the Ulster Hall, Mr McCrystal wondered if it would not have been better to obtain an injunction against the Northern Govern-

ment to restrain them from trying to create a revolutionary situation in Belfast.

He wished, he said, to pay a special tribute to that body of Protestants who were already forming the hard core for the final fight for freedom. [News item]

Belfast became increasingly nervous.

I vividly recall that September week, in which 'Napoleon's Nose' loomed large.

It had been proposed to organize a 1798 commemorative rally on 'Blitz Square' in the heart of the city – the very place where my father and I had once seen the 'Fenian' being kicked to death. But because of the real threat of retaliation by Orange mobs, the police objected, and so did the Minister of Home Affairs. Processions were also forbidden. This gave my father the idea that the rally should be held instead on 'Napoleon's Nose,' on the spot where Wolfe Tone met the leaders of the United Irishmen before the rebellion. The police didn't move to prevent this gathering on a windswept, vertiginous spot. My brothers and I made our own way there, in time to join the rally. There were exaggerated reports of 15,000 rallying there, but it was more like 500, most of them having wound their way up the Sheep's Path, or clambered over the heather from other directions.

After speeches the crowd, mostly composed of young men, sang 'Who fears to speak of Ninety-Eight' and 'A Soldier's Song' led by a piper.

District-Inspector Briggs, Antrim, and six constables had taken up positions on the summit at five p.m. and at 7.30 p.m., when the meeting was due to commence, less than 100 people had gathered. They had climbed the hill by various routes – Sheep's Path, Bellevue, and Ligoniel.

Mr C. McCrystal, Chairman of the Commemoration Committee, who presided, said the ban by the Minister of Home Affairs was an insult to the citizens of Belfast.

When the meeting had concluded and the audience was about to disperse, the sound of bagpipe music was heard far down the hill. A procession of 300 young men and women headed by a colour party carrying the [banned Irish] tricolour and a green flag and accompanied by four pikemen, was observed making the ascent from Cavehill Road direction. A second meeting was held . . . [News item]

I was fired by the atmosphere on that dying-summer evening. High above the nervous city a ring of heavily armed policemen surrounded the pikemen, the flag-bearers, the zealots and the merely curious, Protestants and Catholics, young and not so young, heated by their climb, or their patriotic fervour, or their outright hostility to the whole event – and my father in the thick of them, spouting history to a cold wind. I walked past a couple of twitchy policemen, giving them a grim, your-end-is-nigh look, and stood near the edge of the cliff overlooking the city, my short grey school trousers flapping about my knees under a reddening sky. In my exhilaration, I felt that my father was passing the pike to me; that it was my destiny to lead a future band of United Irishmen which would rid my suffering country of the Saxon foe for ever. I wanted to shake my fist at the stubborn city below and to sing, 'God Save Ireland, cried the hero!', and to make 'them' tremble. But I didn't. Instead, I picked up a small stone and hurled it into the twilight, frightening myself with vertigo.

As children, we had become a bit different from our peers by then. Eighteen months in a southern Irish boarding school had subtly – and temporarily – altered our accents. Secondly, we had a stepmother. Stepmothers were a great rarity back then, certainly in our Belfast neighbourhood. It was she who rescued us from the boarding school.

The boarding school was St Mary's College in Dundalk, a cluttered, peat-smoky market town in County Louth. It wasn't my father's first choice. He at first tried to place us with a convent in Lisburn, closer to home, but the Mother Superior, I believe, formed a bad impression of the McCrystal boys as they smashed the school's tennis balls out of sight while she was discussing boarding arrangements with my father. I am not sure why Dundalk was his next choice; possibly because the Gaelic paper he edited, *An t-Ultach*, was printed there, requiring him to visit the town anyway. As a border town it had – as it has today – a significant number of people who belong to, or ardently support, the IRA. It also had, and still has, quite a few 'travelling people', or 'tinkers', as they formerly were known. Dundalk, like border communities, north and south, was noted for what we today might describe as an 'underclass', and also for its 'cute hoors' – con-artists, cattle smugglers, flash-Harrys who, as my father would say, 'would have the eye out of your head before you could say "Jack Robinson", even if you were wearing goggles'.

'Did I ever tell you', he said – his usual introduction to a long anecdote, 'of the time Bobby Storey and I and another chap were sitting in a Dundalk pub, warming ourselves at a pot-bellied stove over a Guinness and a half-'un [half-glass of whiskey]? Well, in came this big tinkerman with a terrible thirst on him. He went to the bar and said to the curate [barman], "Give us a pint of your best, curate." The curate said, "That'll be ninepence; let's see your money first." "Don't worry yourself, I'll have the money for you soon enough," the tinker said. And with that, he marched up to us and said: "Are ye bettin' men at all?" We wondered what on earth he was up to, but Bobby nodded and said we were indeed. So your man started pulling off his woolly sweater – a big, thick, dirty-looking thing; Bobby swore he could see fleas hopping out of it. The tinkerman held the sweater up and said: "For ten shillings I'll eat that garment. What d'ye say, gentlemen?" We knew we couldn't lose. I put a ten-shilling note on the table. "Each!" said your man. "Ten shillings each!" The curate agreed to hold the thirty shillings. "Give us a bowl and a spoon," the tinker said next. The curate gave him the bowl and the spoon. "Right!" said the tinker, and he dropped his sweater on to the top of the pot-bellied stove. It was nearly red-hot. The sweater shrivelled into a big black cinder. The tinker picked it up, put it in the bowl and crunched it into powder with the spoon. He then proceeded to spoon it into him, washing each mouthful down with my pint, until it was all gone. He got the money, more than enough to get drunk on and buy another second-hand sweater into the bargain.'

The Dundalk college was run by priests belonging to the Marist Fathers, a religious order founded by a Frenchman early in the nineteenth century. It specialized in foreign missions, blunting the appetite of cannibals and being the first to announce the 'true faith' to the Maoris of New Zealand. They employed, I imagine, similar tactics in trying to tame us. I was not desperately unhappy there. At my father's suggestion, I had learned to box in Belfast. I had a weak punch but could duck and weave, and stamp and snort impressively. Consequently I was not bullied. Colm was less content. He missed our mother much more painfully, I think, than did his younger brothers. He also had a stammer, for which he was taunted mercilessly.

But Brendan, who really was far too young to have been sent away from home, must have wondered what he'd done to deserve what he got. This included severe beatings for wetting his dormitory bed. The spectacle of his punishment and that of others his age was quite traumatic for the older boys. But my stoical little brother took the pain and humiliation without flinching very much, his face and knuckles having gone deathly white as he stood in his pink-flannel nightshirt (I had one too), after receiving six strokes of the cane on his buttocks from a sadist in a dog-collar. I watched, trembling, not so much at his pain as in fear of him blubbing dishonourably. Naturally, my impressions of the place have been magnified by time, but to call it a harsh environment is not to overstate things. I was thrashed for accidentally spilling altar wine from a cruet on my first trial as an altar boy. A boy called Daly was expelled for climbing a wall to kiss a town girl. Another boy called Greene fainted outright at the twelfth vicious stroke of the sadist's cane without having shed a tear for the gratification of the man belabouring him.

At night, muffled sobs would break out across the dormitory; by day the cubicles of the school lavatories ('the jacks') resounding to heartrending cries from *les enfants perdus*, while in the junior study hall of an evening, secret monodies dripped into letters home. Even the pupils could be harsh with one another. There was a big lump of a lad from the Irish midlands, whose middle name was, like mine, Mary. Every time he fumbled a catch on the football field, a chorus would go up: 'Mary, Mary, quite contrary!' Usually he grinned and bore it, for he was good-natured and unaggressive. But one afternoon I heard him, alone in the boot-room, weeping over his moniker.

I don't suppose there was anyone he could turn to for relief. The priests expected one to put up with bullying, being (many of them) bullies themselves. I don't believe they showed much concern at what we handed out to three French war refugees who came to board. The French pupils wore very short, tight-fitting, *knitted* trousers, compared with the baggy-to-the-knees garb worn by the rest of us. This, along with their imperfect English singled them out for special treatment by their peers. On one occasion, my brother Colm 'persuaded' one of them to drink a bottle of ink, claiming it was from an Irish vineyard. Some priests, I fear, were a bit suspect in certain ways. There was one who made the rounds of our dormitory hours after lights-out. He was in his early thirties and affable enough, but the boys tended to give him a wide berth, fearing a call to his room. I never heard of anything untoward having happened there, other than the experience of one of my classmates, who told me that the priest had bounced him up and down on his knee, saying, 'Have you ever given any thought to becoming a priest? Ah, I'm sure you must have thought about it sometimes! Would you like a bit of chocolate? Of course you would – you're a good lad. Don't I know your mammy and your daddy well!' I couldn't believe it. This was the priest who seemed to enjoy thrashing boys with a cane while in their pyjamas, and had strange nocturnal wanderings. Occasionally, I had observed him in the darkness of the junior dormitory, slowly and silently wending his way among the beds. One night, I was awakened by a slight movement of my bed. Through half-closed eyes I saw the dark-robed figure merely a few feet away. He seemed to have trouble with his breathing. What appeared to be a white handkerchief fluttered in the vicinity of his waistband. I squeezed my eyes shut, pretending to be asleep. After an interminable minute or so he glided away. Other boys also claimed to have seen him, though a few were certain it was the college ghost.

I cannot say whether the Marist experience strengthened my character, or inflicted harm. Some of my English journalist colleagues who also suffered as prep boarders have assured me that they will never incarcerate their own children thus. One described how an uncle had recently revealed on his death-bed that he had been buggered as a boy by his English headmaster (a Jesuit priest). This victim's nephews, aged nine and eleven, once were called into *their* head's priestly study for a shattering message: 'Your mother's dead. Now get back to your classrooms.' But while it was widely suspected that dreadful abuses occurred in some English public schools, it was rare to have them exposed in the boarding schools of Ireland.

My father could have known nothing about the bizarreries of boarding schools. In any case, he had no alternative to sending us to one. We felt distanced from him, though not abandoned by him. We knew that he loved us. And he was always prompt in his responses to our letters home on college notepaper. Almost invariably, these read: 'Dear Daddy, I hope you are well. I am well. Please send ten shillings for the tuck shop. Your loving son, Cahal óg. P.S. I am working hard.' Recalling the canings, the awful food ('Stickjaw' puddings, black-rimmed bread, rancid butter, dodgy meat and cold gravy), the boils on our necks and rashes on our legs, I like to think that my Dundalk college was the 'Institution' Thackeray visited during his stay in Dundalk while writing *The Irish Sketch Book*. Certainly, the 'arrangement of school business' which he sets out is uncannily reminiscent of the schedule that regulated life at St Mary's.

As Thackeray observes, 'Classics, then, these young fellows do not get. Meat they get but twice a week. Let English parents bear this fact in mind; but that the lads are healthy and happy, anybody who sees them can have no question; furthermore, they are well instructed in a sound practical education – history, geography, mathematics, religion. What a place to know of would this be for many a poor half-pay officer, where he may put his children in all

Hours	Monday, Wednesday and Friday	Tuesday and Thursday	Saturday
6 to 7	Rise, wash, &c.	Rise, wash, &c.	Rise, wash &c.
7 to 7.30	Scripture by the Master, and prayer.	Scripture by the Master, and prayer.	Scripture by the Master, and prayer.
7.30 to 8.30	Reading, History, &c.	Reading, History, &c.	Reading, History, &c.
8.30 to 9	Breakfast	Breakfast	Breakfast
9 to 10	Play	Play	Play
10 to 10.30	English Grammar	Geography	10 to 11, Repetition
10.30 to 11.15	Algebra	Euclid	
11.15 to 12	Scripture	Lecture on principles of Arithmetic	11 to 12, Use of Globes
12 to 12.45	Writing	Writing	12 to 1, Catechism and Scripture
12.45 to 2	Arithmetic at Desks, and Mensuration	Arithmetic at Desks, and Mensuration	
2 to 2.30	Dinner	Dinner	Dinner
2.30. to 5	Play	Play	The remainder of this
5 to 7.30	Spelling, Mental Arithmetic and Euclid	Spelling, Mental Arithmetic and Euclid	day is devoted to exercise till the hour of
7.30 to 8	Supper	Supper	Supper, after which the
8 to 8.30	Exercise	Exercise	boys assemble in the
8.30 to 9	Scripture by the Master and prayer in School-room	Scripture by the Master and prayer in School-room	School-room and hear a portion of Scripture read and explained by the Master.
9	Retire to bed.	Retire to bed.	Retire to Bed.

The sciences of navigation and practical Surveying are taught in the Establishment, also a selection of the Pupils, who have a taste for it, are instructed in the art of Drawing.

Dietary

BREAKFAST – Stirabout and Milk, every Morning.

DINNER – On Sunday and Wednesday, Potatoes and Beef; 10 ounces of the latter to each boy. On Monday and Thursday, Bread and Broth; 1/2lb. of the former to each boy. On Tuesday, Friday, and Saturday, Potatoes and Milk; 2lbs. of the former to each boy.

SUPPER – 1/2lb. of bread with Milk, uniformly, except on Monday and Thursday: on these days, Potatoes and Milk.

confidence that they will be well cared for and soundly educated!'

Almost exactly a hundred years later, we 'healthy and happy' lads would be organized for long walks on Saturday afternoons, sometimes through the Dundalk streets (where we could stop and buy fruit, or dry dates, or a local tooth-rotting confection called 'Peggy's Leg'), and sometimes beyond the confines of the town. I thus got to know bits of Louth's coastline and hinterland. I became friendly with a couple of day-boys who lived in the Cooley Peninsula, an enchanting place a few miles north of Dundalk. On our first summer vacation from boarding school, my father took us to Warrenpoint, a seaside town beyond the peninsula and on the Northern Ireland shore of Carlingford Lough. We boarded the small open passenger ferry across the lough from Warrenpoint to Omeath, on the shore of the Irish Republic, and watched northerners get drunk on southern whiskey. My father hired a horse-drawn jaunting-car to explore the roads of Cooley, a scenically unspoiled peninsula whose mountains are reflected in its encompassing coastal waters. To me, it seemed to pulse with a kind of sacred mystery, though this may have been due to a large, off-road grotto called Calvary, where statues raised martyred eyes in supplication. In the late 1970s, I drove my father back there and we found that little had changed. However, there seemed to be a great number of Belfast accents and mobile homes in and around Omeath. The local people were slightly less affable in greeting strangers than my father had remembered. He attributed it to 'the end of the peasant culture, and about time too'.

In 1991, a few months before he died, I again returned to Cooley, alone, in order to write about an incident that would, I feel sure, have left him pained and confused, had he been alive. The Cooley Peninsula is a triangle bounded by Carlingford Lough, Dundalk Bay and, to the west, a fomenting territory which the British press has nicknamed 'Bandit Country'. I had never associated the peninsula itself with 'bandits' – i.e. IRA terrorists. This fairly remote expanse has been largely ignored by travellers between Belfast and Dublin, though, as I have said, it is popular with summer day-trippers. The main road, on the south side of the mountains, skirts Dundalk Bay before swinging north-east at Rathcor, a patchwork of small fields and barns, cottages, muddy tracks and rough roads stained by cattle. IRA arms dumps have been found in the vicinity.

A few hundred yards further on is a large modern bungalow where a lean, curly-haired farmer, Tom Oliver, lived with his wife Bridie and their seven children. Two months before I arrived, the IRA took Tom Oliver away from here and blew half his head off in a six-bullet 'execution'. The murder of this ordinary farmer achieved something quite unique: it provoked, for the first time in the Republic of Ireland since the Troubles began, an open rebellion by a community in which the IRA had flourished on a mixture of local intimidation and romantic loyalty to a half-understood cause. Two weeks after Tom Oliver's murder, all but a few of the 7,000 people of Cooley attended a rally in the local Gaelic football stadium to support calls for the IRA's removal from the area. Hundreds of people from counties Down and Armagh travelled across the border to add their voices to that of the throng. Southerners from Dublin, Drogheda and even Dundalk itself, where the IRA caroused at night, turned up, swelling the protest to an estimated 8,000 angry souls. At long last, the people felt, they were standing up to those who had killed, maimed, extorted, and generally made ordinary life a misery. It may never be known why Mr Oliver, aged forty-four, died in such brutal circumstances. He had paid his nightly visit to his ailing mother and his mother-in-law, and had driven in his old blue Ford to a field in Rathcor to help one of his cows give birth. On the way, he stopped at a neighbouring farmer's house to borrow 'pullers', a kind of jack used to drag the calf from its mother's body. He never began the task (the calf was found dead next morning). Instead, he was bundled into a vehicle and taken off the peninsula. He was tortured, then stripped, and dressed in the standard IRA execution garb – a boiler-suit – and shot six times in the head. His body was dumped over the border, in South Armagh's 'Bandit Country'.

I wondered if my father would have been sickened by the details. Would he have declined 'to enter on my list of friends' the persons who demolished Tom Oliver with as much sensibility as Cowper's wretch who 'needlessly sets foot upon a worm'? Bridie Oliver's brother identified the body. 'Whoever they were, they thumped him and thumped him to get him to say what they wanted him to say. After the post mortem, a priest said it looked like they'd dropped concrete blocks on every bone in his body, but I don't think they did that; they just thumped him senseless till he'd have no idea where he was or what he was saying. I'll never forget, as long as I live, the screams of Bridie and the children when they went to the morgue, or the awful silence of the people who went into the yard outside to wait for them coming out.' Would this account of extreme barbarity have shamed my father into renouncing his former association with the predecessors of the organization that could sanction such brutality? Would he have been swayed by the killers' excuse: that Tom Oliver was a police informer? I have no sure answers to these questions. As the Troubles progressed in Northern Ireland, I noticed my father becoming less opinionated, less voluble, about what was happening. It may well be that he was silent in deference to my own view that nothing that had happened in my native land could justify murder, and that Ulster folk had the right to remain British if that is what they wished. But, since my father had never been in the habit of deferring to anybody, I cannot press that theory with great conviction. I prefer, rather, to think that he was experiencing something close to disenchantment with what was gratuitous brutality calling itself 'The Struggle'. He continually worried about the increasingly violent divisions between Catholics and Protestants and was, I believe, facing up to the likelihood that wells of nationalism in Ireland had become the drowning-pits of socialism. I regret very deeply that he was not alive to hear the words of Bridie Oliver, when I visited her again in 1995. I sat at her kitchen table, drinking her coffee, gazing out of her window at the cows in her pasture, and piny slopes rising into a cloudless autumn sky. 'I can understand how people want to forget, to let wounds heal,' she said. 'But how can you forget when the intimidating behaviour goes on and on?' Her two eldest daughters endured aggression from IRA sympathizers at local discos. 'Some of the things that are said you'd hardly believe. One young man even said to my daughter: "Sure he wasn't your father, anyway." My eleven-year-old is having a bad time. She can't bear to be in the house alone. She wakes up in the night with these terrible fears and has to come into my bed.' I could only nod in sympathy. There was nothing I could say to her that might give comfort. She and her children had become victims of an IRA atrocity on their own land, on their own doorstep, in their own little family unit.

Leaving her, I climbed to a point where I could look south to the town of 'cute hoors', and then north across Carlingford Lough to Warrenpoint. The air was sharp and clear, enabling me to make out the terraced houses on the distant promenade. I remembered our boyhood summer there, between the death of my mother and the acquisition of my stepmother.

I was nine, I think, when we went to Warrenpoint. We stayed at a seafront house. It had been rented by a woman called Nora, who had two very young children. I do not know whether my father had known her before, or had simply found the house by responding to a newspaper's holiday ads. A dark-haired, vigorous, pretty Irishwoman, Nora was married to an Englishman who had decided to remain in London while she whiled away the summer in Warrenpoint. She and my father seemed to hit it off immediately. I too was excessively fond of her. She asked my brothers and me to call her 'Auntie Nora', and we gladly obliged, for she casually and naturally filled a vacuum created by our mother's death. Nora was a fearless swimmer. She was said to have crossed the lough to Omeath (and perhaps back again, for all I know), freestyle. One evening when the sea was high and surging over the wall of the municipal swimming-pool, she clamped me to her chest with one arm and kicked off, on her back, into the waves. I ought to have been frightened, since I had not yet learned to swim, but I wasn't in the slightest. Nora and my father had many things in common. She was the daughter of a member of the Dublin parliament and was on speaking terms with many of the people my father knew. I believe she was in love with my father. She invited him – and us –

to spend Christmas with her in Newry, where she had temporarily taken over a large house on a hill – again without the company of her husband. There were occasions when I was puzzled by an unexpected arrangement of things: her physical closeness to my father on a sofa, as they drank whiskey and sang Irish ballads; the presence of *his* things in *her* bedroom; the way her fingers lingered while straightening his tie. There was nothing indecorous or overtly specific that might disquieten a child who had lost his own mother not so very long ago and constantly needed confirmation of his father's affection for him. It was simply a sense of intimacy which I had not witnessed in my father since my mother entered hospital to die. I think I derived great comfort from the arrangement, as I trust my father also did. Three decades later, I bumped into people in London who happened to be friends of Nora. They told me she had recently died. When next I saw my father in Belfast, I told him the news and asked why he had lost touch with her.

'Did I never tell you what happened?' he said. 'She came up to Belfast a couple of times. Don't you remember that day she arrived in Ponsonby in a mink coat?'

I did remember. It was after we had returned to Belfast from Newry to pack for our second term in Dundalk. I remember that I was with neighbours' children not far from our front door. She appeared, as though from nowhere, looking faintly upset. She was fumbling in her handbag and dropped one of her kid-gloves on the pavement. I picked it up, catching her wonderful perfume, and called: 'Auntie Nora, your glove!' She smiled, took the glove and hugged me (an act that embarrassed me in front of my friends). I asked if she was coming into our house to see Daddy, unaware that she had already seen him and was in fact leaving. She seemed on the verge of tears.

'She wanted us to get married,' my father explained. 'It wasn't possible, you see. She was a married woman. It would have meant divorcing her husband. Out of the question! Can you imagine? Both of us, Catholics! We wouldn't have been able to lift our heads again.'

I digested this information sullenly. How could he throw away such a wonderful opportunity to transform a loving 'aunt' into a loving mother? I thought: What a waste! But by then, I soon came to realize, my father's heart was elsewhere.

Months later, when we were home (I think for Easter), my father brought Theresa Cassidy to Ponsonby Avenue to meet us. She was taller than him and beautiful, had brown velvety eyes and a laugh that tinkled like a silver spoon against fine china. She played the piano and sang to us as we gulped and belched our way through bottles of fizzy lemonade and cream buns, bought specially, I imagine, to soften us up for what was to follow. Then she left. Next morning, a Sunday, my father called us into his bedroom and asked us to get into the bed beside him. How would we feel, he asked, about having 'a new mammy'.

'You mean, her last night?'

'Yes, Miss Cassidy.'

The bedroom still contained some of my mother's possessions: a holy picture, a small holy statue, her hairbrush and comb, her tortoise-shell hand-mirror. The wallpaper on the bedroom walls had been chosen by her. Her fingers had silenced the morning bell of the small, blue metal alarm-clock now ticking in our ears. She had lain where we now were lying, on linen sheets she had hemmed herself. The room seemed filled by my mother's presence. Was there space for someone else?

I don't think Colm was terribly enthusiastic. Brendan didn't seem to mind, one way or the other. I still had yearnings for Nora, but consoled myself that Theresa was a bit of a stunner and seemed to be quite jolly and kind.

'What do you say, Cahal óg?' my father said gently.

'Mmm . . . Yeah, OK.'

'Not "yeah"; yes! And don't say "OK" – it's American slang,' my father said.

Theresa's family were from Derry City. Her father had owned a pub, but outpaced his customers in the emptying of bottles, went bust and died. The family came to live in Belfast, in a shabby part of the predominantly Catholic Markets area, where they were referred to behind their backs as 'empty beggars' – because, I think, they were well-spoken, neatly dressed and kept themselves apart. 'Fur-coat-and-no-knickers', was another typical Belfast judgement aimed at them before, gradually, they regained a modest degree of prosperity they had lost.

One afternoon, as I worked at my books in the junior study hall in Dundalk, the boy beside me elbowed my ribs and gestured towards the window.

'A film star!' he whispered.

My father and Theresa were walking across the quadrangle, arm-in-arm. My heart thumped and I jumped to my feet. In her going-away honeymoon clothes she *did* look like a film star.

'Sit *down*, McCrystal!' somebody roared, but I had already bolted from my desk and was racing across the quad to greet them. Colm and Brendan followed. They took us to lunch (roast pigeon, which I pretended to enjoy) at a Dundalk hotel, before resuming their train journey to Dublin. That was our final term in Dundalk. My stepmother wanted us home.

Theresa was gentle, but unused to children (she never had any of her own). Nevertheless, her patience with three who were well on the wild side can only be described as saintly. Her piano-playing was imperfect, but she sang well. No one passing our open window of a summer evening could fail to hear arias from Puccini, Verdi and Bizet, or her Gounod's *Ave Maria*. She encouraged me to attend performances of the Carl Rosa Opera Company when it came to Belfast. She took up painting with more enthusiasm than talent, every stroke of her brush earning inordinate praise from my father, whom she adored and in whom she could find no fault. We played pranks that exploited her gullibility and staged tantrums that sent her fleeing to her bedroom, leaving us sniggering in triumph. She was excessively religious and quaintly discerning.

'I think that new postman's a Protestant,' she announced to my father at supper.

'How do you know that?'

'He's got a Protestant face.'

My father laughed so hard he spilled his tea. Not quite grasping what the joke was, my stepmother laughed too, tears streaming down her face, enjoying being at the centre of her husband's humorous attention. She laughed at anything mildly naughty. Once she sang for us something from her own childhood: 'There was a little hen, which poolied in the yard/ The frost came on and froze it, and made it slippery and hard.' My brothers and I looked at her in pretended dismay. She laughed and laughed, covering her face with her hands, shaking until her whole body was sore. On another occasion, my father happened to use the quaint expression, 'athwart the door'. As soon as he said it, I was sure my stepmother was about to giggle herself into a coma.

'What's the big joke?' my father said. 'What on earth are you laughing at?'

Her face was twisted with mirth. Every time she tried to say something, laughter locked her tongue. 'A . . . Ath . . . Athwa . . .'

'Athwart? Is that it?' my father said, as she continued to squeak and squeal with hilarity.

I butted in. 'It's that other word Mammy's thinking of. The one that rhymes with athwart but begins with "f",' I said helpfully.

'Eh?' said my father leaning towards his gurgling wife and feigning severity. 'You don't mean to tell me . . .' But she was off again into another paroxysm.

In assessing the postman, she was making a point frequently and seriously made in Northern Ireland. Some Protestants claimed to know who was a Catholic, merely by looking at one; and vice versa. It used to be said: 'You can tell a Catholic by his dirty neck.' There had been truth in that at one time: Catholics were poor, had no running water, no soap, no idea of hygiene, just as they had, as often as not, no tenure. But there were other subtle indicators too. The people on Falls Road (Catholic) and the people on Shankill Road (Protestant) have much in common, not least their poverty and their propinquity. But their accents, though equally harsh in tone, are nevertheless slightly different. The Falls Road accent has a slight rural lilt to it, probably because country Catholics, dispossessed of their farms or intimidated into flight for other reasons, moved to the city, congregating there in their own communities for self-protection. The Shankill accent is more self-assuredly urban, yet more touchy. Also, there was in people's perceptions a so-called 'Irish face' (dark hair, strong eyebrows, long upper-lip, ill-at-ease look) that signified 'Fenian'; and a so-called 'Planter face' (fair hair, small mouth, mean eyes, self-assured look) – the face descended from the Scots who had taken part in the colonization (the 'Plantation') of Ireland under James I – that suggested 'Prod'. When in doubt, and really needing to know, ask a Belfastman his name. The 'O' in O'Reilly or the 'Mac' in MacLaverty might sound Catholic, but you cannot be sure. One of Northern Ireland's last prime ministers was a Protestant O'Neill. The Scottish 'Mc' abounds.

One then presses on by asking what school a person went to. Given the segregated educational system, the answer should leave no room for doubt. So my stepmother's remark about the postman was all part of a game that almost everybody played – and perhaps still plays – throughout the province. The game has an element of self-torture in it.

We called her 'Mammy'. She was a great cook. She baked the best apple-pie in Belfast. If I or my brothers farted, she made us stand for half a minute in the back yard until malodorous no longer. I like to think she civilized us a little.

7

PANGS OF HUNGER, PANGS OF SEX

Our first summer following my father's marriage to Theresa Cassidy was spent in the Gaeltacht – the Irish-speaking region of Donegal, a county where fierce republicanism has long blended easily with sentimental legend. We spent two months there, in Gweedore, a place of streams, loughs and bogland, all dominated by Errigal – at 2,500 ft, the highest mountain in this most rugged and inspirational county. Historically, Donegal is part of the nine counties of Ulster, but it – along with Cavan and Monaghan – was lopped off when the new political entity of Ulster came into existence in 1920, under the Government of Ireland Act. The legislation therefore placed the most northern county of Ireland south of its border. When one travels in Donegal, one quickly notices that while the currency, school system and official institutions are those of the Irish Republic, the voices are those of Northern Ireland, indistinguishable from the accents of Derry, just to the east across the Foyle estuary. Vowels in Donegal Gaelic are short, as they are in Belfast but not as in, say, Galway or Dublin. Seán is pronounced 'shan', not 'shawn'. Like anyone who has spent time there, my father loved Donegal. Five years before I was born, the travel writer H. V. Morton described it as 'surely the most enchanting place in Ireland.' Ending a Donegal visit in 1849, Thomas Carlyle confided to his diary: 'In all Ireland, lately in no other land, saw no such beautiful soul.' Our holiday was for two whole months. My brothers and I were accommodated in a farmhouse owned by a family called Diver. It backed on to a duck pond and, beyond, a rough expanse of brown peat-bog alight with bright-yellow whin bushes. The front of the house faced a narrow country road. Across the road was a salmon river, the Clady – fast-flowing peaty shallows that paused every now and then for an exploratory swirl into deep pools before leaping noisily seawards again. My father and stepmother came up from Belfast for a few weekends, staying at a hotel overlooking the Atlantic. One of the objects of the holiday was that we should become fluent in Gaelic. We fell quite short of achieving this. Most of the time, we ran wild.

Theresa, who was good with a sewing-machine, had made blue-and-white cotton swimming trunks for the three of us. It was a mile-and-a-half walk to Bunbeg harbour to watch the salmon leap a high, natural weir on their journey up the Clady to spawn; and another half-mile to the long, broad golden beach where we swam and collected tiny, delicate sea-shells that seemed more appropriate to a tropical coast. Sometimes we got a lift in a breadvan owned by a cousin of the Divers. He told us about the Great Hunger – the Irish potato famine of 1845–52 – and the calamity it brought to the West of Ireland. He stopped the van one day and pointed to the sand dunes and the beach beyond.

'Hundreds sleep there beneath the sand,' he said in Gaelic, repeating it in English for me. When my father joined us a couple of days later, I asked him if it was true. It was. 'People won't easily talk about it', he said, 'but there's hardly a family in Gweedore that didn't lose brothers, sisters, cousins. Some got decent burials, but there wasn't enough room in the churchyards.' Much of the poor land in the north and west of Ireland consisted of a few inches of soil, with solid rock underneath. The earth simply wasn't deep enough to receive a corpse. Very often it was easier to remove the remains to the beach and bury them there. 'They're under the sand right enough,' my father said. My stepmother shivered.

About ten years before he died, my father and I went through Donegal into County Sligo and County Mayo. We talked about the graves over which the ocean had thundered for almost a century and a half, and the survivors who had sailed the same ocean to find relief from poverty and persecution. 'People don't need books to remind them of the famine', my father said as we sat on a hill overlooking Clew Bay. 'It traumatized the entire race. That trauma's stayed in our blood. It determines the set of our shoulders as we look back, and it taps us on the shoulder when we look forward.' At least that is what I think he said. The point he went on to make was that although the Irish Famine did not spark a revolution at the time, it conveyed a potent justification for a revolution later. It rankled. Catholic families who were persuaded to convert to Protestantism in return for sustenance became known, down successive generations, as 'soupers' – those who 'took the soup', i.e., who abandoned their religion for food. Sometimes one family member would take the soup, while other members refused, leading to bitter family chasms and feuds that never healed.

In 1995, Ireland sought appropriate ways to commemorate the 150th anniversary of the potato blight, the consequences of which included massive depopulation, torrential emigration, civil discord and an abiding distrust of British governments. To understand why Anglo–Irish relations are never happy for long – and why British Ulster and Irish Ulster are so often locked in disharmony – you have to understand what my father's words mean, especially at a time when Britain and Ireland are desperately engaged in seeking to ameliorate the collective memory of that tragedy; to try to remedy, once and for all, a persistent, centuries-old blight on their relations. 'As far as the Famine goes,' declares Terry Eagleton, the Oxford professor, in *Heathcliff and the Great Hunger, Studies in Irish Culture*, 'we are dealing with the most important episode of modern Irish history and the greatest social disaster of nineteenth-century Europe – an event with something of the characteristics of a low-level nuclear attack.'

Talking to those whom the late, lamented Flann O'Brien described as the 'plain people of Ireland', one has sensed, on the one hand, a desire not to stir things up against Britain during a 'peace process', on the other, a need to acknowledge the enormity of the calamity that most are convinced Britain did insufficient to assuage. In the summer when my father and I stayed in Mulraney, a tiny, straggling community on the north shore of Clew Bay in

Mayo, we met a local hotel manager who had lost many ancestors in the famine. He was reluctant to tell me what he knew, but later sent me a book, dog-eared and yellowing, and printed on cheap paper. Written in 1957, it was called *Annála Beaga Pharáiste Bhuréis Umhaill* ('A Short Account of the History of Burrishoole Parish'), the area where we had been staying. The chapter headed 'The Famine' said:

We have very little documentary evidence of the sufferings of our people in that hour of darkest tragedy. But the old people of fifty years ago who had seen the horrible thing with their own eyes have told us harrowing tales. They have told us of men and women and children dying by the roadside, their mouths green from the nettles and grass they had eaten in their overpowering hunger; of others dropping dead after partaking of a meal of porridge which proved too much for their stomachs long without food; of women carrying their dead husbands on their backs to the graveyards; of others, too weak themselves to carry their dead, burying their beloved ones somewhere near home. Dead vagrants, and they were many, were buried simply by pulling the sod fence down over them to cover them where they had died. Not one woman, but many, ill with fever, took the body of her husband who had died in the bed beside her of the same fever and buried it in the cabin floor. Then she, too, lay down to die.

All over the parish the graves of the famine victims are scattered, sometimes in single graves, now and then several together. How many lie buried in the strand at Mulraney we could not count. Who they were God alone knows. There they rest, the fever of life over, the ebbing and flowing tides ever murmuring their requiem.

The strand, or beach, is a golden hem to a skirt of green clothing hills that rise above a bay of stunning beauty. Modern bungalows perch above the road that follows the shore. During the day, sheep descend from the hills, cross the road and nibble short, tough grasses between the road and the beach. In the early evening they return to their rocky mountain pasture, often when Clew Bay, and its hundreds of islands and its promontories, are incarnadined by the setting sun. Having read the parish history, I cannot walk on Mulraney strand without feeling the kind of great emptiness that one experiences on traversing a wasteland.

Before the famine, the population of Burrishoole was more than 12,000. By 1850, it was 4,000, the number of families having dropped from 2,700 to 890. Most had succumbed to starvation, typhus and cholera. Many had been evicted. The parish history says: 'Lord Sligo flung some 40 families on the roadside in Treenbeg and Treenlar and thereby created his Treenlar Farm . . . Sir Richard O'Donnell was also active. He declared he would not leave a Catholic between Knocknabola bridge and the river of Newport . . . Sligo and O'Donnell are gone and the hated Catholics are back again on the lands of their forefathers.' Among the absentee landlords was the Earl of Lucan, who owned 60,000 acres and whose descendant, in the 1970s, made absenteeism a different kind of art form.

The terrible events of 1845−52 helped reduce Ireland's population from a pre-famine 8.2 million to the 1871 census figure of 4.4 million. Starvation and disease claimed 1.5 million lives. Another million emigrated, mostly to the United States. Pressed by what they had seen, or by landlords determined to reduce the number of tenants on their land, another million-plus followed within the next couple of decades. The exodus drained the countryside, particularly in the west, and brought fresh afflictions to the towns, not least in Belfast and Derry, focal points of the Troubles. Neither rural Ireland nor political Ireland ever fully recovered. The potato blight struck first in Ulster − specifically the fields of County Fermanagh. And although my native province weathered the famine years more successfully than did the west and south-west, it still suffered greatly. In west Ulster, including Donegal, some parishes lost more than half their people. Many of the survivors fled eastwards where the famine was less severe. 'Catholics in large numbers began to arrive in some areas that had been overwhelmingly Protestant for almost two hundred years − notably Belfast,' wrote Liam de Paor in his 1990 book, *Unfinished Business* (Professor de Paor, a

Dublin historian and archaeologist, was a long-time friend of my father). In County Donegal, despairing eyes turned to Derry.

I learned a little of all this in my two boyhood summers in Gweedore, long before the Republic of Ireland had begun to achieve her present prosperity. A stranger from Belfast could see the evidence all around: cockle-shells, mussel-shells, limpet-shells, half-buried by time in a thistle-field, testifying to a starving family's attempt to forage in the sea; a surviving practice of stuffing mattresses with dried dulse, to save straw for livestock; hundreds of ruined cabins, their broken thatch green-black with age; a preponderance of villagers in Bunbeg, Bloody Foreland, the Glenties, Ranafast, whose cousins were all overseas – in Scotland, England or North America.

Two young men from Derry came to stay with the Divers while we were there. They were in their late teens or early twenties. Their fathers had been in the (old) IRA, and they sounded like IRA men themselves. I can't be sure; I was too young to absorb the nuances in their conversations with local teenagers. They came and they went, without manifesting much of a holiday mood. Someone mentioned that their families had left Gweedore for Derry a hundred years earlier. My brothers and I gave them little enough of our attention, as we learned to swim in the Clady's deep pools, ride ponies bareback across the bog, set fire to whin bushes, and make ourselves sick on sweets and experimental puffs on Woodbine ('Five, please, they're for my daddy,' we told the shopkeeper down the road).

The summer months brought children from all over Ireland to the Donegal Gaeltacht. Every day, they were expected to attend classes for a couple of hours and avoid the use of the English language. The school was really a small hall, built on a slab of bog rock and overlooking Gweedore Bay. The McCrystal children bunked off so often that I think an assumption finally prevailed that we did not exist. Most of the lessons, in any case, were devoted to reciting prayers in Gaelic (which I already could do), and to rambling, and often boring stories that always began with the same sentence: 'He was living by himself in a little thatched cottage in the crook of the glen . . .' The only attraction was what we quickly identified as a glut of 'wee scaldies'. I fell for one of them, a slender girl with tanned skin, freckles and hair that fell to her waist. She did not fall for me, however. I was far too bashful to approach a girl. I had to be content with admiring her from a distance, especially when she emerged from her cottage to wash her hair at the roadside pump. Once I almost offered to work the pump-handle for her, but in the end lacked the courage. The only time she spoke to me was to ask for my older brother's name. Later, I saw her often with Colm, giggling with infuriating intimacy. Girls fell for Colm almost as soon as his eyes landed on them.

Ireland – or its Catholic clergy, at least – in those days imposed strict sexual discipline on its young people. Great emphasis was placed on prayers to the Virgin Mary, also known as the Blessed Virgin. Virginity was regarded as a precious condition, and guarded accordingly. Girls who neglected to do so, even on a single occasion, tended to be shunned, even by randy boys who, when push came to shove and kiss came to grope, backed off at the thought of having to seek absolution in the confessional, a place often quite as dismaying as the imaginary, penitential box, manned by Nazis, that Colm conjured up for me in childhood. My father once recalled confessing, as a youth, to 'impure touching' of a girl's body.

'Upper or lower?' snapped the priest.

'Upper, Father.'

'Hmn! Over her clothes or under her clothes?'

'Over, Father.'

'Did you take pleasure from it?'

'What . . . ?'

'Did you have impure thoughts?'

'Well, em, ah . . .'

'Did-you-pollute-your-own-body-which-is-the-very-temple-of-Jesus-Christ? Well, *did* you? I can't *hear* you. *Did* you?'

My father told me he could hear the sound of heads turning in the confessional queue outside. 'It wasn't the shouting that bothered me. I had a feeling he was taking an unholy interest in the details.'

The same thought had struck me more than once. As a (I think) fourteen-year-old, I went to the 'Cappy' with a pretty Quaker girl who lived just off Cave Hill Road. We sat in the rear stalls and I put an arm round her shoulders. I then touched one of her 'bee-stings'. I expected her to slap my hand and move it away. Instead, I felt her breath on my cheek as she turned to ask, in a delightfully innocent way, if I would marry her. I took fright, and removed my hand, the whole afternoon spoiled for me. In my next Confession, the priest was censorious about my associating intimately with a 'non-Catholic' of the opposite sex. Nevertheless he was remarkably keen to know about my progress with her.

'And then . . . ?'

'No, Father, that's all.'

'Is that it? Did you not touch her between the legs?'

'No, Father.'

'Or interfere with her clothing down there?

'No, Father.'

It must be tough on a priest who, while trying to abstain from fleshly pleasures himself, has to sit in a darkened confessional, hand cupped to his ear, as half his congregation sorrowfully parades its fumblings, erections, and ejaculations before him. It is enough to drive a man to drink. It very frequently does.

Protestant boys were raised with no less a sense of virtue than Catholic boys. But they did seem to be a bit more relaxed about sexual matters. When I became an adult, I learned from Protestant friends and colleagues that 'going all the way' was by no means unusual when they were young teenagers. Honesty, hard work and loyalty to the throne were hallmarks of Protestant virtue; 'keeping your body pure' was the impossible duty imposed on us Fenians. Masturbation – or 'pulling your wire' in the local argot – was a mortal sin which, unexpiated by confession and repentance, meant eternal damnation. It used to be argued among us that you would receive priestly forgiveness more readily after spilling someone's blood upon the ground, while crying 'God save Ireland!', than if you had spilled your own seed upon the same ground. I grew up with Catholic boys who, in sexual frustration, did very eccentric things. One, who lived in Ponsonby Avenue, told me that while walking over Cave Hill he experienced such desire for relief that he poked a hole in the turf of one of the slopes, jammed his penis into it and rode the mountain until the onanistic spasms had been exhausted.

'Weren't there people about?' I asked him, incredulous. 'What if . . . ?'

'A man and a woman did see me, but they shot off in a hurry. If they'd said anything, I'd have pretended to be having an epileptic fit.' My adolescent friend was – is – of a pleasant, easy-going disposition. He has been happily married to one woman all his adult life, is a proud, affectionate father, holds a steady job and attends Mass on Sundays. I wonder if the mountain tamed him.

On our Donegal holidays, our spiritual welfare was the responsibility of a Father McGettigan, a middle-aged cleric who had no illusions about the virtue of his charges. At night he patrolled the narrow roads in his black Austin, switching off the engine at the crest of hills and coasting silently down them, his head swivelling in search of courting couples. My father laughed about the priest's night raids. 'When I came here as a young man, there was a big, stone-faced P.P. [parish priest] who went up and down the roads and boreens half the night with a blackthorn stick. He jabbed it into every hedge, every bush, every hay-stook, hoping to catch young people at it. He was always in a terrible rage about something. And if he didn't find anyone at it, he'd knock the heads off all the weeds and thistles he passed on his way home. I think there were some things that preyed on his mind.'

More liberal attitudes prevail in Donegal today. Nobody talks about entering 'the occasion of sin' or making a big deal out of fornication. Rural Irish priests, having lost the battle against condoms, have had to look for other things to condemn, and the only thing that has been playing for a generation past has been the Troubles. But, on my trips to Donegal, I occasionally come across minor tragedies, half-remembered and seldom related, among the elderly; melancholy stories punctuated by little sighs of what might have been had the parish priest left his blackthorn stick at home. In the year the Troubles began, I was in Donegal on holiday, and went to a wake – the first in the county since I tried, as a child, to steal the pennies off the old dead woman's eyelids. I watched an old man drinking alone, staring alternately at the corpse of another old woman and at the turf smouldering in the hearth. Then he quietly headed for the door. There was a purposefulness about his departure. Other mourners called out '*Slán agat!*' (Goodbye) as he strode into the summer evening. But he ignored them – as though he had pressing business on his mind. Someone confided to me that the departing guest had been an old IRA man. Someone else explained that the woman in the coffin had been the light of his youth. Years later, recalling the episode and trying to imagine what their lives and their relationship had been like, I wrote these lines:

DONEGAL WAKE, 1969

> *Maeve's dead.*
> *Grave's dug.*
> *'Nuff said.*
> *Glug-glug . . .*
>
> Sláinte!* But how can I ignore
> Maeve's apron on the kitchen door?
> She hung it there, damp, stiff with flour
> (A whiff of mint and milk gone sour),
> When asked to, fifty years ago.
> She breathed: 'Gently . . . gently, Randal!'
> And lay down on the bed, aglow;
> Watching me blow out the candle.
>
> > *Eyes prick:*
> > *Ice-cold*
> > *Heart's trick,*
> > *I'm told.*
>
> A fortnight after my demob
> I thought to marry; our desire
> Having become an endless throb

In haystack, house and dungy byre.
You assented. And we defied
A Church that turned its back upon
Those consanguineously tied,
And thereby crossed our Rubicon.
    For this
    No Mass?
    Then kiss
    My ass!
Falcarragh, Burtonport, Dungloe,
(Wet weeks in each), and Loughanure
For nine cold, hungry days, and so
Love took the road of lost allure
That led, for you, to Liam *buí*,†
Who sang in Father Phelan's choir;
And led to civil war for me
And years and years behind the wire.
    Flu kills
    Galore.
    Liam trills
    No more.
'No more for me; I have to drive
To Bloody Foreland.' There the sea
Scours cliffs, and reckless seabirds dive,
And one dank pub half-beckons me.
I have no thirst, no thought, no care,
And stumble down the sodden sedge,
And pause on a basaltic stair
To catch her voice beyond the edge.
    'Gently,
    Randal.
    Gently,
    Randal.'

    ★ Good health!   † blond [pronounced bwee]

It may strike some as a paradox that Catholic priests may condemn parishioners for sexual peccancy, while colluding with others involved in the business of killing. If so, it is not an uncommon paradox: the imams of Islam, for example, approve of amputation, decapitation and stoning to death. But what is different about those members of the Irish clergy who support the 'struggle' is that they tend to do so covertly or ambiguously. To come out as a terrorist-priest would be to invite immediate censure and perhaps unfrocking. I know of at least three Ulster priests who have been thus 'silenced'. My father once explained the priestly dilemma to me. 'There has always been a tradition of rebel priests in Ireland. In the years of "hedge priests" [official suppression of Catholicism meant that religious instruction had to be conducted in secret], the clergy and their flocks formed a deep bond and mutual reliance. The priests witnessed the humiliations their people were subjected to. They couldn't very well condemn them when they tried to overcome the humiliations. Even after Catholic Emancipation [1829], when the hierarchy favoured conformity with English rule, the parish priest and his curate would take a relaxed view of republican activities among their parishioners.'

I gathered as much from Father Kavanagh's book about the 1798 insurrection. On the title page are the following lines:

> The Tribune's tongue and Poet's pen
> Must sow the seed in slavish men;
> But 'tis the soldier's sword alone
> Can reap the harvest when 'tis grown.

If that sounds less than peace-loving, one ought not to be surprised. In Ireland, from time immemorial (it has seemed), bellicose priests have been in the vanguard of contesting movements. Belfast Protestants had 'roaring' Reverend Hugh Hanna in the nineteenth century, as well as Ian Paisley in the twentieth. Battling clergy on the Catholic side go further back, creating a litany of martyrs who have set an example for some priests of today. There are even ballads

in their honour. One priestly victim of 1798 was a Father John
Murphy who, in this translation from Gaelic,

> . . . was taken,
> In his retreat to Castlemore.
> He was brought to Tullow and used most basely;
> With faggots blazing they burned his bones.

In his second period of widowhood, in the early years of the
Troubles, my father accompanied me often to Donegal. We would
drive north out of Belfast to Derry, then west through Letterkenny,
a hilly market town nine miles over the border. Like Dundalk –
like *all* border towns – communication is on two levels: hub-
bub and *sotto voce*. It is a prosperous town, typically ambitious,
in the atmosphere of 'New Ireland's' rapid economic growth,
for inward investment. And, as Donegal's largest urban centre,
Letterkenny is sensitive to criticism, especially about sugges-
tions that it is an IRA town, even after clandestine arms dumps
have been unearthed a few miles outside it. One summer, my
father and I did a pub-crawl on the main street. Increasingly
deaf, his voice went up in volume as his Guinness went down in
volume.

'You'll find IRA men here all right,' he confided in a shout that
silenced the other customers. Nobody looked round, but I watched
the faces at the bar tilt upwards to scan a mirror behind it. Their
eyes were on us, strangers in town; one with a Belfast accent, and
the other with a pronounced British taint to it.

'What's wrong?' my father yelled.

'You're shouting a bit loud,' I grated into his 'good' ear.

Two men in the late twenties or early thirties, pulled chairs up
to our table and smiled amiably.

'Are yiz lookin' for someone?' one said, still smiling.

I shook my head, but my father shouted: 'I was just telling the
son here . . .'

'Yiz are on holiday, is that it?'

'Aye,' my father said in loud exasperation. 'I was just telling the son here . . .'

The second man leaned forward. He spoke slowly and carefully so that my father caught every word. 'Wouldn't you be better telling him what you're telling him somewhere else?'

My father gaped at him. He addressed the men in Gaelic, saying something about the great times he had spent in Donegal, his favourite county. I think he was presenting his credentials, his bona fides. The men, no longer smiling, did not seem impressed. We left and crawled no more. In the car, bound for Gweedore, I asked why he never wore his hearing aid. 'Old Man Vanity,' he said, dismissing the notion.

Then, 'Did I ever tell you about Brian Merriman [the eighteenth-century Gaelic poet]?'

'Often.'

'Ah, but did I ever tell you what he said? *Táim in achrann dhaingean na mbliadhnta/ Ag tarraing go tréan ar laethibh liaithe* – "I'm in the strong grip of the years/ Drawing violently on to the days of greyness".'

'And that's how you feel?'

'I'm beginning to.'

Merriman was said to be almost unique among Gaelic poets in acknowledging that women in Ireland got a pretty raw deal from life. 'He wrote a bit bawdily about it,' my father said, 'but you couldn't argue with him, though the Church, not surprisingly, banned him for years. It never ceases to amaze me that a country which pays such reverential homage to women could treat them so shabbily.' I gave him a sideways look and laughed.

'What's that for?' he said, genuinely puzzled.

'Well, I'm listening to you blathering on about prejudice against women, and both of us know that you never carried a shopping-bag in your life. And you never washed a sock, or wielded a broom, or cooked a meal . . .'

'Of course I cooked a meal. After your mammy died . . .'

'I meant an edible meal – not one with green potatoes because you used baking soda instead of salt, or meat with Camp coffee poured on it because you thought it was HP sauce.'

That killed that conversation dead. Yet he was right: there was something strikingly paradoxical about the Irish attitude to women. Three goddesses of pagan days gave Ireland her most ancient names: Éire, Fódla and Banba. More recently, the country was referred to, in poetry and song, as Cathleen Nî Houlihan, Róisín Dubh (Little Dark Rose), and Síle ní Ghadhra (Sheila, the daughter of the hound – i.e., Cuchulain, the legendary Hound of Ulster). In all its incarnations, Ireland has been represented by a woman: a captive warrior, a martyred virgin, a *sean-Bhean bhocht* (poor, old woman), or, as James Joyce would have it, 'the old sow who eats her own farrow'. Distant Irish migrants tend to grow misty-eyed about their old Irish granny, rather than their old Irish granddad.

The reality, however, has been that, until comparatively recent times, women in Ireland have been second-class citizens and, in many instances, mere drudges. The prejudice against their empowerment as citizens has been as dark as any of the prejudices found in Ireland. It seems to persist most strongly in the north. When I look at the Unionist leadership I see no women. When I glance at the list of nationalist MPs, I see no women's names. Sinn Féin's top ranks are male, apart from a couple of women who appear from time to time at the leader's sides and are described as 'aides', or 'personal assistants'. Merriman's greatest work was *The Midnight Court*, a mock-heroic epic, satirical and feminist, which lampoons sexual mores, priestly celibacy and male chauvinism. I recalled it when I was in Tralee, in County Kerry, some years ago to observe a melodrama that was searing Ireland's collective conscience, bringing little credit to anyone. It was known as 'the Kerry babies case', a story with strange religious and political overtones – the kind used by Ulster Protestants to bolster their claims that the South was a backward, priest-ridden place. Yet both north and south of the Irish border, it provided a diversion from prejudices that were violently setting Catholic against Protestant and terrorists against the security forces. But essentially it was about the fate of two baby boys. One was Joanne Hayes's, dead within minutes of delivery in a field, then dumped in a well on the family farm; the other, found horribly stabbed to death on a lonely Kerry beach at Slea Head, was never identified. Within days of my arrival, I was confirmed in my belief that the prejudicial arts are still practised on my island, however much new legislation liberalizes the rules about abortion and other private matters. And in saying this, I should make the point that social rigidity on such questions as abortion is more unbending in Northern Ireland than in the Republic. Some say the role of women in Ireland has eased since the Kerry Babies affair, prompted by the election, in 1990, of Mary Robinson as Ireland's first woman president. But a half-blind dog can see that women, north and south, are still denied the reins of real power. The island has much of the paraphernalia of modernity and sophistication: expensive cars, shopping malls, credit card economy, high educational standards, a well travelled population, and so on. But beneath this glitter, intolerance, such as was so vividly exposed in what became known as the Kerry Babies Affair, continues to work its corrosive effect.

The road to Slea Head in County Kerry spirals into cloud that nearly obliterates Conner Pass, a treacherous defile through the Dingle peninsula. The journey into this stony waste, passing great clusters of prehistoric beehive dwellings, demanded extreme caution. Winter torrents had broken the road in places and there were worrying traces of an earlier route now fallen into the sea. Rounding a sharp curve, I was jolted by a sudden and memorable confrontation: four figures, life-size and blindingly white against the black cliff, broke through the mountain mist. At the foot of a concrete cross, three Marys venerated a bleeding Jesus and maintained an anguished watch over savage, treeless Slea Head, Ireland's westernmost extremity. Beyond, the uninhabited Blasket Islands vegetated in the murk. Below, the Atlantic boiled over jagged rocks. It was at this place, if an early statement she made to the Irish police can be believed, that the infant son of Joanne Hayes was hurled on to the waves in a plastic fertilizer bag a year before.

Slea Head is a good hour-and-a-half's drive from the Hayes farm at Abbeydorney, six miles north of Tralee, the county's chief town. Joanne was tiny (not quite 4ft 8in), with a pale, sharp face and black, curly hair. She was twenty-six and unmarried. She had had three pregnancies, of which one produced a healthy glowing daughter and another ended in miscarriage. The third, according to twenty-five police officers, ended in murder. Ireland was spellbound as the harrowing story – Celtic in substance, Gothic in flavour – of the baby's death and the police methods of investigating it unfolded daily before a special judicial tribunal. It was played out by an assortment of tragic, evasive and sometimes comic figures against a rancorous background of political and ecclesiastical manoeuvrings. It brought into unusually sharp focus the desperation of unmarried women and the anxieties of a Catholic Church increasingly jealous of its power – even as that power was showing visible signs of waning.

Apart from the allegations of murder, and the way they were followed up, the story cannot be said to be unique. It was a love story that went badly wrong for reasons neither uncommon nor hard to fathom. The number of rural marriages in Ireland had been declining for many years. In one western village, parish records showed a drop in local marriages from fifty-one in 1920 to four in 1970. The traditional practice of men marrying late in life – for economic reasons connected with multiple divisions of land among sons – had virtually alienated young women who, on the whole, refused to marry locally. Girls had left the countryside in far greater numbers than had men. The disproportionate number of bachelors in the remoter communities was striking. Girls who stayed at home or returned home having failed to find a husband elsewhere resigned themselves to spinsterhood with or without a sexual fling (sometimes difficult under the watchful eyes of a small community).

I had been aware of these conditions, even as a child on holiday in Donegal. The women there sought jobs in Derry or, failing that, in Glasgow. Sometimes they returned 'in disgrace', to have their babies either at home or secretly in an isolated field. These things were whispered about, or referred to circumspectly, so as not to cause scandal. In Donegal and in other remote parts, farmers at the plough occasionally turned up the remains of an infant conceived in passion and disposed of in panic. The frustration of women forced to end their days as spinsters or to wait to be asked by a man long past his prime has an old and lingering tragedy in Ireland. And the poignancy was brilliantly grasped by Merriman (in translation):

> The women of Ireland in misery sitting
> So that if the men remain as they are,
> Oh, we will be forced to abduct them, alas!
> When at last they desire to marry a wife
> Is when with them no girl would lie;
> When 'tisn't worth being beneath them prostrated
> Block-stiffened, sapless, worn-out ancients.

The Midnight Court describes how the poet, dreaming on a riverbank, meets a woman who represents Ireland's unmarried females. She invites him to attend a court where frustrated women berate him for his bachelorhood and flog him mercilessly. It was easy to find echoes in the Tralee court, a high-ceilinged room with teak furniture. There the anguish of Joanne Hayes unfolded in minute and often excruciating detail, filling some 15,000 pages of testimony, shocking the spectators, drawing sobs from witnesses and sneers from their inquisitors. It was the extent to which unspeakable intimacies were wrenched from a traditionally wary people that made the case unique. When the tribunal ended it failed to solve the central mystery of the macabre affair, but long after the central characters have ceased to exist, it will be savoured and analysed like Merriman's poem.

The two Kerry babies were born within a day or so of one another. The first was found by a jogger on the White Strand, a beach near the small Kerry town of Cahirciveen on the southern shore of Dingle Bay, almost directly opposite Slea Head on the northern shore. At 8.30 p.m. on a Saturday in April, John Griffin, a local sheep farmer, bounded over a dune and glanced at what he thought was a doll, wedged face-down in the rocks at low tide. He jogged on, but decided to take a closer look on his way back. It wasn't until he touched the skin with his finger that he was sure it was a corpse. The baby was bruised and had been stabbed twenty-eight times. A plastic fertilizer bag was found near by, thought to have been wrenched off the dead infant by the sea swirling over the rocks. Griffin's discovery was referred to in the Tralee tribunal as the 'Cahirciveen baby'. Griffin told the tribunal chairman, Justice Kevin Lynch – a Kerry man himself – that he alerted the *Garda Siochana*, as the Irish police are called.

Faced with a particularly gruesome infanticide, the police followed some bizarre avenues of investigation before requesting help from colleagues in Dublin. They sought out families where pregnancies might have resulted from incest. They asked the local gravedigger to keep watch for a repentant mother turning up at Cahirciveen cemetery. The parents of a fifteen-year-old girl whose diary contained references to rape were interviewed. They carried out a nationwide check on private clinics for information about Kerry-based pregnant women. They questioned people about romances broken in the previous nine months. Chemists were checked for women asking for tablets capable of inducing abortion (then forbidden under Irish law). Tinkers were interrogated, as were hippies scattered along the famous scenic route known as the Ring of Kerry. They even raised the possibility of black magic having been involved in the child's death. Just after midnight on the day before Griffin found the body of the Cahirciveen baby, Joanne Hayes felt hot and flushed in the family farmhouse. She had been ambivalent about the child she was carrying. A few friends at the Tralee sports centre, where she was a receptionist, had been aware of the baby's imminent arrival, but Joanne believed she had managed to conceal the pregnancy completely from her family. Only her thirty-year-old sister Kathleen suspected because several months earlier 'Joanne tripped on a bramble bush and fell, and I noticed a bump'. Joanne told the tribunal about the slight pain she felt might be birth pangs as she sat in the uncomfortably hot kitchen wearing only a short-sleeved nightdress. Kathleen was preparing for bed. Their widowed mother, Mary, aged seventy, was already in bed with influenza. Joanne walked from the kitchen into the night air to cool off. Still clad only in her nightdress, she crossed a yard soiled by cattle and went into a field. There was hardly a breeze. The undulating road beyond was free of traffic. She leant against an ash tree.

'I was outside, a bit down from the house,' she told the hushed courtroom, her thin Kerry voice expanded by the microphone on the witness stand. 'I was standing up when I gave birth to a child. I just pulled the umbilical cord and it broke.'

I could see that her own words distressed her. But that was nothing compared with her ordeal under cross-examination by barristers representing members of the *Garda Síochána* when she became hysterical, broke down and had to be sedated. Her story came in gasps and sobs. She placed her six-pound infant and the afterbirth under a haycock, she said. Next morning at dawn, she put the dead baby in a plastic bag and placed it in an old disused well along a ditch not far from the farmhouse. The tribunal decided to name it the 'Abbeydorney baby'. Had it lived, she would have named it Shane.

The baby's father, Jeremiah Locke, was a married man and barely over 5 ft. He was also the father of Joanne's little daughter, Yvonne. She said she 'just happened to fall in love with him'. Her hopes that he would leave his wife and set up home with her had been dashed by Jeremiah's wife becoming pregnant, too. Her defeat was that of the witness in *The Midnight Court*.

> Where is my fault that she's chosen before me?
> And what is the reason that love is not given me,
> When I am so graceful, so modest, so excellent?
> . . . At dancing, game and race and gathering,
> Bonfire, gossiping, drinking parties;
> Fair and market and Mass on Sunday,
> Seeking notice, to see men and choose them.
> I spent my wits in a useless hunt . . .

But there was worse. Joanne Hayes became the prime police suspect in the Cahirciveen murder inquiry for what seemed understandable reasons. She was unmarried. She consorted with a local man. She had been pregnant and was no longer so. Where was her baby? She was asked to go to Tralee *garda* station where, she told the tribunal, she was questioned for hours, in a manner which would break the spirit of many a hardened criminal, let alone an unsophisticated farmer's daughter whose only contact with police had been to say 'Hello, Liam' to the village bobby. In the end, she was taken on to a detective's knee while another detective took down her statement. 'What have I done?' she cried. 'I am a murderess!' She was arrested and charged with the murder of the Cahirciveen baby.

According to the statement, which she said she made under prompting and duress, the baby was born *indoors*. There she struck it with a bath brush and in a frenzy plunged a carving knife into its body. Her two brothers Ned, aged twenty-eight, and Mike, twenty-seven, who had looked after the 60-acre farm since their father died ten years earlier, drove the tortuous road to Slea Head and, within sight of the phosphorescent crucifixion tableau, dumped the baby in the sea. It all seemed to fit. The assumption was that tides and currents and ocean winds carried the dead infant across the bay to Cahirciveen. Joanne Hayes was remanded in custody to Limerick gaol, and thence to a psychiatric hospital to await trial.

Eventually, of course, after precise directions to her brother Ned, Joanne's baby – the Abbeydorney baby – was found where she had tried to tell the police she had put it. The police then concluded that she had given birth to twins. Forensic evidence suggested, however, that the Cahirciveen baby was blood group A, while the Abbeydorney baby and its parents were blood group O. The police thought again: Joanne Hayes must have been impregnated by two different fathers on the same night. Legal minds began to boggle at this gynaecological improbability.

The public prosecutor's decision to abandon the trial in the light of these developments did not end Joanne's ordeal. The Irish

Minister for Justice set up a tribunal of inquiry into how the police charges came to be preferred and into allegations by the Hayes family after the charges were dropped. That summer, Justice Lynch presented his report which criticized some police procedures but fell considerably short of the disciplinary recommendations many – including the Hayes family – had expected. Already, Joanne Hayes had been stripped naked by tribunal barristers and exposed publicly to anatomical examination worthy of the most painstaking gynaecologist. Twice she left the witness stand to be sick. She described through sobs her first two ordeals – the birth and the arrest – even as she endured her third, the inquiry.

'You know,' asked counsel for three superintendents, 'there is a medical phenomenon – I will explain it to you – called puerperal lunacy?'

Joanne shook her head.

'Quite common. In your fever, in your temporary lunatic state, you got the knife and stabbed the baby.'

'No. It is all *untrue!*'

'You didn't know if the baby was born dead or alive?'

'It was dead.'

'Then what had you done?'

Her voice rasped into the microphone. 'I abandoned it.' She wept.

'You said you gave birth to a child outside. Did the child cry?'

'I don't think so.'

Hadn't she panicked and killed it by putting her hand on its neck? Wasn't that what happened?

'I pulled the baby by the neck when I was pulling him out.'

'You held him by the neck as you pulled him out. Didn't you realize you were killing your own baby?'

There was silence, then a sob. 'No.'

'You had no intention of allowing that child to be alive in the world after it left your body!' Counsel's delivery was heavily censorious, as though he was a parish priest rebuking sinners.

'That's untrue.' Joanne Hayes, huddled in a woolly jumper and anorak, was like a distraught teenage girl unable to find words of sufficient vehemence.

'And that's the reason you went out of the house into the field to give birth on that terrible, awful night!'

She choked. Her response was an expression of sheer misery; a precatory sound, begging mercy, appealing for their understanding, their sympathy for a life irreparably bruised by bewildering events. It stunned the courtroom spectators into a clenched silence. The policemen stared at their feet.

'That's not true,' wailed Joanne Hayes. Her despair echoed Merriman's lines from 1786:

> . . . At the witness table standing straight there.
> Her speech hindered by the bosom heaving,
> Without sound in her silence and worn by feeling.
> 'Twould be easy to state that she wished for death;
> Heavily fell her tears without let,
> As she stood at the table, straight as a quiver,
> Beating her hands and squeezing her fingers,
> While tears in a downpour she was weeping . . .

The aggressive questioning reflected the impatient indignation of the Irish male who was, in a sense, also on trial. The *gardai* and all the barristers were men. She was given little quarter there. As in *The Midnight Court*, there were a

> . . . Conceit of lawyers and jeers from great ones,
> . . . Legal clouds and a bad law's appearance.

Counsel for the police to Joanne's lover, Jeremiah Locke: 'Sure, wasn't she having sexual relations before she met you and while she was with you, and maybe she is still having relationships with one or more men!'

During the several days she was pinned to the tribunal witness stand, carloads of flowers arrived for Joanne Hayes. Women picketed the courthouse carrying placards critical of the inquisition. They shouted their protests and began to look just a bit disruptive. The judge issued a mild warning. While testifying, Joanne twisted a religious figurine in her fingers and clutched medals that had been blessed by priests. Women all over Ireland purchased Mass cards, entitling the diminutive witnesses to have Masses offered up on her behalf, and sent them to her home.

The house where Joanne Hayes was born is a long, low building with thick walls painted reddish-brown and cream. Behind the house, washing flapped in a cold breeze coming off the Stack and Glannaruddery mountains to the east. Nobody answered my knock on the front door and I walked round the back to find Ned tossing the dregs from a teapot into the yard. I was invited in. Ned was plump and puffy-faced, as was his mother, Mary. He was bleary-eyed and explained that one of the cows had calved in the night, requiring a long vigil. The family was at Mass. Ned picked up Yvonne, Joanne's daughter, hugged her and dandled her on his knee. Religious pictures hung from three walls. Ned turned on a television set above a cupboard containing empty plastic fertilizer bags. The Bishop of Limerick was on, sternly persuasive about the folly of the government in trying to make contraception legal in Ireland.

Yvonne ran to her mother as the family came in. She clearly enchanted the household, including Mike, who was painfully shy. Mary Hayes eased herself into a chimney nook beside a turf-burning stove. One of her three sisters was a nun, another a priest's housekeeper, whereas the third, Bridie Fuller, a frail ex-nurse in a wheelchair, was an embarrassment. Bridie, recovering from a stroke, had told the tribunal that Joanne had had her baby *inside* the Hayes farmhouse, that she herself had assisted at the birth and cut the umbilical cord with scissors. She insisted that her sister Mary, and other family members, had been around for the birth. The family sought to have Bridie certified as unfit to give evidence. Mary Hayes was indignant. 'There wasn't a baby born in the house,' she told me. 'God, glory be to Him, knows that and if I've to go before Him this minute, I'm telling the truth!'

Joanne talked about the grilling she had received from the police. 'They wouldn't believe me. I begged them to get me out to the exact spot [at Abbeydorney]. No, he wouldn't. Detective O'Carroll said that he wouldn't be made a fool of by a cheeky strap like me. He said he was going to bring the baby from Cahirciveen and I could identify it. They wouldn't take me [from the police station] to Abbeydorney because they said all I wanted was to get some fresh air and clear my head.' They were 'roaring and shouting' at her, calling her a murderer. When she felt sick, a detective threw a newspaper on the floor, telling her to be sick on that. Another detective said that Ned had made a statement that she had killed the baby by stabbing it in the chest. If Joanne didn't 'tell the truth', her mother would be charged with murder and Yvonne put in an orphanage. This detective kept banging on the table and slapped her twice on the face. She asked for a bible on which she might swear she was telling the truth. It was not produced.

In custody, she wrote to a friend: 'I had to make a false statement because they told me that if I didn't my mother would be jailed and Yvonne would be put in an orphanage . . . I don't mind being punished for what I did, but I didn't want to be punished for the baby at Cahirciveen.'

But at the tribunal she *was* punished, even though I had to remind myself that she wasn't on trial, that she was actually the complainant. They questioned her virginity before she met Jeremiah Locke. They dragged her back again and again to the early hours of the day her pregnancy ended, through the birth pangs, the delivery and the disposal. 'Not only were you not satisfied with stabbing the baby, but you beat it with a bath brush,' thundered counsel for the police. A recess was requested, and Joanne ran down a corridor to the toilet. She vomited. She sobbed and could not stop sobbing. A doctor told Judge Lynch she was hyper-ventilating, was nauseous and had a pulse rate of 120. Lines from *The Midnight Court* intruded again.

It tormented my heart and left me foolish,
Left in my thoughts and my spirits drooping;
Deflated and sick I am and weakened,
Pitiable, defeated, lamenting and weeping . . .

In the Dublin newspapers, only one other topic competed with the Kerry Babies Case for space: the government's Bill to make contraception legally available to the likes of Joanne Hayes. The *Irish Times* mentioned condoms in three headlines on one page alone. It ran an editorial, 'Sex and the law', which suggested there was an element in such cases 'of the ancient concept of woman as the temptress, the root of all evil. The law, no doubt about it, is based on a masculine concept of life.' Irish bishops went on television, lobbied politicians, and issued ferocious reminders that the government Bill would gravely harm Irish family life. Across the land, alarm bells clanged in bishoprics and belfries. Catholic morality, hitherto underpinned in the Irish Republic by a Constitution that gave the Catholic Church a special place in affairs of state, and in Northern Ireland by sectarian tensions that made one side compete against the other for God's favour, was seen to be under fire on all sides. A form of national shock juddered through towns and villages, then subsided.

Before I left, a girl who worked at a Tralee hotel told me excitedly that her mother had just been on the phone from Asdee, a village twenty miles up the road. Her mother could hardly get the news out. There had been a 'manifestation' in the village church, St Mary's. Three children, aged between seven and twelve, had left their school playground to enter the church, where they reported seeing movement in the hands and eyes of two statues in a corner. 'I saw Jesus moving,' said the youngest child, Elizabeth Flynn. 'His hand moved and he called me. Then I saw the eyes of the Blessed Virgin move.' Thirty other children flocked into the church from the playground. They saw it too. The acting Bishop of Kerry was informed, and the diocesan vicar hurried to Asdee to question the witnesses. They said they were keeping 'an open mind'.

I too hurried to the unremarkable, featureless village. I met the local curate, Father Michael O'Sullivan, a soft-spoken young man who was struck by the 'amazing consistence' in what the children had reported. He himself wouldn't use the word 'miracle', but, since God often worked in strange ways, he did not rule out some connection between the business in Tralee and the manifestation in Asdee. I went inside the small church. A crowd had assembled around a candelabrum. They lit fresh candles and recited rosaries. The street outside was thronged with new arrivals, awaiting their turn to see the statues. Within a day, Joanne Hayes had been ousted from the front pages of Irish newspapers, her place taken by an illusion. Religion in Ireland showed itself capable of moving mountains of metal type. Subsequently, I learned that Ms. Hayes had courageously reclaimed a dignified life for herself without having to leave the family homestead. She is well regarded in the community.

Yet what, I wondered to myself at the time, would the Protestants of Ulster make of such things? At the very least, they reinforced their prejudices against the Roman Catholic Church, but for some they were a confirmation of what they had been taught to believe all along: that the area below their border was a place still rooted in the Middle Ages, and that the Catholic nationalists in the north would bring Ulster down to the same level given half a chance. And nowhere is that half-chance so resolutely resisted than among the Protestant farmers on the northern side of the border.

8

THEODICIC BELLMEN

It is not surprising that dwellers on or near the Irish border become twitchy. The IRA's 1956–62 campaign is often referred to as 'the border campaign'. In my childhood and youth, the border roads were places of almost palpable tension even when empty. The border was manned by customs posts on either side, as well as security forces. Smuggling was a two-way operation: livestock going south; spirits and clothing going north (though, depending on market conditions, these flows could be reversed). Some families occasionally went to Dublin by train, and returned, all twice their normal weight and wearing several sets of clothing. British Customs officers were more thorough than those of the Irish government. I always had the feeling that the authorities in Belfast had a visceral dislike of the idea of any Northern Ireland citizen travelling south. At one stage, in the 1950s, they introduced an irksome system requiring every motorist heading south to be equipped with a triptyque, a special permit. This was abandoned after complaints from loyal Unionists, who had urgent reasons for driving south, among them the acquisition of cheap whiskey, gin, stout, cigarettes and pipe-tobacco. Whenever I travelled south – to attend St Mary's College Old Boys dinner-dances – my father would say: 'Watch out for the B-Specials [auxiliary police] on the [northern] border roads.' The warning was not given lightly. The B-Specials were so notoriously and venomously anti-Catholic that they would shoot a Catholic's dog if given the opportunity. Once they took pot-shots at a Catholic bishop's pet dog. Most were farmers and farmers' sons, who liked nothing better than a good hunt, especially when disposal of the quarry had divine sanction. On at least two occasions, my father was stopped at the border on his way home from Dundalk, Drogheda or Dublin where he had been on Gaelic League business. Like all fluent Gaelic speakers, he wore a *fáinne*, a ring of gold, on his lapel. This didn't necessarily identify him as a Catholic, since a great number of Protestants had also chosen to learn Gaelic. But it suggested that he almost certainly was, and a nationalist to boot, which, in the average B-Special's eyes, amounted to the same thing. All that happened to him and the driver of the car on both occasions was that he was searched, shoved and slapped around. But it was an indignity that no human being should expect to endure while on a legitimate journey in his own land.

Such things helped explain my father's unrelenting antipathy to police officers. I'm fairly sure he inherited some of it; the thuggish attack on his Shakespeare-spouting father would have been part of that inheritance. Events in Willowfield Gardens would have reinforced it. I have never known him to be rude to policemen, but I have observed his face freezing up if one approached to check his or my driving licence. Catholic policemen (never a significant proportion of the Royal Ulster Constabulary at the best of times) sometimes nodded and smiled at him on leaving Mass on a Sunday, but he never nodded or smiled back, even when they were the parents of my school-fellows. One school pal was Ronnie McMullan, an amiable and loyal comrade who lived two streets away from us. His father was an RUC inspector, a stiff-backed, impassive man, diligent about his religious duties and the welfare of his children, all of whom were stable, bright and fairly outgoing. Inspector McMullan, despite his blank expression, would look at you with a warm, friendly gleam in his dark eyes, and I never felt uncomfortable when he came to his door in response to my knock. But because of my father's attitude to 'peelers' I felt uneasy, even in those brief contacts with him. I also felt a sense of guilt about my reserve – so much so that I cannot recall ever talking to Ronnie about his father or his father's job.

I was about nineteen, I think, when a cousin (a daughter of my father's blind brother, John) married a handsome, cheerful young constable. My father received the news as though he'd been knifed in the back. 'Damnable, damnable,' is what he said, as though some awful disgrace had visited our family. I thought this pretty rich at the time, given that my father had been, for most of his life, particularly the latter part, quite detached from his siblings' lives and the doings of their children. Consequently, I have first cousins whom I haven't seen for decades, and first cousins whom I have never seen at all. I have no doubt that he was fond of them all; it's just that he – and possibly they – seemed to have no great need for tactility, or visual presences, or even written correspondence, to reinforce or demonstrate that fondness. A couple of years later, the young man resigned from the force to embark on an alternative career. Immediately, my father began speaking of him with forgiveness and affection, making him welcome at Ponsonby Avenue.

My own early hostility to 'peelers' was not entirely due to my father's visceral dislike of them. As a Catholic, I grew up in an anti-police culture as intense and as natural as I have encountered since in the East End of London or sections of the Bronx in New York. This culture did not always spring from rabid republicanism. It sprang in the main, I think, from the fact that the police constable had, in days gone by, represented or enforced an authority that tipped rural people out of their houses for non-payment of rents, smashed poteen stills, pounced on cattle smugglers and salmon poachers and – worst of all – infiltrated communities, the better to exercise that authority and make the miserable lives of Catholic nationalists even more miserable. The prejudice was effortlessly absorbed by children. On Hallowe'en nights, my friends and I would ambush Sergeant Kelly, a fat RUC man, as he wobbled up Ponsonby Avenue on his ancient black Hercules to curtail our use of fireworks (which included the dangerous practice of putting 'bangers' in letter-boxes). A rocket would be placed in an empty milk bottle, and aimed at him as he pedalled and puffed up the Ponsonby slope towards us as we dared him forward. 'Smelly Kelly has a big fat belly!' we yelled. Once, a rocket hit him in the stomach, knocking him off his bicycle. We cheered and ran.

As I grew older, I gradually lost much of the prejudice towards the RUC that my father and my environment had imparted to me. It did not leave me entirely, though. Frequently, the Ulster police force would disgrace itself with brutal – and clearly sectarian – onslaughts on Catholics, especially if the latter were on a march in support of human rights. Their use of torture on hooded republican suspects in the 1970s has been well documented, piling even greater ordure on the force's reputation. But later my feelings towards the force came to accommodate a certain respect and a great deal of sympathy as they tried, desperately and at considerable sacrifice, to fight terrorism without further alienating the Catholic community. Their task of maintaining law and order in Belfast has been hard enough, as religious ghettoes choose to rely on paramilitary 'punish-ment squads' to suppress crime, rather than beckon in the RUC. But the pressures of maintaining peace in the countryside must be far more acute, given the risks of ambushes on narrow lanes, booby-trap bombs, and other traps. Along Ulster's border with the Irish Republic, the telephone poles carry placards demanding the disbanding of the RUC.

Not long before the IRA's 1994 ceasefire, I travelled along this wiggly dividing line and spoke to people on its northern side. In Crossmaglen, in south Armagh, the IRA had warned residents a few days earlier that they risked becoming casualties by not hurrying to and from school with their children. The warnings in letter-box leaflets, were linked to terrorist threats against the local British Army base. The border – 288 miles of it – is like a dangerous serpent; its head in one sea and its tail in another, joint-creation of man and nature. It twists across the island from its eastern origins in Carlingford Lough, flops through a second, freshwater, expanse – Lough Erne – in the Ulster-Irish midlands and, having almost reached the Atlantic, turns sharply northward to plunge into Lough Foyle. It has been attacked, defended, penetrated, temporarily sev-ered, bombed and blocked with amazing regularity. It is both source and focus of intercommunal hatred, destruction and paranoia. Attempts to slay it – or move it elsewhere – have failed again and again. Driving along it, you have to follow roads that are now in Northern Ireland and seconds later in the Republic. In commercial terms it ceases to exist (as a result of the European Union's abolition of customs boundaries), but in every other way it perseveres, with or without the tall security posts, and with or without the 'peace process'.

For Protestants such as Roy Harpur, more or less isolated in their south Armagh farmhouses, the idea of scaled-down border security is quite frightening. He lives in two shadows: that of Slieve Gullion, a prominent mountain, and that of the gunman. He and his wife are patently decent, God-fearing and forbearing, but they worry about what life will be like in the event of a settlement of the Troubles. Naked sectarianism does not disappear at the stroke of a pen. Over a belly-busting lunch in the farmhouse kitchen, Mr Harpur described for me what the last quarter-century had been like. 'I can't remember the half of the terrible things that have happened. I don't know what joy anyone could get out of it, irrespective of their feelings.' On one occasion, he got a call urging him to leave his house – 'It was a tit-for-tat for some Roman Catholic neighbours who had been threatened by loyalists. That Sunday, three Roman Catholics were murdered across the road. The next night [the local IRA] murdered ten Protestants on their way home in a minibus . . . I always thought nothing could surpass the IRA in brutality, until I met a policeman [who] described things that loyalist extremists do to their victims.' Sometimes the bigotry seems imbued with fundamentalism. 'As a man said to me the other night, either the end of the world is approaching or this country is on the brink of a religious revival.'

Family traditions and notions of 'heritage' motivate most border farmers, even though some feel time may be against them. There is an unwritten rule that, if Protestants wish to leave, they should try to avoid selling the land to Catholics. This policy is less an act of conscious bigotry than it might seem. Border Protestants have an enhanced sense of heritage. They believe that if they sell to Catholics, they are as good as transferring British territory to the Irish Republic. Harry West, an elderly Fermanagh Protestant who had served in the Unionist government, before it was discredited and prorogued, agrees. His nine-bedroom house is on a hill over-looking, on one side, the runway of a tiny airport; on the other, Lower Lough Erne. The house is open to Catholic and Protestant alike, he told me during my border journey.

'We recognize we are in the minority – by about 8,000 – in County Fermanagh,' he said. 'We accept that and have learnt to live with it.' He recalled inviting a former British Secretary of State for Northern Ireland, Roy [now Lord] Mason to stay overnight. 'Roy and his wife and daughter arrived; there was a great gathering, and the crack was good. He got me into a corner and said, "Would I be right in saying this is a mixed bunch?" "Yes," I said. "It always is." "I never would have believed it," he said. So I told him: "There are some Roman Catholic people in this area who are as good loyalists as we Protestant people."'

I thought back to 1960 when I was twenty-four and West had just joined the Northern Ireland Cabinet at Stormont. The border was unsettled then too. Economic difficulties in the statelet had created uneasiness in all sections of the community. People were asking questions about unemployment, industrial growth, the adequacy of Lord Brookeborough's Unionist government. Less than four years earlier, irregulars of the IRA had initiated a campaign of terrorism along the border, bombing British military installations in County Fermanagh. Similar acts of terrorism continued for another two years both in Northern Ireland and in Britain. But the IRA's activities caused no shock-waves in Belfast. All the campaign did was to take people's minds momentarily off the economic malaise. The government of the Republic of Ireland publicly con-demned terrorism as a means of achieving the incorporation of the six northern counties into its territory. In February 1962, the IRA announced that it had abandoned its campaign to reunify the island by force. Tensions slowly subsided.

Seven years later, the renewal of the campaign did much more than renew tensions. Many Protestants have left their border farms 'because they were being shot at'. Some have moved to Scotland. Mr West believed the border 'is creeping our way'. I met other Protestants who were genuinely fearful of ending up in the Irish Republic, even though many of them have relatives who have farmed across the border without difficulty since the island was divided. The border air has always had a smouldering whiff to it. There never has been a 'demilitarized zone', only road-blocks, craters caused by dynamite, demolished bridges. No other restrictions were placed on law-abiding citizens of either side, visiting and doing business with each other. Yet today's bright intercourse is often conducted in the shadow of yesterday's memories. You sense it when talking to Harry West. He was appointed Agriculture Minister in the Stormont government by the man who, as Sir Basil Brooke, boasted that he would never tolerate having a Catholic in his vicinity. Mr West is an affable man who is seen as a relic of the old regime. His heart lies nostalgically in those far-off days when a 'Protestant parliament for a Protestant people' brought a kind of tyranny to a third of the population. When we talked about Brookeborough's resignation in 1968 and death five years later, Mr West fiddled with his teaspoon and confessed with a sigh: 'I don't mind telling you I dropped a tear . . .'

More than 150 years ago Thomas Davis, the Irish essayist of Welsh extraction, wrote of his hope that 'as Orangemen become more enlightened, they will more and more value the love of their countrymen, be prouder of their country, and more conscious that their ambition, interest, and even security are identical with nationality'. My father's sentiments always were a kind of echo of that. But I don't think he ever managed to see things through the Protestant prism. Until he was too feeble to express it, his view always was that Protestants had nothing to fear from a united Ireland; that discrimination in a separated Ulster would not be followed by recrimination in a re-absorbed Ulster. But he did not – could not – quite grasp the idea that Protestant Ulster wished to retain its *status quo*, not so much through its contempt for, or suspicion of, Irish Catholicism, though these prejudices were frequently and vehemently expressed, as through an unassailable desire to be British. Further, a great many Ulster Catholics, feeling relatively unburdened by the yoke of history or nationalist preferences, would be happier ruled from London than from Dublin.

Nationalism in Ireland, as elsewhere, is a sword more often than it is a ploughshare. Undoubtedly it is an uplifting and cherished emotion that binds us together in moments of adversity, providing material for consolidating our individual roles within society. It confers on inadequates feelings of adequacy; the paltry, diffident 'I' becoming the proud and confident 'We'. It creates not only the group but the instinct to defend it. It encourages the concentration of individual pugnacity in deadly form. Just as it fuels wars, it can feed resistance to peace. In its heightened, arrogant form – patriotism – it nourishes an exaggerated esteem of the achievements within the group, and dislike and depreciation of those outside it.

My father was well aware of these things. He often said that patriotism was a word that fell most sweetly on the ear, but could leaden the heart and spread poison to the soul. It could, I heard him say, make even educated – not to mention self-educated – persons temporarily indisposed to analyse dearly held convictions and sanctified emotions. He understood all this very clearly. But it was, I cannot avoid thinking, a comprehension arrived at from the Irish patriot's standpoint: that while the idea of a united Ireland was largely wrapped up in misty distortions and mythical suppositions, it was still validated by the rules of natural justice and territorial completeness. On those (fairly rare) occasions when I tried to talk to him about Unionism's sense of *terra patria*, his 'good' ear lost some of its receptivity and his eye darted away. This puzzled me occasionally, for I had always known that he professed to be sensible to the fears and aspirations of those of his fellow-countrymen who wished to call themselves British rather than Irish. He regulated his life so that he could eschew bigoted gestures. When many Belfast

Catholics confined their bread purchases to the bakery of Bernard Hughes, a Catholic, we stuck with the Co-operative Bakery, probably because of the Co-operative movement's links with socialism. As children, we would justify our choice by chanting (outside adults' hearing): 'Barney Hughes's bread, /Sticks to your belly like lead. / Not a bit of wonder /It makes you fart like thunder.' My father declined to patronize exclusively shops owned by Catholics. To do so, he said, would be an act of discrimination. So when I would say to him, 'Ulster should remain British, if Ulster people are happier that way,' it rankled slightly with me that he did not concur with enthusiasm. If my father – a man of peaceful nature, sense of fairness, reined-in emotions, and ability to examine all facets of a problem – could not quite bring his ear to the other fellow's larynx or his eye to the other fellow's lens, transcending his own preferences, then who could?

Many thoughtful Protestants concede similar deficiencies. Fred Cobain, a former Unionist mayor of Belfast, once said to me: 'We Protestants are captives of our own mentality. We need to create institutions where Catholics and Protestants can get together. That's how we can be free.' He did not think the Orange Order was the answer. Many people think, rather, that the Orange Order is the question. However beneficently that organization has tried to present itself, most people see its fiery colour as the torch of hatred rather than the lamp of freedom.

For all the fine silk that goes into its brilliant banners, the Orange Order has more than its fair share of rough-grained men and roaring priests. Despite its members' pledge of loyalty to [Protestant] Church and Monarch, it has long been associated with private armies and civil disobedience. Not a year passes in which it neglects to celebrate William, Prince of Orange's 1690 rout of the Catholic King James by marching triumphantly through, or close to, Catholic neighbourhoods. Paradoxically, the banners they carry are emblems of compelling beauty, wrought with great devotion, even if hoisted with defiance and bigotry. Each of the hundred or more lodges has its own distinctive banner, commemorating ancient battles, where

Protestants and Catholics died fighting each other on their own soil, and less ancient ones, such as the Battle of the Somme, where they died fighting on the same side on foreign soil. As the Orangemen tramp city streets and country roads, resolutely facing the past, the silken banners ripple with further ironies. Among them is a dismaying exaltation of the now defunct B-Specials – whose excesses against Catholics before the latest Troubles helped to pile ignominy on top of hegemony, and contributed to the collapse of the Orange citadel, Stormont. Another oddity is that while many Orange lodges carry temperance banners, few of the marchers beneath them are sober at the end of Orange Day.

The lodges may be an anachronism, but they remain the self-appointed custodians of Ulster Protestant history, just as the IRA and Sinn Féin regard themselves as the Keepers of the Cause for Ulster Catholics. My father used to compare the Orange Order to the Ku Klux Klan. I would not go that far, but I think he was referring to their ridiculous apparel, their intolerance, their rejectionism, their fundamental certainties and their desire, as expressed in lines I wrote some time ago, to:

> Flagellate dissenters whose caution is absurd;
> Let Borborygmus swell the Written Word.
> Preach in Orange Portadown, Portaferry too;
> If they won't give credence, take their blood in lieu.
> Holy-watered fingers plunging in our eyes,
> Theodicic bellmen timing our demise;
> Fulminating Islam, decomposing Marx,
> Zealots of the Talmud, and Christ in the Ozarks.
> Pulling up the drawbridge, drawing down the blind,
> List'ning for Al Daawa on the screaming wind.
> Hail the Millennium with miracles wrought,
> To unify all in a Commonwealth of Nought.

Both Orange and Green propagandists can and do point to iniquities in each other, often with justification. The jabbing fingers, far from being admonitory gesticulations calling for accommodations by 'the other side', are really points of emphasis against accommodations of any kind. Years before World War II occurred, an eminent German sociologist issued for the benefit of his countrymen a book entitled *Warlike England as Seen by Herself*, containing extracts from British writings indicating the lengths to which the United Kingdom was prepared to go in subduing other races and seizing their territory. In every case, these extracts were characterized by omissions, distortions, modifications, additions and falsifications, deliberately intended to mislead the reader; but all had the appearance of good faith and plausibility.

Similarly, in Northern Ireland, I have come upon distortions, themselves not always of great account, yet manufactured in a mind so teeming with prejudicial pettinesses that no chance was to be missed in putting the other side 'in their place'. An example of what I mean can be found in the Northern Ireland street directory published by the *Belfast Newsletter*. Under every town's 'institutions', local churches are listed. In nearly every case, the Catholic church is mentioned last – after the Church of Ireland, the Presbyterian church, the Methodists, the Congregationalists and the Baptists – even in towns where Catholic churchgoers are in an overwhelming majority. The only occasions on which they are not to be found at the bottom of the list is when they just manage to edge ahead of tiny mission halls and Jehovah's Witnesses. The propagandists of republicanism and loyalism hoodwink their respective constituencies. Fear and death occur in speech with conditioning regularity, causing people to brood upon –

> towers of dread foundation laid
> Under the grave of things.

From such deceits spring acts of murder, ruthlessly executed and calmly excused: terrorism – defended by Robespierre, in a classic phrase, as 'nothing more or less than prompt, severe, and inflexible justice'.

Often I wonder what would have happened to me had I stayed in Northern Ireland. Would I have been able to breathe the prejudicial air without becoming addicted – or without choking? I do not know. As I write these chapters, I sometimes pause to ask myself the question: how can you be so sure that you are not addicted, or, at the very least, tainted to the extent that every observation you make, every assumption you draw, every expression you interpret, disqualifies you as an honest, worthwhile chronicler? Perhaps it is no use claiming that I have lived away from it all for so long that the 'taint' no longer curbs my observations, my assumptions, my interpretations; it might well be argued that my very virtual absence from the centre of things since 1964 makes my appreciation of them out of date and worthless. Again, I do not know. I just wonder whether, had I not left for London, I could have continued to traverse Napoleon's Nose, as my father did, without thinking in sectarian expletives, as he didn't? Again, I do not know. When I was a child, in Holy Family church, I sang:

> *Tantum ergo sacramentum*
> *Veneremur cernui,*
> *Et antiquum documentum*
> *Novo cedat ritui.*

It was the great hymn of the Middle Ages. At the time, I had no idea what it meant, even when broadly translated into English ('Down in adoration falling,/ Lo! the Sacred Host we hail,/ Lo! o'er ancient forms departing,/ Newer rites of grace prevail'). It was precisely the kind of sanctimonious gobbledegook that was capable of feeding the prejudices of Protestant acquaintances, even those whom I considered 'friendly'. But it brought tears to my eyes; and, to my heart, a willingness to be martyred for any cause that might come along, so that I could prove to Christ that I was – to use the words of the Confirmation ceremony – a 'strong and perfect Christian'. As I sang it with half-closed eyes, diffusing the shimmer from the altar candles into a great backdrop of light that became part of my very being, I wished that a statue would move for me, and that life might be one, long, joyful holy war.

9

CHARLES ATLAS, KAY STARR, ANGELA, SHEILA AND THE CASEY SISTERS

My piety then was no weaker and no stronger, I suppose, than the feelings of my Protestant peers whenever they too were moved by excessive religiosity. These feelings politicized us, intensified our respective brands of nationalism. That did not make us unique, of course. Religion and nationalism have fused elsewhere as driving-forces to delusion and hatred. Notably and recently, we have been repelled by it in former Yugoslavia. But what depresses me, as it sometimes did Charles McCrystal, is our steadfast unwillingness to learn anything at all from the past other than a justification for continuing as before.

Intense nationalism led to anti-Semitism in nineteenth-century Europe, and pushed the Austrian *Kleindeutsche* into Lutheranism – the Prussian religion – and into renouncing international, conservative, Habsburg-aligned Catholicism. In the idiom of nationalism, people made themselves *Romfrei* ('Rome-free'). The phrase *Los von Rom* (no bond with Rome) was a political slogan in the early 1870s, just as something very similar was to become a political slogan in Ireland early in *our* century ('Home Rule is Rome rule') and persists today ('No pope here!'). It buttressed national patriotism and deepened the division between the *kleindeutsch* camp and the mainstream of Austro-German democratic nationalism, intensifying the feeling of persecution – of being in a political ghetto – among the *Kleindeutsche*.

Little-Ulster-at-bay embodies what the *Kleindeutsch* movement embodied: extreme rancour, indignation and feelings of having been betrayed by its own side; reluctance to discuss and compromise; ambivalence towards order, authority, property and equality; pre-occupation with conspiracy; a view of the enemy as degenerate, contemptible, and entitled only to hard knocks and short shrift. Nineteenth-century pan-Germanism, on the other hand, manifested many of the things that Irish republicanism represents in Northern Ireland today, not least its insistence on the necessity of unconditional surrender and of total solutions and pride in violence as an expression of integrity – not to mention physical coercion, contempt for conventional political parties, a partiality for conspiratorial organiz-ations.

But piety for me was intermittent, easily transgressed or dissolved by mundane matters such as student friendships, the pursuit of pubescent girls and summer holidays. On leaving the Dundalk boarding school, I returned briefly to Holy Family school in New-ington in order to sit the eleven-plus examination. This got me into St Malachy's College, yet another institution run by priests who believed that spiritual hygiene could be achieved through corporal punishment. I opted for Greek, Latin and Irish – languages that did not greatly enhance my communicative powers when I became a foreign correspondent. But I enjoyed the college very much, even though my achievements there were of only moderate distinction. And I fear that, when I left five years later, the words on the school crest, *Gloria ab intus*, were not deeply engraved upon my record.

St Malachy's college had been a diocesan seminary since 1832 when it was surrounded by fields that stretched northward to Cave Hill and southward to Donegall Street. The building had belonged to a Belfast merchant, Thomas McCabe – and here again the 1798 Rebellion crops up. McCabe had been associated with some of the Belfast leaders of the United Irishmen. In the years preceding their insurrection, he was suspected of treason. His jeweller's shop was wrecked by a mob of soldiers which left only one pane of glass unbroken. Ordered shortly afterwards to participate in the loyal illuminations for the King's birthday, McCabe placed several candles behind the single, unbroken pane, his silent flickering comment on the meaning of loyalty in Belfast. He also changed the wording of his signboard to read, 'Thomas McCabe, an Irish slave, licensed to sell gold and silver'. When I joined the college, its president was Very Rev. Patrick Kerr, nicknamed 'Patchy' because of his baldness. My Latin teacher was John Cassidy (nicknamed 'Hopalong') who had unusual difficulty in getting us to pronounce certain syllables. One warm summer afternoon, when all the classroom windows were wide open, he asked us, one after the other, to run through the present tense of *dico* ('I say'). None of us could manage *dicunt*, the third person plural, which amid nudges and sniggers, would come out as 'di-coont', or 'di-cyunt', or 'dicuw . . . unt'. Hopalong grew more and more exasperated with us. He mopped his brow and swished his cane.

'How many times do I have to tell you?' he roared, his voice carrying across the quadrangle. 'It's di-*cunt* . . . *cunt*! . . . *cunt*! . . . *cunt*!'

Unfortunately, Patchy chose to walk past the open windows at that moment. He came to a halt, eyes widening, jaw dropping. A moment later, he opened the classroom door slightly and nodded to Hopalong. 'I say, Mr Cassidy, may I have a brief, private word?'

The college's spiritual director was Rev. Desmond Wilson, who later went to live in Ballymurphy, a strongly republican housing estate in west Belfast, where he was widely regarded as 'a Sinn Féin priest'. But it was another priest, probably the bursar, who ordered that pictures of nude statues illustrating our new Greek readers should be removed before the books were distributed, lest our young minds be corrupted by the sight of marble testes photographed in grainy black and white. This meant that, in learning about middle and passive imperatives, we could translate the sentence, 'Persuade Socrates to train the boys in wisdom,' but were spared an image of Aphrodite with her marbled nipples showing, or even of Apollo with his figleaf. However, a lay teacher, a large Cork man called Maurice Drinan (like my father, a prominent member of the Gaelic

League), compensated for the censorship by drawing a bull's testicles on the blackboard in a rudimentary attempt to explain to us the 'facts of life'. Hysterics ensued, as we stuffed hankies, pencils, blotting paper – anything – into our mouths to prevent ourselves from cackling out loud.

Another layman on St Malachy's staff, a physics teacher, David Kennedy, joined my father on the 1798 Commemoration committee. I was slightly intimidated by the fact that so many of the 45-strong teaching staff were acquainted with my father and therefore expected greater things of me than I was able to provide or promise. But generally speaking, although I was not prepared to put in very much effort, I had a smooth enough run through my college years, with just enough cramming to avoid ignominy. My place in class never rose above seventh, and my school reports did not lie: 'Intelligent pupil, but his [English] literature mark is perhaps flattering. Answering here was very mediocre'; 'Bad mark. Does very little work. Could do well' (ancient history); 'Has lost considerable ground, because he is not taking his work sufficiently seriously. In a precarious position' (maths). Students who lunched in the college canteen benefited from the creations of 'Miss Carina M. Davey, I.M.A., Cordon Bleu (Paris)'; those who found the creations disagreeable were treated by the college nurse, Sister Mary Attracta. There was a shrine to Our Lady of Lourdes in one corner of the grounds, and handball alleys in another. St Malachy's College had debating groups, Irish language groups, a Legion of Mary, a 'pioneer total abstinence association', which I joined, and a water polo team, which I also joined (though not many years were to pass before I abandoned both water polo *and* abstinence). The ivy-walled front of the college was approached by a long private avenue that ran down to Antrim Road and, just across it, a tuck shop. A block away on the north side of the college, our neighbours included an Army barracks. On the west side, our playing-fields and running track backed up against the high wall of Crumlin Road prison. In very hot weather we had our lessons on a grassy bank at the foot of this wall. While our Latin teacher droned on about the Britons begging for peace . . . *Interea suos remigrare in agros iusserunt* . . . we listened hard for penitential sounds or grappling-hooks from the other side of it.

During my St Malachy's years, we summered in Portstewart, in County Derry. I have a clear memory of the day my brothers and I first stepped from the sooty train at Cromore Halt, our eyes raking the green sweep of Ulster countryside for a glimpse of Atlantic surf. There was no sign of it. Had we got off at the wrong station?

We were bundled into an equally grimy taxi, its belching exhaust matching the departing locomotive's spread of filth. 'But where's the sea?' I whinged.

My father, puffing his pipe up front, turned: 'What sea?' he said, winking at the driver. Our stepmother, crushed in the back of the pungent cab, smiled reassuringly at her adopted brood. The smile that welcomed us when we came home finally from boarding school comforted us now. I said no more.

Cromore Halt lies behind a rise in the road that runs down to Portstewart. Within minutes we had fumed our way to where the sky began to drop, revealing in descending order the wind-streaked sea, the rocky coves, the neat harbour and even neater houses and shops of what was to become, after that first exhilarating plunge among them, the favoured resort of my youth. My first Portstewart summer was followed by four – or was it five? – more. Portstewart cheered me out of the forlorn forties, into the (relatively) florid fifties, providing me with novel sensations, some good, others less so. I performed my first high dive, suffered my first migraine attack, ate my first entire box of chocolate marshmallows (*before lunch*), saw my first jellyfish-sting victim, cheated my first fruit machine, trembled in my first romance. I emerged from those years with a swimmer's crew-cut, and deltoids desperately cultivated from a borrowed Charles Atlas course ('Once a seven-stone weakling, this man has the world's most perfectly developed human body!'). As I endeavoured, in the privacy of Portstewart's acres of sand dune, to coax my abdominal muscles into a prominence greater than my ribs, I was convinced that the reconciliation of perfection and individuality would somehow be effected in me; that, were it not for a crop of pimples that sun and salt and fingernails had failed to scour away, girls would, in the end, succumb.

Going back in 1988, in search of resemblances to those distant experiences, intent on overcoming the incompetence of human recall, was, I began to realize, sure to summon some unexpected refluent that would vex and well as please. I was not wrong.

Cromore Halt was closed and its station house in the process of being sold. The doors were nailed shut and some roof slates missing. There was a restaurant near by, the Galvey Lodge, which had a 'Cromore Halt Dining Room'. It had luggage racks. If Bushmills whiskey was consumed in sufficient quantity, it would sway. The bathing boxes were gone from the Herring Pond where Colm, Brendan, I and our friends swam when the moon was large and the water high, and the waves crashed over a little basalt reef to drown the shrieks of our spumescent frolics. At one end of the promenade, the Montague Arms Hotel, where Catholic priests could hit the bottle in peace, causing no scandal, was now a mere wine bar with living quarters for students above it. The students were from the University of Ulster at Coleraine, about ten miles up the River Bann from its estuary a couple of miles west of Portstewart. At the other end of the promenade, overlooking the harbour, the Carrig-na-Cuile Hotel had become an old people's home. On a grassy rise above Port-na-Happel swimming creek, a small square of concrete was all that remained of the *cabane de clairvoyance* of Gypsy Rose Lee, all soothsaid and long dead. Further down, close to the weedy rocks where Protestant french letters were said to float, her successor was in place: Madam Amadine, plump in her blue hut, palming fivers to beguile day-trippers with the allurements of her surmise.

It is edifying for a writer – for *anyone* – to turn from time to time from the fountain of discovery to the cistern of memory; for the tones of childhood to sound through life's swell of mingled melody and earnest encounter, the diapason of one's maturity. The tones of my Portstewart remembrance sounded from two chief sources: an amusement arcade juke-box and a piano in Tinsley's Café, both among the shops lining the promenade. While I thumped pennies out of a faulty fruit machine, the juke-box thumped *its* treasures into me. I can still hum Frank Chacksfield's 'Blue Tango', chance a few bars of Kay Starr's 'Wheel of Fortune' and Frankie Laine's 'Rock of Gibraltar', and recall our travesties of Jimmy Young's 'They Tried to Tell Us We're Too Young' ('They tried to sell us horses' dung'). The arcade had moved a bit up the promenade, where its fruit machines were less pervious in 1988, and the music was, to me, all travesty. Near the Montague Arms, a house in which we stayed, *Bonne Bouche*, looked exactly as it had been nearly forty years ago. So did other accommodations that had sheltered us: in the Diamond, Harbour Villas, Atlantic Circle. But Tinsley's Café was no more. The rows of tables, the pastry counter, the ice cream machine, the jars of sweets had vanished. They, and the battered upright piano around which we teenagers clustered summer after summer, had been replaced by TV sets, video recorders and hi-fis.

A salty wind from a distant Donegal headland loudened the bay and pressed me against the plate-glass as I tried to unravel from these new entanglements of Hitachi, Sony and Aiwa the plurality of sensation I had experienced there: the thrill of entering, wet towel and trunks under my arm, spondulicks in my pocket and lust in my heart, heading for the big table beside the piano, where my pal Maxie – Kevin McAlindon, yet another policeman's son, and now one of Ireland's largest wine importers – played 'Greensleeves' and 'Twelfth Street Rag' and a shard or two from *The Glass Mountain* soundtrack, surrounded by Angela and Sheila and the lovely, laughing red-headed Casey sisters, all regarding him, to my dismay, in worship.

'Are you lookin' for something particular?'

My disappointment must have shown. A woman in a duster coat was at my elbow, eyeing me with what seemed to be concern. I said I was looking for Tinsley's.

'Ach, it's gone these many years,' she said. 'But Mrs Tinsley still lives above the shop.' She pointed. 'Ring yon wee bell there.'

And so it happened that I again met Margaret Tinsley, alert in her seventies, widowed. Charlie, her husband, was ten years dead. A musician himself, he loved youngsters to bang away on the café keys, intervening only to correct their fingering. The piano survived. 'I couldn't let it go,' she said. 'There are so many nice memories . . .' I nodded my approval. 'So I got Jimmy Dempsey, who runs the TV and video shop down below, to store it for me in his home.' It turned out that his home was behind a low wall where we used to swim at Port-na-Happel, and where the surge and gurgle of dark water will now always drown the tinkle of the Tinsley piano.

We went through names from my youth. As Margaret Tinsley filled in the gaps, I was stunned by the finality of desolation that the litany bestowed.

'Of course I remember Angela,' she said. 'Wasn't my engagement ring made in her father's [Belfast] shop! . . .' Angela's pale, open face returned. We must have been fifteen, maybe sixteen, walking hand-in-hand along the cliff path skirting the walls of a castellated convent, a half-moon steady above and ashimmer below. In a doorway, locked on nuns and against male opportunism, my elation was rewarded with a single kiss. One of her brothers was studying for the priesthood. Another brother was a Marxist republican and (as I learned later) a man highly regarded by my father. Back in Belfast, on my way to play water polo at the Falls Road swimming-pool, I visited Angela in Divis Street, where her father's jeweller shop was. She wore a green school uniform. She seemed much more interested in her homework than in me. I never saw her again.

'. . . Sheila? Aye indeed, from Coatbridge in Scotland. Lovely girl, lovely family.'

Appallingly clever, the black-haired, brown-cheeked Sheila, daughter of a Belfast doctor and a Scottish judge, could outswim us all and never got cold in the Portstewart water. My own fingers and toes used to blanch within ten minutes of immersion, and I yearned to subdue my shivers against her glowing skin. But she let me suffer, and I suspected she had a preference for Maxie. I don't believe *he* got very far either.

'. . . Hadn't you heard? It was awful. Two of the Casey girls were shot dead in their father's office in 1975 . . . Belfast . . . Sectarian murder . . . Their brother too!'

And there was an onrush of something like Wordsworth's

> sorrow and despair
> From ruin and from change, and all the grief
> The passing show of Being leave behind.

Every summer, their family took the same house, painted yellow and with a long, neat lawn sloping towards a children's bathing-pool beneath the convent wall. I looked out through Mrs Tinsley's drawing-room window to identify it across the rolling bay. The house was still there, freshly painted. I could not summon up the sisters' images; only their fun and their freckles and the giggles of one of them when Colm called out: 'Colette, Colette, we'll get you yet!'

I asked about Una Fitzpatrick, a tall, slender girl whom I didn't know well, and whose two brothers became priests; one shy, the other a great turn in a sing-song. Mrs Tinsley told me that Noel, the shy one, had been murdered as he gave the last rites to a dying victim of the Troubles. The other brother was Raymond, a priest based near Lurgan, in County Armagh. I decided that I would visit him whenever an opportunity arose.

Saying farewell to Mrs Tinsley, I walked slowly along the sea side of the promenade, watching the gulls swoop over the little harbour. It is hard to apprehend the fragmentary composition of memory. Memory's instrument is the imagination, and the imagination is driven to the indulgence of a 'dream', a passion for unity and order. But in the salt air of Portstewart, passion was defeated by experience, imagination baffled by history. I walked past *Bonne Bouche*, with its brightly painted garden seat below the front window, towards the Diamond, passing between two Christian churches – one Protestant, the other Catholic. The fragments of unity and order that were embedded in my Portstewart experiences and in my general existence in those far-off days now seemed a long way out to sea.

Yet for all that, the resort remains a source of joy. The only tears it ever squeezed from me came not from grief or disappointment, but from the blinding whiteness of its sunny promenade. As I walked down it once more, blinking wetly in the afternoon sun, I saw well enough that the town was very much as I remembered it, its inhabitants just as agreeable. I stayed at a guest house not far from the derelict station – an agreeable change from those earlier accommodations, which had been cramped, rumpled from their weekly turnover: night shelters. Urgency did not drive me from the place, as it once drove me from the lodgings of my youth when guests from Lancashire sang hymns after high tea, sending me fleeing to the devil in the amusement arcade. A two-mile strand curved gently westward from a golf club to the Bann mouth, its swirling waters so treacherous that we were forbidden to swim there. The beach itself is safe and, thanks to the National Trust, stays spotless, the dunes preserved, and the tide, in its big surfing surges, cleaner than almost anywhere in the British Isles. The dunes are so extensive that it was easy for me, as a boy, to imagine I was crossing a desert, on my sunburnt way to a far-off *kasbah* where languorous girls in diaphanous garments reposed upon silken sofas.

There was little else on our minds then. No bombs exploded, no bullets flew, no threat of revolution rushed to engulf us like the wild, white surf. My father (probably under my stepmother's influence) had gone a bit 'arty', abandoning waistcoats and taking to dark-brown and bottle-green rayon shirts. Yet even lovely, loosely knit Portstewart gave off little whiffs of sectarian preference which the sharp, saline breezes could never quite obscure. Although my brothers and I were happy to ignore the occasional lines of demarcation, we were well aware that some hotels, like some guest houses, were staunchly Protestant and others traditionally Catholic and that, for a time at least, the Herring Pond was a Protestant bathing place, while Port-na-Happel was a place for Catholics. Nevertheless, the resort always seemed more than capable of alleviating stress, accommodating the diverse and minimizing trouble.

Some years later, when the Troubles were at their height, a Fleet Street colleague drove his rented car on to the Portstewart beach and escorted a local girl into the solitude of the dunes 'for some intensive, in-depth research' (he said). The task consumed hours. Afternoon yielded to dusk, and dusk thickened into night. The tide flowed and ebbed. Research completed, my colleague searched in vain for his hired car. Pacing the beach for half-an-hour, he eventually spotted the tip of a radio aerial poking skywards from the wet sand. Since the car's fate was too complicated and embarrassing to explain, he told the rental company it had been hijacked by paramilitaries, a common occurrence. The firm had no difficulty believing him and promptly provided a replacement.

On the promenade, Christians still gather with brass and sheet music to praise the Lord. The summer pulse hasn't really changed in four decades. Portstewart fairly swarms with visitors: well-off farmers from mid-Ulster, professionals from Belfast, Scottish excursionists. The faces I observed, on hobbling pensioners and on their tugging grandchildren, might have been sketched from my youth. Conversation remained full of the bland warmth in which Ulster folk wrap themselves for fear of unwanted controversy or causing offence to visitors. Going back was a transcendent exercise, at times dependent neither on memory nor on fresh perception. It was the kind of pilgrimage which can replace nostalgic clarity with sudden confusions. The diapason sometimes may hurt the ear. But one continues to hear the rhapsody.

10

AT THE LAKESIDE DIES AN ANCHORMAN

It was not until 1990 that I got an opportunity to visit Una Fitzpatrick's surviving brother, Raymond. He died subsequently, but seemed in good health when I met him in June that year at Aghagallon, just outside the town of Lurgan, where he was parish priest. His younger brother, Noel, he told me, had been shot dead in Ballymurphy, a west Belfast housing estate, in 1972, as he went to the aid of a wounded man.

'I wouldn't say he was murdered, though. Noel was killed by a shot from the [British] Army, almost certainly accidentally. The priests who were in the parish with him at the time agreed that he was shot just before he reached the wounded man and as he took out of his pocket the holy oil stock. If you've ever seen one, you will know that it could look for all the world like the barrel of a revolver, especially in the dusk and at some distance. I never wanted to know who exactly it was that shot him, for I didn't want some mother mourning over her son shot in retaliation. And even if it had been known, my brother would have forgiven him, as he'd done some months before with a driver who smashed into his car, landing him in hospital. Noel went to the court afterwards and pleaded with the judge not to send the man to prison.'

He asked about my family, and if I had any regrets about leaving Northern Ireland. I shook my head slowly. Had he heard of the McDonald murders? The McDonalds were two brothers, stepsons of my mother's older sister Ginny. So far as I'm aware, they were uninvolved in politics of any sort, concentrating their efforts on making a living from their garage in North Belfast. It was there that they were killed in one of a series of sectarian murders which swept Belfast in the 1970s and 1980s. 'So the answer to your question, Raymond, is, no, I have no regrets about leaving,' I said.

Raymond made me tea in the kitchen of the parochial house. We moved upstairs to his living-room to reminisce about Portstewart and mutual acquaintances. Now and again, I noticed, he would glance out of the window, as though anticipating someone's arrival. There was no sense of dread or any real tension that I could put my finger on. The house was silent, but for the two of us. There was no sound of movement into or out of the church next door. Yet I thought I detected in him a slight wariness in his regard of the narrow country road beyond the church. A fine Northern Ireland historian, A. T. Q. Stewart, observed in an essay ('The Narrow Ground') that 'the Ulsterman carries the map of . . . religious geography in his mind almost from birth. He knows which villages, which roads and which streets, are Catholic, or Protestant, or "mixed". It not only tells him where he can, or cannot, wave an Irish tricolour or wear his Orange sash, but imposes on him a complex behaviour pattern and a special way of looking at political problems.'

Raymond and I mulled over these observations as he drove me in his car down winding roads and lumpy countryside to the south shore of Lough Neagh. Many people waved to him. He waved back. He also waved to those with blank, unresponsive faces whose eyes, nevertheless, darted quickly from him to his passenger and back again. We were in 'Bigot Country', and this made me feel nervous sitting beside a Catholic priest on sparsely trafficked roads. Six years later, Aghagallon was propelled into the national news when a Scottish-born Catholic taxi-driver was found there, slumped in his vehicle and shot in the head – a local sectarian 'reprisal' for Catholic attempts to block an Orange Twelfth of July march through a nationalist suburb of nearby Portadown, a fiercely loyalist town – so loyalist, in fact, that its residents occasionally have not hesitated to attack the RUC if they considered the police to be too accommodating to Catholics. Many of these Catholics can be found in the town of Lurgan, a few miles away. In one Lurgan neighbourhood, the IRA holds sway – clear enough from the republican murals and slogans.

It has been like that ever since I can remember and, I'm sure, since my father could remember. Before I left Northern Ireland for London in 1964, I had been to Lurgan quite often. I liked the town, though there is nothing particularly attractive about it, other than its public park, landscaped in the eighteenth century. As far as I am aware, it played no part in, for example, the 1798 rebellion, concentrating instead on damask weaving, which had started a century earlier. In fact, the only fame the town achieved was as the burial place of the racing greyhound, Master McGrath, which won the Waterloo Cup in 1868, 1869 and 1871. The word Lurgan yields nothing of greatness either, meaning simply 'strip of land'. James Logan, one of the founders of Pennsylvania, emigrated from the strip of land in 1699. George Russell, the writer, painter and propagandist (whose famous *nom de plume*, 'Æ', was abbreviated from an earlier pen name, 'Aeon'), spent his school days there and has a street named after him. There used to be a Lurgan Castle, built in the seventeenth century when English and Scottish 'planters', or colonists, settled there. The castle is now known as Brownlow House (after the family who received land grants from James I) and functions as an Orange Hall. A large Protestant church – Christ Church – occupies the centre of the town. There was – still is, I believe – some middle-class mixing, but a high level of separate and parallel leisure provision among the working class. There is a Protestant Mechanics' Institute and a Catholic Working Men's Club; an Irish National Foresters (Catholic) and a Masonic Lodge (Protestant); and two religiously segregated old people's homes. My father used to go to Lurgan every year to examine young people in the Gaelic language at Irish festivals there. It had, he said, a 'strong nationalist element' of whom the local loyalists would never cease to be suspicious.

Between Lurgan and Portadown, a new town, Craigavon, was built after I had left Northern Ireland for London. It provided – or was supposed to provide – a kind of neutral ground where citizens could shop and stroll without drawing each other's blood or spitting in each other's eyes. But since it was on Protestant turf and named after the first Unionist prime minister of Ulster, nationalists found little neutrality to celebrate. Some, extreme republicans, may even view it as a potential bomb target. In 1984, when I was on assignment in Northern Ireland, I met a Protestant loyalist from Craigavon who told me the IRA 'have studied the new town so well they know it like the back of their hand – and the back of mine too, for that matter!'

This man had travelled to Belfast with two companions from Portadown to meet me in the north Belfast flat of George Seawright, a Unionist councillor whose contribution to the Ulster debate was the trigger of his own demise. At a meeting in the City Hall, Councillor Seawright proposed that Catholics who objected to 'God Save The Queen' being played at concerts should be incinerated – 'the whole lot of them. The priests should be thrown in [the incinerator] and burned as well.' In his home, he was subdued and polite, gently removing a gun from a shoulder holster and placing it on the mantelpiece, careful that it was pointed away from me. His wife made tea and sandwiches. Shortly afterwards, friends of his from south Armagh arrived in the flat. They talked (in a corner diagonally opposite me and, they must have assumed, beyond my hearing) of a big meeting in Portadown and a 'final solution'. One of them mumbled something to the councillor. It sounded like 'That stuff's on its way.' But I could well have been mistaken.

All this conspiring may well have been to impress a journalist. If so, I was indeed impressed. I was unable to finish my sandwich and was glad to leave. South Armagh loyalists, like south Armagh republicans, have short fuses, long memories, and big powder kegs. Listening to them behind the steel shutters of Seawright's neat-and-tidy flat, I barely resisted a sigh of despair at the fixity of their ideas and language: 'Fenians', 'Fuckers', 'Score a couple', 'Smack them hard', 'Sly bastards', 'Chop his bollix off'. It wasn't simply bombast for my benefit. A year after this encounter, Seawright got nine months in prison for physically attacking the then Northern Ireland

Secretary of State, Tom King. A further two years on, Seawright was shot in the head by republican terrorists as he sat in his car on Shankill Road. He died two years later.

'I thought of writing to his widow to express my sympathy,' I told Father Raymond on the way to Lough Neagh. 'Should I have . . . ? You know, she was a nice, hospitable sort of person who obviously loved her silly ass of a husband . . .'

'Well, hmmn. Mightn't she have thought it intrusive, since clearly you were no friend of the deceased? Maybe you're best not drawing too much attention to yourself. There're a lot of hard men about.' He pulled the car off the road, coasted down a narrow track and switched off the engine. He glanced briefly from left to right over his shoulder.

'Ah, there's not much harm in anybody around here,' he said – I suspect for my benefit – as we got out of the car and looked out over the water of the lough. 'I once read about a lecturer who argued that all sensible men professed the same religion. When he was asked what that religion might be, he said that no sensible man would ever tell.'

I laughed. 'He was a sensible man.'

We pulled in at a beauty spot called Oxford Island. Raymond said: 'Now, isn't that tranquillity? Have you been here before?'

As it happened, I had been there before – with my father years earlier. We had played ducks-and-drakes with small, flat stones, skimming them across the surface of the great lake and wondering if we should hire a boat for the day. We didn't, because it started to rain, and we sat in my car until the sun emerged again. The subject of religion (omnipresent in Ulster) had come up yet again. I had wondered aloud why religion, perhaps the vaguest of all the important nouns in the English language, could commit people to such clearly defined acts as murder as well as self-sacrifice. My father's voice entered its recitation mode, as he dredged up a mouthful of Ruskin. 'Our national religion is the performance of Church ceremonies, and of soporific truths (or untruths) to keep the mob quietly at work while we amuse ourselves.'

'I agree with Ruskin,' I'd said. 'But isn't it a bit cynical for a pious man like you?'

He ignored the mockery. 'No, because Ruskin was referring to religion at a certain level – its utilitarian level, where it's exploited as a class instrument, a political instrument. There is a purer level of religious practice, mystical and essential, that can't be traduced by what Ruskin had in mind. Ruskin knew that too – he was just having a go at the hypocrites and altar-lickers.'

I repeated that exchange for Raymond's benefit. He laughed, and sucked his teeth when I asked him what there was about religion in Ireland that made it a lethal instrument. Then he shook his head. 'It's not a lethal instrument at all. Christianity doesn't kill, though I grant you that people professing Christianity do kill for what they *imagine* to be religion. What happens – and certainly happens here – is that a veneration for the remote past and long-accepted assumptions reaches a dangerous intensity. It's a kind of ecstasy that you do find in some religious practice, but it's not actually religion. If people *call* it religion, it's only because they don't know what else to call it.' As we walked to his car, he nodded at the waves lapping the shore. 'There's a lot of history there. If the lough could speak, it could tell us a quare few terrible stories.' We then left Oxford Island quickly and drove to where I had parked my car.

'God bless you and take care of you where you're going,' he said, as black, low clouds drifted over the sun, bringing a likelihood of rain. I never saw him again, though I was soon to return to Oxford Island.

I drove to the north of the county, to write about a funeral. It was the interment of Patrick Boyle, aged fifty-nine and unemployed, in Annaghmore. So far as could be ascertained, he had respect for human life and aversion to brutality, holding these things to be essential to the ethical foundation upon which the structure of any civilized state is built. The pointlessness of his extermination by the loyalist Ulster Volunteer Force was something to ponder as rain thundered on black umbrellas in the tiny Annaghmore churchyard, drowning sounds of grief as Mr Boyle was lowered into the deluged earth. It hammered on the church roof, deafening a sodden congregation to the young, ruddy-faced curate's words. 'The question on everyone's mind is "Why?"' As they straggled out into the downpour, the elderly parish priest offered comfort. 'The corpse it rains on is a happy one,' he said, mystifyingly.

The grave filled in and the mourners gone, a friend of the Boyle family sat with me in the empty church and attempted to answer the curate's question. The Boyle family, he said, lived in a small Roman Catholic enclave just across the narrow road from the church. The surrounding countryside, largely Protestant, was nicknamed 'the murder triangle' in the 1970s, but there had been no recent killings. 'I swear to you,' he said, 'nobody around here is looking for trouble. It's been really peaceful lately.' The day before the murder, Mr Boyle had slipped and damaged his ankle at a wedding. The following night he limped into his kitchen to help his wife prepare lunch boxes for their four labouring sons. Two miles away, a Protestant couple sat in a white Peugeot van, parked at the roadside. 'They were reading their bible,' Mr Boyle's friend said. Two men interrupted their reading, one of them yanking open the door and saying: 'If you're that religious, you better pray, because we're going to shoot a Provie' – meaning a member of the Provisional IRA. The couple were forced to lie on the floor of the van, which was then driven off by the unidentified men. These men used walkie-talkies to communicate with a third party, saying things like, 'Phase one completed' (after hijacking the van), and 'Phase two completed' (after chopping through a roadside telephone cable with an axe in Annaghmore). Phase three must have been the attack on Mr Boyle. The men fired guns through the sitting-room window, then kicked open the front door. Mr Boyle, a portly man, could not move fast enough on his injured ankle to avoid the bullets. Two of his sons escaped injury, overlooked by the gunmen in their haste. A third son was shot in the arms and legs. A fourth was shot in the stomach.

The family friend said: 'The Boyles were all for snooker and darts and never into republicanism or anything like that.' The UVF issued a statement admitting the murder, and adding that it was 'a mistake'.

Another 'mistake' brought me to Armagh again before the year was out. Part of my visit was spent in Lurgan that October so that I could talk to a young woman, Lynn Hughes, about Denis Carville, the man she had intended to marry. What she had to tell me was without doubt one of the most terrible of the 'quare few terrible stories' that Lough Neagh harbours. It has made sinister the Oxford Island beauty spot where I had strolled first with my father, and later with Raymond Fitzpatrick. At one point I feared Ms Hughes would faint as I coaxed her into recalling her ordeal.

Oxford Island is actually a peninsula, ringed by gently wooded slopes. Where brambly glades open into a public car park there is a red sign saying 'Dangerous Place' – a warning to swimmers. It was to this dangerous place that Lynn Hughes and Denis Carville drove before midnight on 5 October. And it was from here that she fled, alone, less than an hour later.

She stumbled through the dark, keeping to the metalled path that curved away from the lake shore to the main road. His blood had soaked through her white T-shirt and chilled against her shoulder and chest. Clouds obscured the moon, turning the lake surface behind her gun-grey. Occasionally, her brown ankle-boots hit the grassy verge and she swerved to regain the path. She called his name, but the sound strangled in her throat. She tripped, almost fell as she clattered across a metal cattle-grid. A car approached, its headlights dipped. She slowed to a walk, thinking: 'Oh God, it's them!' But the car passed by, and she ran on. She had covered three-quarters of a mile.

There was a house on a dark lane to her right, light coming from a chink in a curtained window. She jabbed at the doorbell. A man appeared uncertainly behind the glass of the door. He shouted a question and could barely make out her reply. He heard 'Help!', then 'Ambulance!' Nervously, he told her to go to a side door. She tottered the few paces to where the other door was now being opened. A man stared out at her bloodied clothes. An accident?

She fought for the words. 'Denis' . . . 'shot' . . . 'ambulance' . . . 'please help' . . . In the lighted hall, the man, whose name is Vincent Mitchell, studied the girl as he phoned for an ambulance and the police. She told him her name. She was young and pretty, with black hair and dark, intense eyes. Her shirt and jeans were sodden with blood and she was in shock. Mitchell's wife joined them. They gave the visitor something to drink. Lynn was sitting beside the phone when the police called back. An officer questioned her, trying to confirm this wasn't a hoax that could lead the police into a terrorist ambush. She screamed at them to hurry, then turned to Mitchell: 'Can I phone my daddy?' What Lynn Hughes didn't know, or couldn't bring herself to acknowledge, was that Denis Carville, the young man she planned to marry, was dead.

It was a few weeks after the event when she described for me what had happened. She had not recovered much from her ordeal; perhaps she never will. Her hands shook as she puffed on a cigarette. She couldn't sleep without the light on, she said. But she recalled events calmly, and when I offered at one stage to break off our conversation, she shook her head and gazed at me steadily with sad brown eyes. She was eighteen then, and lived with her father, a retired textile worker, and her mother, a chicken pro cessor. Her street had run-down terraced houses near the town centre. Her father, with only one eye and disabled by serious lung complaints, seldom left home. Her mother worked nightshifts at the processing company. Lynn's shift at the same plant was from 5.30 p.m. until midnight, except Fridays, when she finished at 8.30 p.m.

Denis Carville had a white Ford Fiesta 1400. He washed and polished it twice a week, and, behind the wheel, thought himself, at nineteen, a dashing figure. Beneath the bonnet, he had rigged up a speaker. In Lurgan's shopping streets, he liked to slow down behind strolling girls and boom into his microphone: 'Hello there! How's about you!' He hoped to trade in the white Fiesta for a black one. 'Black shines up better,' he said. He had a good job at a timber company which makes doors and windows. His boss, Greg McCarten, admired his spirit and his kindnesses. Denis toiled alongside Irvine Moorhead, a deaf mute, and worked out ways to communicate without mutual embarrassment. Moorhead, in his late thirties, married and with children of his own, enjoyed the younger man's company as together they completed window frames and assembled doors. They scrawled notes to each other so that Moorhead could join in banter about girls and cars among the workforce. In his office, McCarten said: 'I've known Denny's da' for twenty years – we used to do sub-contract work together. When the da' came to me two-and-a-half years ago and asked if I would give Denny a start and said he's a good lad, that was enough for me. He *was* a good lad. The best.'

Denis Carville was born on 13 September 1971 in Taghnevan, a Lurgan estate built by the Northern Ireland Housing Executive, an organization which has tried to achieve a Protestant-Catholic mix, to prevent ghetto-ization. His father, also Denis, and his mother, Jean, produced two other children: Michael, six years older than young Denis, and Una, four years older. Young Denis's first recorded ambition was to be as tall as Michael. 'He was small for his age,' Jean said. 'I used to make pencil-marks on the wall to show how fast they were growing. But it wasn't until Denis had his tonsils out that he started to shoot up and put on weight.' She opened an album and nodded at a photograph of Michael's wedding. 'Look, he was Michael's best man. I think he just made it – maybe half an inch taller than Michael.'

As the Troubles progressed in Northern Ireland, the Housing Executive's plans were thwarted by increasing acrimony between Lurgan's communities. Catholics, making up about forty per cent of the town's population, moved to 'safe' neighbourhoods. Protestants also sought security among their own. Although Taghnevan became one hundred per cent Catholic, the Carvilles moved away, buying a semi-detached house on Parkview Street, directly opposite St Paul's Catholic church. Apart from that upheaval and a few incidents in which Catholic homes in strongly loyalist areas were burned down, the Carvilles had no real cause for anxiety. 'The Troubles never annoyed me,' Denis senior said. 'We're not interested in politics in the slightest, so there was no reason to be afraid.' His younger son went to the parochial school across the road. 'He was mad about bicycles, so I bought him bicycles. He loved dogs, so he had to have dogs – a Jack Russell and an Alsatian. When Toby, the Jack Russell, died, Denis built him a coffin with an electric saw, put the dog in a blue blanket and put him in the coffin with a bone and a couple of biscuits. He wrote "Toby Carville" on the top of the box. We had a little funeral and buried him at the back of the shed where I keep my pigeons. He talked about nothing else but Toby that day.'

Jean cut in: 'He had a tremendous appetite. On Friday nights, it was usually pizza or spaghetti bolognese. And he would eat his way through sweets and chocolates and lemonade after that. He never liked falling out with me. Once we had words, and he left the house without saying, "Mammy, I won't be late," like he always did. But he came back in a minute and smiled and said it. And I said what I always say – "Cheerio, watch yourself. I'll see you later."'

At eleven, Denis Carville transferred to the secondary school near by. He wasn't an outstanding student. His sole ambition was to leave, start work and drive a car. On his very first day, he bunked one of his classes. His father said: 'A teacher saw him up in town and phoned me. When Denis went back to the school, the teacher said, "Your father wants to see you." And when he got home and saw my face, he said, "What have I done now?" I said, "You were playing the teacher up this morning." He looked at me and said, "Oh, I was just trying her out. Everybody does that with a new teacher." We threatened to stop his pocket money and take away his snooker cues, expensive ones which I'd bought for him – he was spoiled, you know, but I couldn't refuse him anything. Would you like to see them?'

Denis Carville's father led the way upstairs to his son's bedroom. Above the narrow single bed, a window overlooked the church. Neatly laundered shirts and underwear were piled on the bed. At its foot, a portable television rested on a video recorder and a small cabinet holding tapes of popular Westerns. 'He would come in from work, take his dinner up here on a tray and watch *Neighbours* and *Home and Away* and use this snooker cue to switch channels,' the father said. He unzipped a bag and removed a cue. 'This cost me £150,' he said. I glanced around the small room and into an open cupboard that bulged with teenage jumble: roller-skates, barbells, shoes no longer fashionable, a guitar never mastered, ties never worn, pictures of dogs. On a shelf I spotted an Irish harp, six inches high, crudely fashioned from balsa wood and roughly varnished. Some strings were broken. On its base an inscription was etched: *Long Kesh 1973*. Long Kesh, later renamed The Maze, is a prison where terrorists are held. Mr Carville anticipated my question: 'It wasn't his. I won it in a raffle years ago. There were thousands of them around after internment was introduced in Northern Ireland. It was meaningless to Denis. He wasn't into that sort of thing. His interest was girls.'

Jean laughed: 'I remember when he was eleven and came home saying he had a date with a girl called Nicola. He went upstairs and came down smothered in Brut. I asked him where he was taking her. He said they were meeting over the fields. After he'd left on his date, I walked over to see what was going on. I found them sitting in the long grass, a yard apart, talking. That's what he called a date.'

Despite his lack of academic enthusiasm at the all-boys school, Denis Carville's final report, in 1986–87, was not discreditable. Maths: 'Works well in class'. English: 'Very co-operative, mature attitude'. Geography: 'Excellent pupil. Works well always'. Life skills: 'Very responsive pupil'. His former headmaster, Gerry McCrory, recalled young Carville as 'the anchorman in the class, stable, well liked by the other children . . . I think the school had a moderating influence on all the boys. There never was a pupil demonstration here even when the Troubles were at their worst. We prayed for peace and all who were deceased, irrespective of faith.'

Faith was central to the Carville family. Every Sunday, Denis and his sister attended 8.30 a.m. Mass, invariably sitting together. 'He never exactly lived in the chapel, like some Catholics do,' Jean said. 'But he did what he had to do. He had as many Protestant friends as Catholic friends.'

Una said: 'He was no angel, and we shouldn't make him out to be one. He had the odd beer and he smoked cigarettes. He was really very ordinary and had no secrets from me. I knew what he was thinking. I understood him.'

Jean said: 'He loved bright clothes – very trendy, never anything formal. On the day of Michael's wedding, he was in his hired tails and he said to me, "Mammy, run out and see if there's anyone outside. I don't want them to see me in my penguin suit." I took a look outside and gave him the all-clear, and then he ran to the car.'

On Friday, 5 October, Denis Carville was wearing blue jeans, a white cotton shirt, a black leather bomber jacket, black suede boots, a watch on a bracelet strap and, tucked inside his shirt, a gold Celtic cross. He had carefully blow-dried his light-brown hair to straighten a stubborn curl where it overlapped his collar. He bounced downstairs, having eaten pizza and chips and had a nap. He grabbed a biscuit from a kitchen drawer and chewed it while calling to his mother: 'Mum, I won't be late tonight.' She replied, as always: 'Cheerio, love. I'll see you later. Watch yourself.' He slid into the white Fiesta and roared off to Victoria Street, half a mile away, to join Lynn Hughes.

Denis and Lynn had first met at a dance in Lurgan's Ashbourne Hotel a few months earlier, and spent some Friday evenings at the Centrepoint Disco or at Lynn's parents' house. Occasionally they would drive to Newcastle, a County Down resort in the shadow of the Mourne Mountains, or to Tanaghmore Gardens, the Lurgan park, which had a wishing-well and a goldfish pond – or to Oxford Island. That's where they went on 5 October.

Lynn said: 'He used always to ask me, "Will you marry me?" I thought he was joking, but three weeks before this, I said yes. He hadn't told his parents yet. We agreed to get engaged at Christmas. He joked about me having fifteen babies after we got married. But we never really thought about the future – just about having a good time.'

The white Fiesta pulled into a darkened marina and parked near the edge of the lake. A few dozen yachts bobbed gently on the water, sail-ropes clinking against their masts. It was a perfect place for 'a good coort', an Ulsterism for courtship. But they stayed only fifteen minutes. A minibus full of what Lynn thought were Boy Scouts arrived and their boisterous shouts invaded the privacy of the marina. Denis Carville drove towards the point of the peninsula where the car park was deserted, except for a taxi which immediately pulled away and headed towards the main road. He squinted through the gloom but failed to read the taxi company's name on the roof. 'What's a taxi doing here this time of night?' he wondered aloud. He turned off the Fiesta's engine. On one side of the car there were bushes and trees; on the other, a long, low building containing public toilets. The wall of the building had a crudely drawn mural of two swans flying into a yellow sun. Black rainclouds passed over Lough Neagh and silence closed in.

The tap on the window on the driver's side came between ten and fifteen minutes later.

'He had a woollen hat pulled over his face,' Lynn said. 'I saw his eyes through the holes he'd cut in it. He said: "You have three seconds to open the door." Denis opened the door. I could see only one man. There might have been others further back, but I couldn't say for sure. It was awful frightening, because he'd tapped the window with the barrel of a gun – a long gun, a rifle maybe. His voice seemed nervous, a young voice. It was the voice of someone in his twenties, I think.'

The masked man again addressed Carville. 'Are you a Catholic?'
'Yes.'
'What chapel do you go to?'
'St Paul's.'
'Have you your driving licence?' Carville produced it.
'Both of you, turn your heads away.' Lynn and her boyfriend turned away. There was a short pause.
'Tell me the name of your parish priest, Denis.'
Carville was panicking. He couldn't remember the priest's name.

He said the priest had married his brother and buried his grand-mother, yet the name won't come. The masked man waited. Then he said: 'Have you any medals, Denis? St Christopher medals, things like that?'

Carville shook his head, then remembered the Celtic cross on the chain around his neck. He pulled it out.

The masked man studied it carefully, then said: 'Keep your head turned, Denis. We are going now.'

Lynn said: 'That's when he did it. I didn't know Denis was hit. I thought they were shooting the windows through. That's what it sounded like. They say there were two shots, but I only heard one. I think that's what happens; the shock of the first blocks out the sound of the second. I kept calling to Denis, and he wouldn't answer. I thought he was waiting for the man to go. There was warm stuff running over me. I thought it was paint. I turned Denis to me and realized what it was. It was very dark. I didn't realize he was dead. A couple of seconds later I got out of the car and ran. I didn't even know if they were still there. I just took the chance and ran.'

Father Brian Brown was the curate at St Paul's. He was thirty-five in 1990 and, like Denis Carville, had been a joiner. This made a special bond between him and the Carville family. He was particularly close to the younger son, who struck him as 'a typical teenager, obsessed with work and coortin' – but very creative, which you can see from his sketches [he did] in school.' Like Denis Carville, too, he had stopped carrying religious medals on his person. 'Years ago, when I was working as a joiner in Belfast, a crowd of young teenagers sur-rounded me and said, "Are you a Fenian?" I'm a country boy, and I had no way of knowing what they were, but I could see the mark of the UVF badges they'd removed from their lapels. I took a chance and, to my eternal shame, I said, "I must admit I'm a Protestant." I was heading towards the Falls Road and this is why they'd stopped me. But when they heard my country accent they must have thought I didn't know where I was – wasn't aware of the geographical barriers in the city. I was wearing a medal at the time; never went out without it. But they didn't search me for it.'

He was in bed when the police telephoned. 'There's been a shooting,' they told him, 'and it's a member of your congregation. Could you come down to the station?' He asked the policeman for a few details. 'You have to be sure that it isn't a set-up. He was able to give me information that satisfied me he was genuine.' The officer met him at the station entrance and took him to the incident room where he met Lynn and her mother. 'I hadn't met Lynn before this. She was lying there covered in blood. I comforted her and asked a few questions. She mentioned the name Carville and said Parkview Street. She spoke Denis's name, and then I knew. She told me about the car and the knock on the window. The police said they'd have to move quickly. It would be on the radio, and Denis's parents would have to be told. A CID man came with me to the house.'

The Carvilles were in bed. Denis senior had retired early. Una's boyfriend, Paddy Maguire, had gone home. Jean Carville lay awake. 'I never sleep until Denis would come in. I would hear Rocky bark when he arrived, because he always fed the dog when he came in.'

When the doorbell rang, she looked at the clock on the bedside table. It was 2 a.m. She thought: 'O God, he forgot his keys.' Denis senior went downstairs. From her own bedroom, Una heard voices as the front door was opened. Perhaps there was an emergency and a neighbour wanted to use the phone.

Denis senior opened the front door. A policeman stood there. 'Do you have a son called Denis?' Denis senior knew immediately what had happened.

'How bad is he?' he asked.

Una left her bed. 'When I went into the living-room, Daddy was slumped in the chair. Father Brown was standing beside him. Daddy said: "Our Denis has been shot dead."'

Jean: 'I didn't come down till I heard Una scream.'

Una: 'The CID man picked me up off the floor. Daddy kept saying to me, "Una, go and get on you [get dressed]!" I was in my night clothes.'

Jean: 'I came in and said, "What's wrong?" And Father Brown

told me about Denis being shot. I asked if he was badly hurt. I remember him saying, "I hope to God they roast in hell!" I immediately phoned Michael, who lives not far away on the Lough Road. He and Patricia have a little baby, Catriona. Father Brown drove me there. Patricia was up with the baby. She was teething. Michael just looked at me. I said, "He's dead, love." He started to cry.'

Lynn Hughes had not yet left the police station in Church Street, where a doctor was trying to calm her. She showered off her boyfriend's blood and put on a change of clothing that her mother had brought. She still had not absorbed the fact that her Denis was dead. She was driven to the Carville home.

Jean: 'When she came here, she looked like an old woman. It was only later, when we got to know her, that we saw what a beautiful girl she was. She was devastated. I gathered her in my arms and hugged her. I think it was harder on Lynn. That wee girl has been through something that for the rest of her days she'll never forget.'

Una: 'She says she feels close to Denis, being here with us.'

Jean: 'She stays some nights here. We take her out. If we go out for lunch or dinner, we take her with us.'

Michael Carville took his mother home. He went to the morgue to identify his brother and returned to his mother. He put his arms around her. 'Mammy', he said, 'it's not the Denis you know.'

Jean: 'But I had to see him. Michael was right. Denis had one bullet through the back of his head that came out through his eye. They'd stitched the eyes up. The other bullet went through the back of his neck and out the side. Those wounds were stitched up too. I looked at him and said, "My God, is that him?" His head was swollen and it wasn't really until Sunday night that the swelling went down and you could see the red mark around his throat where the shirt collar had nipped into his swollen neck. He had a little smile on his face. I would rather be in Denis's place than in the place of the man who pulled the trigger.'

Denis Carville's murder was claimed by the Protestant Action Force, an alternative name for the UVF, which said the killing was a reprisal for the IRA murder of Colin McCullough, a soldier in the

Ulster Defence Regiment (now called the Royal Irish Regiment). There were some similarities in the murders: McCullough had sat with *his* girlfriend in a car just two weeks earlier at the lake shore, about 600 yards from where Carville died. His avengers had warned that IRA atrocities would be answered.

Denis Carville senior told me the police know the identity of his son's murderer. 'They've had him in for questioning,' he said, 'but they don't have the evidence. He says nothing to them.' Others appeared to know the killer's name. In its report of Carville's funeral on 9 October, the Irish tabloid *Sunday World* carried a curious account.

The cold-blooded loyalist killer of 19-year-old Lurgan youth Denis Carville turned up at the young man's funeral on Tuesday dressed as a mourner.

The murderer was spotted standing at the top of the town's Francis Street next to the dead man's home in Parkside Street. The killer was wearing a neatly-cut suit and a black tie!

He was accompanied by another man and they were later joined by a third known Protestant paramilitary . . . Then the killer, along with his two cronies, walked along Edward Street where one of them had parked a car . . . Loyalist sources claim the mid-Ulster UVF intends to kill a Catholic for every Protestant member of the security forces murdered by the [IRA] Provos – using the new hit man who likes to watch his victims being buried.

Shortly before I visited the Carvilles, Lurgan was seething with fear and indignation over yet another IRA atrocity: two members of the Royal Ulster Constabulary and two companions were ambushed at Caster Bay, a few miles along the lake shore from Oxford Island, where they had been shooting duck. All four were killed. A car, thought to have been used by the terrorists, was found burnt out in a republican area of Lurgan. And after my long conversations with the Carville family, I thought about a decision, taken years before I left Northern Ireland for England, to lower the waters of the lough in order to create more agricultural land. How stupid!, I thought. More territory to fight over!

11

'I WANT A HOUSE. I'M A STAUNCH LOYALIST. GOD SAVE THE QUEEN.'

Like many self-taught men, my father was exceedingly anxious that his three sons should go to university. He was keenly disappointed when this failed to happen like clockwork. Colm settled for a printing job and became a works foreman before retiring with bronchial troubles. Brendan, the scholarly one among us, took a degree in education and became a lecturer in a teacher-training college. And I opted for what a Scottish friend once described as the 'adventure playground' known as journalism. But at no time can I remember my father allowing the anxiety or the disappointment at our academic shortcomings to dominate his relations with us. He did insist on homework being done, but he was no fanatic in the monitoring of it. He believed that Brendan was eminently equipped for a career at the Bar, yet showed only supportive enthusiasm when he chose teaching. As a teacher of Gaelic himself, he never once pressed us to learn the language (I was the only one of the three to pick up more than a smattering of it), though when we were children he left illustrated nursery tales, written in Irish, around the house to whet our appetite. He also claimed, years after I had left home, to have left helpful books about procreation lying about; if he did, I never found them, and he certainly never directed my attention to them.

Once we had 'passed the taws stage' (as he put it, meaning the point beyond which corporal punishment would be as ineffectual as it was undignified – for him and us), his method of spurring us on was through praise, not censure. When I had decided on classes on physics and chemistry (believing that I wanted to be a doctor), he talked about the great horizons socialized medicine had opened up for boys such as me. I then dropped both subjects, having been able to achieve only a feeble grasp of them, and took up ancient history instead. Again, my father nodded approvingly. History, he said, was the 'sovereign solvent of prejudice' and 'the herald of reform', a sort of *aqua regia* which 'shakes things up and liberates our thinking'. I do not know if he truly believed what he was saying, or if he said these things to encourage me out of my dithering. He could have said, instead, that history consolidates prejudice and imprisons our thinking – not least in Northern Ireland – but he didn't. He was not a great one for negative observations. When Brendan did particularly well in his school exams (as he did frequently and without apparent effort), my father would beam and say: 'The world's your oyster if you keep this up'. Every time I showed him my unfledged efforts at poetic composition, he would look at me and exclaim quietly: 'Oh yes, that's the best yet!' To assure me that I had made a wise decision in taking up ancient history, he presented me with six beautiful volumes of Rollins' history of the Egyptians, Carthaginians, Assyrians, Babylonians, Medes and Persians, Macedonians, and Grecians, translated from the French, bound in fine pigskin and published in 1828.

Colm became a compositor with the *Irish News* because he was keen to start earning money as soon as possible, though I often have felt he was motivated, unconsciously perhaps, by a desire to walk in at least some of my father's footsteps. My father backed him fully, even asking around about apprenticeships that might soon become available. The McCrystals had had experience with 'the print' since the late nineteenth century, so there seemed to be a certain generational symmetry in his eldest son's choice. But I know that he himself had become quite ambivalent about it.

My father had served 'the print' well, but it did him little service in return. He belonged to the Typographical Society, the printing trade union, but it – like many other working-class bodies in Northern Ireland – was steeped in sectarian prejudice. Every year or so, when pay negotiations were at hand, the society would appoint my father an *ex officio* member of the Belfast branch committee. He had a reputation as a good negotiator, never lost his temper, and knew more about most things than did the employers. Then, negotiations over, he would be dropped again, until the next time his talents were required. In between these occasions, his workmates would continue to festoon his work area with the icons of Unionism and loyalism, knowing that, in doing so, they were slapping him on the face. He had long left this scene of humiliation when the British government imposed on Northern Ireland employers an obligation to ban such provocative displays.

I was slow to make up my own mind about the future. My exam results were good enough for me to be accepted by Queen's University, Belfast, but I had no clear idea of what I wished to do there, or afterwards. I sensed my father's anxiety, even though he applied no overt pressure upon me. He had so often said that joy and sorrow, hope and fear, success and frustration, sympathy and resentment are our teachers, that he could not very well force me to the campus as the only fountain of wisdom. He was, of course, concerned about my lack of serious enterprise; by what he perceived in me to be dilettantish tendencies. It would not have surprised me to learn that he measured my deficiency by the number of parties I went out of my way to attend. These were buns–and–lemonade affairs (no booze at all), with girls who might sit on one's knee and allow themselves to be kissed in the wide range of kissing games we had devised for ourselves. My chum from the Holy Family school, Brendan Hyland, organized the best parties. His mother, tired from her consulting-room, nevertheless cut sandwiches for us, while a cigarette dangled from her mouth. In the big drawing-room upstairs there was a gramophone and Sinatra records. The underside of a grand piano provided minimum privacy for those of us engaged in serious fondling. All the girls at these parties, however, were from convent schools where it was taught that to entertain even the *notion* of fondling, light or serious, was to 'enter into the occasion of sin'. So most of us, I am inclined to believe, remained frustrated virgins until we got married. Some of us who partied at the Hylands' met our future spouses there. One was my friend Joe McAlinden, a publican's son, who married Brendan Hyland's sister, Adrienne. Joe, a pale, quiet fellow, was shot dead in the Troubles by an intruder who climbed through his bedroom window one night on Cave Hill Road. There were times when the parties would be switched to the home of Terry Shields, now a solicitor, who had a zany sense of humour, drove an old (I think) Singer car, which he called Martha, and liked to liven up his gatherings by importing two sisters from Falls Road for whom, we learned with some gratitude, 'sin' was no great occasion. One of them introduced me to the art of 'French kissing', wiggling her tongue down my throat until my tonsils rattled.

'Have you nothing better to do?' my father asked when I came home from one of these parties not long before midnight. 'You won't get on if you keep this up.' And that was about the height of his remonstrance.

My friends and I were a 'gang', I suppose, but in the blandest sense, raising our voices to the Almighty, our lust into unexplored infinity, and our fists to no one. I used to hang around the public tennis courts on Cave Hill Road, above its intersection with Antrim Road, swinging my cheap Pakistani-made racquet (it cost thirty shillings) and smoking my pipe. My father bought his sons pipes when they reached sixteen. He also supplied us with an ounce of dark tobacco. The idea, he said, was to pre-empt addiction to cigarettes. The idea didn't work. I loved the image that I fancied pipe-smoking bestowed on me, but I did not like the nausea that went with it. So I found an alternative. One could purchase cigarettes singly in those days, and I would peel off the paper and stuff the cigarette tobacco into my pipe. I would light up at the tennis courts and try to feel mature. I wanted a new suit of clothes for university; of dark, worsted material that would enhance the maturity. For the suit I needed to earn money. I answered an advertisement for a trainee accountant with Gallaher's tobacco factory (hoping to pick up free samples of cigarettes if I was hired). At the interview, I was given some figures to add up, but failed miserably. The alternative was farm work. The kind of work most readily available for the likes of me was picking potatoes from eight o'clock in the morning till five o'clock in the afternoon.

I was about to head for the potato fields in Comber, County Down (fourteen shillings a day), when Dan Gilbert not only came to my rescue, but launched me on a career. Dan used to referee our inter-college water polo matches. He was also secretary of Bangor Swimming Club and a distinguished swimming instructor. Most important of all (for me, as it turned out), he was a night sub-editor on the *Northern Whig*. He found me a job as a cub reporter with the *Northern Herald*, a small weekly paper in Bangor, County Down, with a circulation of 5,000 copies, whose owner he knew. The editorship had just been taken over by a former *Daily Express* foreign correspondent who was from the north of England. All I had to do, said Dan, was to omit reference to my university plans. So, for three pounds a week and an infrequent byline, I lied.

It was hardly a virtuous start to earning one's livelihood. My father often said that lies are always found out, and that deceit is a form of contempt for others. Lying is a symptom of a deranged mind, he would say. 'Have you never heard of pseudologia phantastica?' I hadn't. My deceit rubbed against my conscience for months, until I discovered that I actually did want to be a journalist and that university would be an unnecessary hindrance to the process. I wrote to the university to say I would not be going up.

Bangor intimidated me at first. Or, perhaps my not altogether successful attempts at small town journalism were to blame. The town was strongly Unionist and Orange, whereas fair-sized bits of Belfast's map were green, or at least mottled. In an odd sort of way, I felt myself to be an interloper. Being a self-conscious Catholic among self-confident Protestants unsettled me. The prosperous, evangelical town brought me, for the first time, into communicative contact with stripe-suited canons, tented gospellers, unyielding Unionists and die-hard Orangemen, not to mention members of the Royal Black Preceptory, a sort of elite Orange group whose very name had a somewhat sinister ring to it. Bangor had, and has, a plethora of Protestant churches. I was obliged to cross their hallowed portals to write my reports about weddings and funerals and choral festivals. I interviewed Protestant vicars and moderators, taking down their sonorous messages in slow and stilted Pitman's shorthand. Some were ostentatiously welcoming when told my Christian name, which I usually had to spell out for them, slowly.

'C-a-h-a-l.'

'Mmm . . . unusual. Irish, isn't it?'

'Yes.'

'Ah, you're not from these parts yourself, then!'

'No, from Belfast.'

'Ah indeed. And do you like our church, Ca-hal? Am I pronouncing it right?'

'Yes, perfectly. It's a lovely church.'

'But you're not of our persuasion – would that be right?'

'No, I mean yes, you're right . . .'

'Ah, live and let live, I always say. God loves us all. Come and see us again.'

The newspaper office was three rooms and a lavatory above a bank on the corner of Abbey Street and Hamilton Road. Shortly after I started, workmen built an Orange arch across Hamilton Road, its centre piece being King William on his white horse. In the course of my comings and goings, I had to walk beneath this bit of triumphalism. I found it annoying at first, but concluded before long that neither the Protestant king nor his loyal mount were capable of afflicting injury on my Catholic person. I began to relax, and affected a spotted bow-tie, uncommon in places such as Bangor at that time. 'I like your wee dickey-bow,' a girl in the nearby cake shop said coquettishly when I dropped in to pick up confections for the office elevenses.

The newsroom, small and pokey, was occupied by four of us, a feature writer, two reporters and a secretary called Dodi who also took classified ads. The editor, Frank Entwistle, imposed his singular stamp on our little *lieu de travail*, with some rigour, a fair bit of understanding and a moderate intake of beer at the darkened end of the working day. Drawn back to Fleet Street after a few months, he left behind a deeply unsettled quartet which had, more or less, coalesced through its successes, its frustrations, its frequent galvanism and occasional oscitation, through the power we (naïvely) imagined we possessed and, most of all, through the person upon whom we entirely relied for that power and on whom we focused for direction, inspiration and reward, day in, day out – the editor. Most significantly of all, I suppose, our naïve sense of power waned – and, with it, the vaguely comforting notion that a newspaper was a solid shelter in which to enjoy a paradox: living off ephemera, without experiencing a sense of impermanence. Entwistle was replaced, of course, by a local man who – unusually – was a Catholic, but who – less unusually – was a drunk. The fact that he was a Catholic and a drunk made me doubly uncomfortable and, I probably would have to concede, vaguely ashamed.

A magistrate, who was also in charge of the local B-Specials, dropped into the office to see the owner who, I noticed, pointed me out as a hard-working curiosity 'of the other persuasion'. At Bangor gymkhanas, the magistrate always made a point of shaking my hand, or clapping my back, and saying 'Well, well, well' with what I took to be bemusement. Looking back, I can recognize that certain clearances were occurring in my mind. I was discovering that Protestants, without their regalia (banners and sashes), were ordinary, decent, warm, honest people who were not out to do me down; they, on the other hand, seemed to be discovering that I, a Roman Catholic, *with* my, more modest, regalia (bow-tie, reporter's notebook), was open, comprehensible, non-threatening – a 'Fenian' who had not yet left his teens, but who was 'getting on', improving himself, without giving annoyance to his 'betters' by getting above his station – or to use a delightful expression I heard from Norman Stone, the Oxford professor of history, 'farting above his bum'. I became drama critic at the local amateur theatre (the late Colin Blakely played there then) and the annual repertory theatre from England. I also learned how to 'angle' a story, to blow smoke-rings and to drink beer. My pay went up from three pounds to three pounds ten shillings.

I was with the *Northern Herald* for eighteen months, having become slightly bored. I remember little of what I wrote in those days, other than features to boost the Blood Transfusion Service or chronicle a 'record day-tripper invasion' in a heatwave. I missed my old friends in Belfast and wasn't making many new ones in Bangor. I commuted daily, the train journeys consuming a large part of my wages. My average working day was ten hours. I often had to work on weekends. Occasionally, the owner asked my help in delivering the papers to shops in tiny hamlets with such names as Conlig, Six Road Ends, Nun's Quarter and Ballywatticock. For this I was paid extra – in chocolate bars: two bars of Cadbury's Milk Tray for two hours of newspaper distribution, with a Mars Bar thrown in if I worked a bit longer at it.

To increase my income, I wrote a few short news stories for the *Irish News* in Belfast. It is possible that I could have got a job there, but I had no wish to be on the staff of a newspaper which was overtly under the influence of the Catholic bishop and his priests, which wrote obsequious editorials about the hierarchy, and which had dumped my father when he went to Russia. Again, my father did not attempt to nudge me into choosing options, but he did urge me to seek advice from one of the few journalists he truly respected. That was John Cole, a Belfast Protestant who was to become one of the great journalistic beacons of our time and who was then a political reporter on the *Belfast Telegraph*. I no longer recall how my father came to know Cole; it may be that they had met through a mutal interest in socialism, or in interview when my father was in controversial mode.

I had some reservations about the *Belfast Telegraph*. It was owned by the Baird family, who had doggedly pursued a pro-Unionist policy. The paper's administrative, editorial and printing floors were strutted by Orangemen and Freemasons. The whims of the Unionist government at Stormont were seldom challenged. I wondered if I ever would be able to function there.

'I think you'll do better there than at the *Irish News*,' my father said. He pulled open a kitchen drawer, searched within it and pulled out a yellowed newspaper which I had not seen before. It was called *United Ireland*, published in Dublin, and dated Saturday 10 October 1891. The faded columns testified to the efficacy of 'Mother Seigal's Syrup' and 'Clarke's world-famous blood mixture'. But most pages were entirely occupied by laments for Charles Stewart Parnell, the Anglo-Irish political agitator and 'uncrowned king' of Ireland who had died in Brighton of 'rheumatism of the heart' in the week before the paper was published. Whipped up by the Catholic clergy, many of Parnell's supporters had deserted him when his affair with a married woman, Kitty O'Shea, was made public.

'Read that,' my father said, as he always did when I was in need of enlightenment. He pointed to an editorial marked in blue crayon (probably by my late grandfather, he said). The editorial was an attack on 'a blasphemous and indecent article' about Parnell – a Protestant – in another publication, the *Irish Catholic*. 'Read that, and you'll know what this country's up against.' The *Irish Catholic* article said:

The death of Mr Parnell is one of those events which remind the world of God. Only a few hours have passed since his mere name was potent with many, and now who amongst the very humblest of our people would exchange places with him who once practically ruled the destinies of this country, as any crowned monarch ever did or ever will. Before the scene witnessed at Brighton on Tuesday night, the heart stands still, and the mind itself seems to pause terrified at the recollection of the awful possibilities which be beyond the tomb. So far as the world knows, Mr Parnell has died unrepentant for his offences against God and against his country, while he still planned the bringing of further discord amongst her people, and while he was yet the tool of a faction steeped in traitorism to Ireland to the very lips. To Catholics the close of the career of Mr Parnell will present itself with a terrible significance. Death has come upon him in the home of sin; he has died and his last glimpse of the world has been unhallowed by the consolations of religion, his memory is linked for ever with that of her whose presence seems to forbid all thought of his repentance. And we know that he passed into eternity with never a sign of sorrow for the insult he offered to morality, and for the revolt which he sought to create in his native land against the anointed prelates and ministers of God's Church. The darkness is pierced by the cry of sorrow, but the light of hope shines not, and there is nought but darkness, drear and horrid.

'This is the language of men calling themselves Christians,' the *United Ireland* editorial said, contemptuously of course.

'It's the language you would have to learn if you joined the *Irish News*,' my father added. That paper has since shrugged off the heavy diocesan hand that had rested on its self-righteous shoulder. But in those days – the mid-1950s – the *Irish News* resolutely faced the altar, bowing and genuflecting when required to do so, which was often. Its reporters, mostly clever people, often humbled themselves at public ceremonies by kissing the bishop's signet ring before daring to ask unsearching questions about the Church's wonderful work collecting for charity or saving souls. So narrow was its gauge that it once ran a headline on the sports pages: 'Catholic Dog Wins Derby'.

I took my father's advice, and before long, John Cole dropped me a line, suggesting that I arrange to be interviewed by the joint-editors of the *Telegraph*, John E. (Jack) Sayers and Thomas McMullan. Sayers, at that time, was trying to goad the Northern Ireland establishment (that is, Unionism and Orangeism) beyond the horizons imposed by bowler brims pulled hard down. He wanted an end to sectarianism, and a new government relationship with the nationalist minority. I think that is why he placed such faith in John Cole, giving him freedom to write objectively about Ulster politics. Sayers, a Methodist of perspicacity, saw writing on the wall, other than the usual 'Fuck the Pope' and 'Fuck the Queen', and was anxious to create an atmosphere in which extremism would find it hard to maintain a purchase. The son of a previous *Telegraph* editor, he had skipped university for journalism. In the Second

World War, he was a lieutenant-commander in the Royal Naval Volunteer Reserve and joined the staff of Churchill's map room in Downing Street. It was said by some that his war service and proximity to Churchill (however impersonal) made Jack Sayers (or 'JES', as his staff called him) a snob on returning to Belfast – and to 'the dreary steeples of Fermanagh and Tyrone', whose re-emergence Churchill anticipated on the ending of the European war. Sayers was pale and reserved, a Brylcreemed man whose eyes seemed shaped by the Orient, who was (oddly in an editor) of very few words in conversation and who preferred to communicate by memo. McMullan was pink-complexioned and extrovert. His face would beam and crinkle between syllables (a Stan Laurel without hair). Both were waiting to interview me on the day I nervously knocked on a third floor door and was ushered into a large office overlooking Royal Avenue.

The interview went reasonably well. They nodded approvingly when I told them what books I currently was reading, and seemed genuinely pleased that I had decided against university. Then McMullan leaned slightly forward, smiling slightly.

'Now, McCrystal, we are aware that you're, ahem, a Roman Catholic.'

'Er . . . yes, that's right.'

'As we have noted from your c.v.'

'Oh! Yes, indeed.'

'And I want you to know that we don't hold that against you. Hum?'

I said nothing, wondering what was coming. My palms had become moist. Sayers was looking at some sheets of paper in his hand, as though uninterested in the turn the conversation was taking. McMullan's face was jovial as he pressed on.

'Your Christian name, Cahal; Irish, isn't it?'

'Yes it is. It means Charles.'

'Charles? Is that so? Hmm.'

His right hand adjusted his spectacles on his nose, continuing upwards to scratch his pink, bald head. He glanced at Sayers, who ignored him. Sayers seemed amused, and now and again he caught my eye as if to communicate the fact that this was all jolly silly, but we have to put up with it. Then the affable McMullan looked at me very earnestly.

'You understand, McCrystal, that the *Belfast Telegraph* is keen to employ Roman Catholics. Do you know Cecil Deeney? You don't? He's here, doing well – he's a Roman Catholic too, you know! Hum?'

I examined the carpet beneath my feet. I was uncomfortable, even though these men were going out of their way to be friendly.

'But – and I know you won't take this the wrong way – there are some people in Belfast who think we're moving too fast in employing Roman Catholics; people who've been reading the paper for years and feel that it reflects their opinions on all sorts of things. You understand? Hum?'

I was beginning to. The complicated nature of the newspaper's new integrationist policy started to unfold for me. I felt peculiarly important. The editors would not be saying these things to me if they were not willing to offer me a job. It looked as though I might succeed in becoming the second 'house Mick', hard on the heels of the first, Deeney – a Derry man five or six years my senior, who was to become one of my warmest friends. I also felt amusement at their difficulty in explaining my parametric future to me without giving offence.

'For example,' said McMullan kindly, 'if you were marked [assigned] to cover the City Hall, you can imagine, can't you, hum? how some Unionist councillors might react to someone with a nationalist byline like Cahal reporting Corporation affairs for a paper which has traditionally supported the Unionist cause – and still does. Some people are awful narrow-minded.'

I nodded slowly, trying hard not to smile. Finally he got it off his chest.

'I've got an idea! Would you consider, er, "Charles" rather than "Cahal" if we decided to appoint you to the staff? "Charles McCrystal". That'd be all right, wouldn't it, Jack?'

He turned excitedly to Sayers, who did not respond, other than to glance at me searchingly. I was by now fairly convinced that Sayers was on my side.

'Well, you see, that could be difficult,' I said. 'That's my father's name, you see, and I'm not sure I'd like . . .'

'Yes, yes, I know, I know,' McMullan rushed on, 'and I'm not saying you would be *obliged* to change to Charles – that is, if you were to join us. All I'm suggesting is that you think about it over the next few days. It's too unimportant to lose any sleep over, but do give some thought to it, and let me know what you decide.'

So I thought it over, jettisoned a syllable ('ha!'), and called myself 'Cal' – a cunningly effective compromise, I thought, until readers' responses to what I wrote from time to time implied an assumption that it was the shortened version of 'Caleb', or 'Calum'. Every so often, I get a letter from Japan, from Murray Sayle, a good friend, journalist and author, with whom I have shared foreign assignments in the past. He always begins it: 'Dear Calvin'. In a way, I was conscious at the time of having sacrificed a portion of what my father might have referred to as my Gaelic identity. But he seemed not to attach great significance to it. 'It sounds the same,' he said. 'It's not as if you're betraying anybody.' In any case, I was what I had scarcely hoped to be: a Catholic reporter on Northern Ireland's largest and most influential newspaper, being paid seven pounds and fourteen shillings a week plus expenses. I think I'd have renamed myself 'Caligula' if really hard-pressed.

In the first few years, I was kept away from politics. I didn't mind at all. I was not yet twenty-one, knew little or nothing about the machinations of government or the parties represented in the Stormont parliament. I had never even bothered to visit the building atop a green hill on the eastern outskirts of Belfast. There was much to learn before I edged into political journalism: the police courts, small-town disputes, storm damage, train crashes, trade unions. Despite persistent feelings of insecurity – which, by then, I had attributed more to being a Catholic amongst Protestants than to being a non-university man – I enjoyed working on the *Telegraph*.

I continued to live in Ponsonby Avenue with my father and step-mother, to whom I handed over a portion of my salary. Within a year, I was earning £15 a week, and had sampled alcoholic drinks I'd never seen at home (gin and vermouth, Jack Daniels, Bacardi, whiskey-sour). I had also become engaged to Stella Doyle, a building contractor's daughter I'd first met at a Brendan Hyland party. Her brother, Jack, had also been a boarder at St Mary's College, Dundalk, though he arrived there in the year after I had left.

Now here's a curious thing. When I first mentioned to my father that I was in love, he said: 'Well, well, that's *great*!' And then, taking the pipe out of his mouth, he asked casually: 'Catholic?'

It was not an extraordinary question in the context of Northern Ireland's religious divide. It didn't jolt me at the time, for it was the kind of question all Belfast parents would have asked in the circumstances – and in all likelihood still ask. I have regarded it, in turn, as an aberrant reflex, an ironic comment and a simple, innocent query. In retrospect, however, I have had difficulty in reconciling it with his concern, which I believe to have been totally genuine, to fuse Protestants and Catholics together. And so I have given up trying to work it out. I'm not sure if a contradiction had surfaced, or if he might as casually have murmured: 'Atheist?' Brendan's view is inconclusive, though dour. My brother remembers minute sectarian traces in my father's response to his brief courtship of Protestant girls before he finally married a Catholic one: nothing critical or challenging, nothing you could put your finger on, perhaps just a flickering shadow that vanished almost before you noticed it. Brendan wonders: 'Was daddy a Nimby ["Not in my back yard"] in this respect?'

Stella was educated at convent schools, including the Dominican College in north Belfast. Her hair was dark and her eyes and laughter sparkled. She had a natural beauty that neither sought nor required affectation. I fell for her at once and have been married to her ever since. She immediately hit it off with my father and stepmother, who were relieved that I intended to settle down, 'cease gallivanting and making an ass of yourself'.

The remark may seem harsh. I was, after all, only twenty-two when I got married after a two-year engagement. I had had neither time nor opportunity to 'play the field' before setting up home. But there was some cause for my parents' concern. Introduced a bit late in the day to strong drink, I found myself taking to it with gusto and without caution. At one journalists' Christmas party, I drank lager after lager, not realizing it was being 'spiked' surreptitiously with vodka by my companions. I passed out, came to, and drank some more. I passed out again. A colleague drove me home to Ponsonby at two in the morning, when the house was in darkness. He opened the front door, shoved me down the hall and disappeared. I remember nothing of this. Next morning – a Sunday – I stumbled out of bed and wobbled downstairs, encountering articles of my clothing on the way down. I had been sick in the bathroom. And on the landing. And in the hall. I opened a door. My father was reading a newspaper, his back to the window. I opened my mouth and said: 'I . . . I . . . Good morning . . . I . . . What . . . ?' My father looked up, his face expressionless. There was ice in his eye. 'Very creditable,' he said, before returning to his newspaper. I slunk away.

Stella steadied me. Her loyalty to me then, as now, has been a commodity made all the more precious by her singularly spirited independence. She would be lavish in her expressions of delight at my modest achievements, and unbridled in her contempt for less modest traits, such as turning up late, numbed by drink. Quick to take offence, she is also quick to forgive. And I have often pondered a paradox: Stella's father was, so far as I could tell, apolitical (natural enough for a Catholic businessman who maintained offices in both Belfast and Dublin), yet she is highly politicized (anti-Unionist, anti-partitionist); I, on the other hand, am an apolitical child of a household that ate, drank and slept politics, yet I can see as many virtues in Unionism as in nationalism and great imperfections in both.

'Where are you going to live?' my father asked when Stella and I had fixed a date for our wedding. I had no idea. Like all young couples, we wanted our own place. But I was not yet earning enough to take out a substantial mortgage on a new house. We had talked about having six children (we settled for three), which would require a bit of space, though not, of course, immediately. In the end, her parents came to our rescue. The Doyles were fairly well-off and had a holiday home at Ballymacormick Point, east of Bangor, as well as their house in Belfast. Her father said we could live at Ballymacormick until we could afford to move elsewhere. The small, single-storey house was halfway up a narrow country road and overlooked fields sloping down towards the sea. A short time earlier it had replaced, as the family's summer retreat, another house called 'Solitude', whose water supply was drawn from a nearby well. The road is pretty well built up now as Bangor has expanded to accommodate thousands of Belfast citizens displaced by the Troubles. The long front lawn of the new place, called 'Ulsterville', was protected by a low wall and a two-posted gate. On one post, a plaque announced the name of the house in English; on the other a second plaque gave the name in Gaelic, '*Teach Uladh*', the words in golden gothic against the shiny, black plate. At the onset of the Troubles in 1968–69, my father-in-law, fearing that the Gaelic lettering might have annoyed loyalist neighbours – despite his membership of the Royal Naval Club and friendship with Lord Glentoran, a minister of the Unionist government at Stormont – removed the Gaelic sign, burying it in a drawer. The even longer back garden had a serpentine fish pond, cherry, apple and pear trees and a large greenhouse. My wife's father employed a gardener, so I was spared the toil of digging or weeding. The year in which we lived there was, despite a hard winter, a happy one. Ballymacormick is a persistent reminder of a relatively untroubled period when sectarianism merely parodied itself and thoughtful Catholics and Protestants seemed anxious to rise above it. Recently, I recalled those agreeable years, in the following lines I sent to my wife's eldest sister, whose memory had been fading as fast as was her health.

Much time has passed, Kathleen, since our first encounter
At the corner of the Ballymacormick Road

And the coastal road to Groomsport: the dead centre
Of our secure world in those days. I think I rode
A bus, walking the remaining two hundred yards
To the corner. I breathed the early summer air,
That had settled heavily over all the Ards
Peninsula. In the adjoining field, a mare
Grazed with her colt. The grass appeared to run right down
Into the distant sea. A songthrush blessed the land
From a hedge of thorn, dog-rose and alder. The town
Seemed far away. And there you were, your outstretched hand
Reaching for mine, as your sister introduced us.
Your laughter was infectious, and in buoyant mood
For tea of scones and apple-pie to boost us,
We ambled upwards to a house called 'Solitude'.

That house is gone; the one succeeding it, a ruin.
The corner where we met back then has been excised
By a second road to Groomsport. Changes blew in
From Belfast and elsewhere. But no one was surprised
By such developments. For years, life just went on
As though the well from which you filled your pail would stay
Forever brimming, and I never would be done
Mending your ever-broken rosary. So pray
Someone tell me just how and why it came about
That we have strayed so far apart since then. I know
I've been away, and you've been ill (and in and out),
And grief has crushed your yielding heart, blow after blow.
But, recalling that summer – and summers after –
I know for certain your spirit cannot be crushed;
Nor can any tribulation curb your laughter,
Or my own memory of it when your voice is hushed.

But of course such nostalgia reflects little of what Northern Ireland actually was in the 1950s and early 1960s before I left it. A half-hearted IRA campaign, which seemed to concentrate on making holes in border roads and blowing up radio transmitters, fizzled out, to be replaced by a civil rights campaign, organized by the Catholic middle class. Great strife was to follow, blighting narrow country roads (hitherto as quiet and unalarming as the one at Ballymacormick) and city streets before and during the most recent Troubles. Yet we were more old-fashioned than we perhaps realized. Old habits of thought yielded reluctantly to new. The Unionist was exceedingly jealous of his established scheme of things. The nationalist had little idea about how to alter the scheme to his own advantage and for long periods seemed happy to torment the establishment with nothing more lethal or more ingenious than a pea-shooter. Both were totally convinced that the secret that would sustain them lay deep in the past; consequently the future had become a nagging irrelevance. They claimed the old as a familiar habit, and spurned the future as a risky adventure. On both sides, sentiments teemed with anachronisms that appeared to embarrass no one. My father was scornful of the Ancient Order of Hibernians, a Catholic national-ist entity that 'merely aped the Orangemen', and the Knights of St Columbanus, which, he said, had 'all the flounce and flummery' of the Masons.

A few years ago, I went to Dublin to interview Dr Mary Robinson, the Irish President, and was particularly struck by her attachment to symbolism in the national psyche. I was quickly convinced that she is a person of great sincerity and an inquiring mind. The symbolism of keeping a light burning all the time in the window of her official residence, as an inspiration to Irish migrants who might be considering a return to their homeland, was a warm and touching gesture. Yet symbols have been Ireland's curse down the centuries: flags, walls, banners, steeples. They provide the leitmotif for what scholars dignify by the term 'continuity of history', but, as historical products, symbols are often handed down from remote periods and with vague origins. They guarantee that our prejudices and conceits, scruples and obligations are seldom of our own cre-ation. And they get in the way as we fumble for advancement in intelligence and insight.

As I settled down in the *Belfast Telegraph* and bought a house in Knock, not far from Stormont, it was clear to me how difficult it would be to unpick symbolism from the political cloth. The first thing I noticed was that the newspaper's elderly, irascible High Court reporter wrote with an Orange pen and was inclined to tap it against a glass of (Dublin-made) Guinness to encourage a high froth. But it also seemed to me odd that the newspaper staff placed unusual importance on past war service. I assume this was due to the fact that Northern Ireland, unlike the rest of the United Kingdom, had no compulsory call-up for the Second World War; therefore those who volunteered tended to advertise their fighting spirit for ever afterwards. Thus, Sayers's survival of the wartime sinking of HMS *Courageous* was a persistent talking-point, though he did not strenuously encourage it. The chief sub-editor's service with the North Irish Horse in the Far East was a source of weekly anecdotes. His deputy retained his Army title, 'Major'. Until Sayers began his liberalizing campaign, such things emphasized the *Telegraph*'s position as the organ of a pro-British establishment.

But the not-quite demilitarized newsroom was nothing compared to Stormont: Captain the Rt. Hon. Terence O'Neill (Minister of Finance, later Prime Minister); Major the Rt. Hon. Ivan Neill (Minister of Labour and National Insurance); Lieut.-Colonel the Rt. Hon. Lord Glentoran (Minister of Commerce); Lieut.-Colonel the Rt. Hon. Alexander Gordon (Minister in the Senate); Major George Thomson (Clerk of the Parliaments); Brigadier Nelson Russell (Serjeant-at-Arms); Brigadier John Calwell (Deputy Serjeant-at-Arms); Major Francis Lyle Harrison (Counsel to the Speaker). After stints as City Hall reporter, High Court reporter and labour correspondent, I joined the *Telegraph*'s reporting team at Stormont. It occurred to me at the time – though I suspect it would have been regarded as churlish to have mentioned it then – that all this ex-brass created an impression that Northern Ireland was governed by a junta – which indeed, in Catholic eyes, the government resembled, having been a one-party, one-religion apparatus for more than half a century. More than forty years ago, Patrick Gormley, Nationalist

MP for Mid-Londonderry, harangued the Unionist benches thus: 'No thought can get into this House . . . save on the old sectarian lines. All the constituencies are cut and dried.

'We are wasting money having elections. All one has got to do is to get a list giving the religious persuasions of the people, total them up, and one will produce the election result. That is not democracy. If the area cannot live naturally, the same as any other political unit, there is something radically wrong with it. If, to keep the peace in the area, the government have to ask for more force, for more men to be hanged, for bigger and better gaols to be put up, there is something radically wrong.'

The anticipated permanency of the Protestant parliament for a Protestant people was even the subject of (possibly unconscious) humour by the people's representatives. In April 1958, on rising to welcome the Queen's Speech-by-proxy to her Stormont Commons, the Prime Minister Lord Brookeborough began as follows: 'I should like in the first place, at the opening of this ninth parliament, to extend a welcome to newcomers on both sides of the House, some of whom are more welcome than others. [*Laughter*] Let us hope that the fusion of new blood and old will result in a healthy and vigorous parliament and make for stimulating discussions on the vital subjects which will come before us.'

Among the vital subjects discussed that parliamentary term was the allocation of houses. The Nationalist MP for South Fermanagh quoted from a local Unionist newspaper in County Tyrone as follows: 'Any Unionist who sells a farm or lets a house to an Anti-Partitionist [i.e., Nationalist] is assisting that Party to win the local government representation in that area at the next election, and their action can only be regarded as treachery to their Party.' The MP then read out what had become a familiarly depressing litany of discrimination against Catholics in public housing. Among the cases he detailed was this:

'Patrick McCusker, of Aughnaskew, Maguiresbridge, County Fermanagh, with his wife and three children, aged four, five and six years, was evicted from his cottage in February 1957. The councillors knew that this family had occupied the house uninterruptedly for nearly sixty years. They were good tenants and good rent payers. Mrs McCusker was the daughter of the first tenant and she had been there for forty-two years having ten children born in the house. The council of that day did not award houses on political grounds. That was before the setting up of this government.

'When Mrs McCusker, by reason of age and infirmity, became ill, her son Patrick, like a dutiful boy, returned to look after his mother. She died some time ago but the council refused a transfer of the cottage to her son. In due course an eviction order was served on the family and they were thrown out on the roadside in the winter weather on a February day. Said Mr McCusker to the people assembled to witness the sad plight, "This is justice for you as we know it here in Fermanagh. May God forgive all of them who had a hand in driving us from our home of fifty-four years." The man selected for McCusker's cottage was James Gardiner, who had a wife and four children, but who lived in Main Street, Lisnaskea, in reasonable accommodation.' Mr Gardiner was a Protestant.

The discrimination was pretty blatant at times. One applicant for a house sent a letter to the local council declaring he was from [loyalist] Portadown and wanted a house in Rathfriland, adding: 'I am a staunch loyalist. God save the Queen.' He got his house.

At first, it was thrilling to report the Stormont debates. But I think my enthusiasm came from being in the convivial company of my *Telegraph* colleagues, all men (no women) of wit and acumen. Our leader was Tom Roberts, successor to John Cole, who had gone to the *Manchester Guardian* – as the *Guardian* then was called – as labour correspondent. Roberts was highly professional and never missed a deadline, but once his duties were over, the *bon viveur* took over. This usually entailed a fast car journey from Stormont to McGlade's on Donegall Street, where we operated an informal 'back office' called alternately 'the blue room' (after the décor) and the 'Theatre Bar' (after the actors and actresses who were supposed to frequent it, but seldom did). Cecil Deeney was Roberts's number two, a prematurely grey journalist who, after a few whiskeys, could be persuaded to sing 'It Happened In Monterey'. The rest of the Stormont team included Trevor Hanna, a short, jaunty chap of my own age, who wore coloured waistcoats and narrow trousers, and Bill McGoockin, who had a strong rural accent and great appetite for work. I cannot recall him ever becoming drunk with us; he may well have been a teetotaller. Although I assume that most of my colleagues were Unionists, they never, so far as I was aware, injected their political preferences into what they wrote. Nor did I detect many signs of bigotry among them. Roberts and the Catholic Deeney were the closest of friends. The Protestant Hanna and I were like brothers. Even when some of these colleagues crossed the line into pro-government or pro-Unionist public relations (Roberts to the Northern Ireland Office in London; Hanna to the Unionist Party machine; McGoockin as RUC spokesman), they maintained – or seemed to maintain – the breadth of outlook which had enhanced their journalism. Another colleague, Dennis Kennedy, who, after a distinguished journalism career in Belfast and Dublin, became a diplomat and then an academic, was a Protestant to whom many a Catholic might gladly entrust their lives and their country. In McGlade's, we planned pub-crawls to Donegal, where we would damage our vocal chords in sing-song and our livers in drink. MPs, including some Stormont ministers, occasionally joined us in McGlade's, as did trade union officials, undercover policemen, businessmen and anyone else who was paid to listen, learn or propagate. On my bar-stool I persuaded myself I was working – that this is what journalists *do* in order to keep abreast of things – but most of it was delusion. I was spending too much time 'working' in McGlade's. When my third son was born I went there to celebrate on brandy-champagne cocktails. After a few of these in the middle of the afternoon, I fell backwards off the bar stool, and was caught by an alert barman before my head struck the floor. One night, driving home glassy-eyed from McGlade's, it dawned on me that even if my liver survived, my marriage might not. So it was a piece of good luck – though forged from tragic circumstances – that pushed me in the direction of Fleet Street. A number of experienced Belfast staff journalists boosted their income by 'stringing' for London and Dublin newspapers. Tom Burns, who had joined the *Belfast Telegraph* from the *Irish Times*, held the *Sunday Times* 'string'. One morning he went swimming in the surf at Portrush, had a heart attack and died. I took over his 'string'.

By then, the merciless throb of Northern Ireland politics had begun to make my head ache. There seemed no end or amelioration to the daily darts of inane pettiness being flung across the Stormont chamber floor. Nothing was going to change these people, I thought, after listening to a fairly typical debate, on what was described as 'the Dungiven Incident'. The best way I can convey the flavour of it is by repeating some of the Stormont exchanges. Dispiritingly, it is a debate that continues to this day. When I first heard it, I was lean and wiry, with fresh skin, taut muscles, clear eye and a full head of hair. As I compare it with the indistinguishable text of the same debates on the same subject forty years later, I am of wider, slacker girth, my skin is creased, my muscles lax, my eye rheumy and my hair almost gone. When I try to look ahead, to forty years into the Millennium and beyond – to, for example, the tercentenary of the 1798 rebellion by the United Irishmen – I anticipate an identical debate droning on, no doubt with the same awful, thudding vocabulary. It was about an Orangemen's march through the largely Catholic town of Dungiven, in County Londonderry. The Orangemen fastened the emblem of their Britishness – the Union Jack – to overhead wires leading to the Catholic church, leaving churchgoers with the option of walking under it (indicating submission), or removing it (and inviting attack).

Mr Gormley: (by *Private Notice*) [I] asked the Minister of Home Affairs whether he can state if he sanctioned a heavy police escort for the Bovevagh Orange Band through the town of Dungiven last Thursday; whether he is aware that such a parade would be provocative; whether further provocation has taken place against the people of the town; and whether he is prepared to apply the law equally to all . . . We are very near the Twelfth of July . . . I am fighting for my people. I am using democratic means. I expect to be treated as a public representative when I come into this House. I have been slighted when I made protests about maltreatment and disrespect I got from the B-Specials. I got no redress from the Department of Home Affairs, none whatever . . . The Union Jack is used as a provocative religious emblem . . . Dungiven has not a big population, probably around 700. I happened to go through Dungiven shortly after this incident . . . There is talk of Protestants and Catholics boycotting one another. That is not going to help: some innocent people are going to suffer.

Mr Topping (Min. of Home Affairs): The incident on Sunday last arose when the attention of the police was drawn to the fact that a Union Jack had been suspended from the overhead electricity wires leading into the Roman Catholic Church in Dungiven. The flag was attached to the wires, about 20 feet from the ground, and it was completely hidden from the main road by trees. The Electricity Board representatives who came out to remove the flag from the wires, in the ordinary course of their duty, were prevented from doing so by a hostile crowd which gathered inside the grounds of the church. The police had no alternative of affording protection to the Electricity Board officers or of removing the flag themselves. The latter could be, of course, an extremely dangerous operation if not carried out with the greatest care. The police, when carrying out this operation, were themselves assaulted by the crowd . . . It must be obvious to all except those interested in the dissemination of party political propaganda that the law of our land is always applied equally and without fear or favour to all.

Mr Connellan (Nat.): Very sensational news.

Mr Stewart (Nat.): – but we have it on record at Westminster . . . that when the people here were coming together it was a case of, 'Start something; get them at each other's throats.' That was the policy.

Mr Minford (U.): Are we supposed to say to the government that there will be no Orange bands or Orangemen walking through the village? We will walk through any village. We will keep the Union Jack flying anywhere we want . . . People who are not prepared to show at least some semblance of loyalty in this country should cross over the border to that land of plenty and Popery.

Mr Diamond (Repub. Lab.): The Hon. Member ought to be interned.

Mr Minford: If that old corncrake would keep his mouth shut. [*Laughter*]

Mr Hunter (U.): The point I want to make is that here is the Roman Catholic Church objecting –

Mr Connellan: No.

Mr Hunter: – to the flag of the country in which it resides.

Mr Stewart: That is not so . . . People object to having it shoved down their throats.

Mr Hunter: As a member of the Orange Order – like so many Hon. Members of this House and like the overwhelming majority of Her Majesty's subjects in Northern Ireland – I would refute and deny completely and utterly that the Union Jack is the political flag of the Orange Order . . . The Orange Order is a religious institution. [*Hon. Members: Oh.*] Just listen to the exclamations of those who do not know about it.

I listened to them all and heard nothing new. What I heard were echoes of the horrible violence of fanaticism from that unpleasant phase in human history known as the Inquisition: the first tribunal at Narbonne, in 1208; the first *auto da fé* at Aragon, in 1314; the incineration of 2,000 males and females at Seville, between 1482 and 1484. Nothing much has changed, I told myself. I heard also the sounds of a later 'golden age' for state executioners when, following Henry VIII's death, English Protestants sought out, flogged and executed English Catholics – and vice versa; when the stake, the execution bloc and the hangman's noose achieved great popularity, because of the novel ways of carrying out some of the 72,000 executions, among them decapitation using a bag of gunpowder. I told myself again: nothing much has changed. I thought that I could not take much more of it.

'It's the insanity, the neurotic affections, the puffing and blowing of these ignorant blockheads,' I wrote to my father. 'Every time I sit in on the Stormont debates, I want to bang my head on the press gallery.' Did he remember, two years before, reading aloud Roy McFadden's poem, 'A Cry' ?

> If I was Samson I
> Would pull this mad house down
> Loud about their ears –
> But I being only I
> With hands like melting snow
> Must thole the fools, and crown
> Joy with a cap of tears.

He replied, agreeing that men's minds and lives were impoverished by the kind of stuff I had to endure at Stormont. But, as almost always, he was uplifted by the idealism he believed would eventually unite Protestant and Catholic in Northern Ireland. He quoted that marvellous Lurgan-schooled Gaelic revivalist, George Russell (Æ), author of such poems as 'The Divine Vision' and 'Gods of War': 'A nation is cultivated only so far as the average man, not the exceptional person, is cultivated and has knowledge of the thought, imagination and intellectual history of his nation. Where there is a general culture its effects are seen in the houses, the pictures, the homes and gardens, the arts of life. Almost insensibly beauty enters the household and what is meant by civilization is apparent.'

I was finding it increasingly hard to believe in my father's optimism. As a labour correspondent, I frequently was in the company of trades union people, men and women as familiar with Marx's editorials in *Rheinische Zeitung* more than a century ago as they were with the editorials in this week's *Belfast Telegraph*. Many of these union people were sincere socialists, with an unyielding commitment to the workingman. But they often showed traces of bigotry – not to me personally, but, in unguarded moments, about 'Fenians' generally. There were, of course, shining exceptions. Four come to mind: Harold Binks, of the Clerical Workers Union, who drank himself to death; Billy Blease, General Secretary of the Irish Congress of Trade Unions, who later became Lord Blease; Betty Sinclair, the communist Secretary of Belfast's Trades Council; and Paddy Devlin, of the Irish Transport Workers Union, who became a controversial politician. Devlin, a Catholic (and no relation to Joe Devlin, my father's other friend mentioned earlier), was one of my father's closest friends who, when Charles McCrystal died, described him as 'an inspiration'.

On a visit to my father, one evening towards the end of the 1950s, I glanced through his copies of *The Bell*, an Irish literary magazine with a radical reputation. In a 1943 issue I found an article entitled 'When Peace Breaks in Ulster'. It spoke of 'the new writers' who 'have no ivory towers and they ask none: like all Ulstermen, despite their other shortcomings such as a lack of the graces, they do not shrink from the maelstrom'. This applied to thousands of non-literary young men and women. The article went on:

Go into our cafés and pubs, workshops and recreation centres, and hear them speak of social conditions, of plans for post-War economic and physical reconstruction, talking knowingly of the Scott-Uthwatt and Beveridge Reports, of British relations with the Soviets, of Northern relationships with the Twenty-six Counties, of the clean, decent world we are all hoping and working for . . . This kind of talk, however unsophisticated and ill-informed, is beginning to *mean* something more than talk. The young are determined to think out the position while the War is on: when peace breaks out again they know it may be too late to prevent a backward slide into the old familiar morass . . . Young Ulster is developing a faith for the future; a blind, instinctive groping towards life, but nevertheless a generous acceptance and appreciation of the contemporary scene . . . Young Ulster is on the march – energetic, enthusiastic, idealistic. The whole problem is to find a unifying social and aesthetic cause wide enough to include the majority, while not unduly clamping down on individualism, so welding together in common purpose all that is best in the resurgent spirit. Out of this dynamism, salvation may come for Ulster: and who knows that, having saved herself by her vision, she will not save Ireland by her example?

Rousing stuff. It seemed my father was not alone in his optimism. On the other hand, this exalted message was published when I was nine. I was reading it, for the first time, when I was about twenty-five. Young Ulster had become Old Ulster, and nothing had changed. Old Ulster is now decrepit Ulster, and I'm still waiting.

12

'ULSTER'S GOLDEN AGE'

The late 1950s and early 1960s were not my father's best years. Colm followed me into marriage, and Brendan was about to do so, removing the sounds of family from the family home. Small disasters occurred. My father and stepmother were invited to meet Brendan's prospective parents-in-law, the Grants, for the first time, and travelled to Helen's Bay, an affluent spot on the south shore of Belfast Lough to do so. The Grants, who owned the Grand Central Hotel, then Belfast's biggest, lived in a large, elegant house. All went well. The Grants were then invited to Ponsonby Avenue.

'Have a seat,' my father said in our parlour to John Grant, about whom the phrase, 'tall and imposing' was no exaggeration. He chose the only chair that was notoriously ricketty. It splintered beneath him, sending him sprawling.

'And do you know why I think Mr Grant's a man to be admired?' my father told me later. 'He picked himself up, looked at me straight in the eye and said, "Would you believe it? That has happened two or three times with chairs in our house recently." I knew it probably hadn't happened in his house at all, but he said it to ease my embarrassment.'

With all three sons married, the house in Ponsonby exchanged exuberance for tranquillity. Theresa took up oil-painting, encouraged by my father. She painted on hardboard (the rough side) because canvas was too expensive. Her 'still life' efforts were highly commended in a Belfast amateur art competition, but her attempts at portraits were, by and large, not a great success. Most of these attempts were directed at my father, either full face or in profile, as he read his books, smoked his pipes or dozed in front of the fire. When she had completed one, he would scrutinize it enthusiastically, holding it close to the window, and murmur: 'Well, that's uncanny.'

'What's uncanny?' my stepmother asked nervously.

'The resemblance – uncanny is the only word for it. It's the best yet!'

Theresa would flush with pleasure at his praise, but also laugh uncertainly, and say things like, 'Oh, you're just saying that, Cathal . . .', before getting him his supper.

They were both very active, going for long walks over Cave Hill or to Glengormley, at the end of the Antrim Road trolley-bus route. They also played shuttlecock in our back yard, which was just long enough for a cramped version of the game. My father gave the yard walls an annual whitewash and Theresa encouraged trees and shrubs to grow in deep, brick-built troughs. Nevertheless, I think their horizons had come in on them. Beyond the yard wall, new flats had been erected on the 'wastey'. New neighbours had moved in. Newington's young generation had vanished, while its old generation was starting to die off. Those of life's ambitions that had not already been achieved had begun to lose their attraction or significance. Having spent many of his years embroiled in controversy, Charles McCrystal now seemed to spend a great deal of his time attending funerals. He continued to read voraciously, and showed no inclination to instal a television in his home until Brendan bought him one. He was still a regular customer at the Communist Party bookshop near the city centre. I knew this because one of my *Belfast Telegraph* colleagues, a Protestant republican called Jack Bennett, told me so, adding that he believed my father to be 'one of the finest Irish socialists I've ever met'. Infrequently one came across newspaper items that mentioned him.

Gaelic Speaker Reads Russian For Lord Mayor
BELFAST, June 3. – When Lord Mayor Cecil McKee received a 150-word telegram from Leningrad inviting him to Russia he could find

no one in City Hall who could translate the Russian language in the telegram.

The Mayor searched the city for a translator and found one in Cathal McCrystal, of Ponsonby Avenue. Mr McCrystal, a printer, took up the study of Russian several years ago.

Now and again when I went to see him, he was attempting a hypnotic remedy for a visitor's 'nervous complaints'. These might include, for example, a phobia about metal objects. My father's 'treatment' (I am very reluctant to use the word, since it implies a remedy he was not medically qualified to supply) involved long, relaxed conversation as well as hypnotism, and I'm not sure he was right to be doing it. He once said to me that the people who came to him refused his advice that they should consult a doctor. 'In any case, it's nothing to worry about,' he said. 'I never put them into a deep sleep. It's more a soothing, confidence-building session. And if their symptoms include physical pain, I wouldn't dream of trying to treat it.' Even so, I still wonder uneasily about his appearing to give willingness and capability equipollence. Being Chairman of the Northern Ireland Hypnotists' Society was hardly a signal for 'treating' anybody for anything. Glancing through them now, I find that some of his books were pretty out of date at the time. One, *Neurypnology, or The Rationale of Nervous Sleep Considered in Relation to Animal Magnetism or Mesmerism*, was by James Braid, a Manchester surgeon regarded as 'the initiator of the scientific study' of the subject. It was published in 1899. Sometimes I have suspected that my father's delvings into diverse subjects such as hypnotism was an unconscious need to compensate for his lack of a college education.

As the 1950s drew to a close, he lost his job with W. & G. Baird, as a result of petty-mindedness. My father had suffered intermittently from haemorrhoids (piles), and always found a reason for not having them surgically treated. The condition grew worse with age. One afternoon when he was in the lavatory at Baird's, he haemorrhaged badly. An ambulance was called and he was taken to hospital. There was nothing terribly alarming in this, and he was sent home that afternoon and advised to rest until the following day. But, picking up his wages at the end of the week, he discovered that the company had deducted a half-day's wages as a result of the medical emergency. Here was an employee who had served the company for more than thirty years, was some years from retirement, who seldom took time off, even with flu, and whose work had never been unsatisfactory. Yet when he missed a single afternoon as a result of illness and hospitalization, he was deliberately penalized. More stunned by such treatment than he had been by the sectarian emblems placed on his work-station over the years, he asked to see the company manager, who explained the deduction.

'In that case, I no longer work for you,' my father said. As he departed, none of his colleagues spoke up on his behalf. The Typographical Association, the union he had helped negotiate many pay deals, did nothing. I suppose he could have sued for constructive dismissal, or perhaps victimization (the company had always regarded his republican and socialist tendencies askance). But I think he was much too shocked to consider it. A week later, I met one of the men with whom my father had worked.

'I'm really terribly sorry about what happened to your daddy,' he said. 'I wasn't in work that day, otherwise I'd have said something.'

His chin trembled and there were tears in his eyes as he shook my hand and walked away. I felt sorry for him, for his addled conscience and for his strange notion of comradely loyalty, because I knew he *had* been in that day. Shortly afterwards, Jack Sayers called me into his office in the *Telegraph*. He was paler than usual.

'I have just learned what happened to your father,' Sayers said. 'He is a man for whom I've had enormous respect, even though I've never met him and don't agree with his views. It's disgraceful, and I'm ashamed.' He gave a final nod. 'That's all.'

Times became rather difficult in Ponsonby Avenue. My father, it sometimes has occurred to me, may have concluded that he had touched life at too many points. One of the qualities women had admired in him was boyishness (arriving at our Portstewart guest house one summer, he was mistaken by the landlady as our older brother; though this may well have been flirtatious flattery). Some of that left him now. He remained sprightly enough, but his sprightliness may have sprung from the soil of misfortune, like wild blossoms that flourish in bleak places. From his family – and I expect from his friends, and no doubt his enemies – he concealed mortification and insult, shrugged and went on as though nothing untoward had happened. His paradoxes kept people, among them myself, guessing. A partisan, he grew to rise above faction; an explorer, he was no opportunist. He remained unpliant and went unrewarded: the lifelong friend of losing causes. One of the principles my father clung to, until his grip on life waned, was that you should 'live fully up to your income and leave nothing behind for next-of-kin to squabble over – unearned income is unseemly'. So he had very few savings. Theresa talked about selling encyclopedias door-to-door, but her husband thought that 'there'd be very few takers around here, not to mention the fact [he laughed] you could rupture yourself'. Within a few weeks he became a reader with another firm, Pitman's. His wages were lower, but it didn't appear to bother him ('You can have too much money, you know'). And although the Baird brush-off left him subdued, intermittently, for some time, he seldom let it show. He beamed happily in the company of his grandchildren, the first of whom – my eldest son (also Cahal, though he prefers to use the same abbreviated form I'd adopted) – was born in 1959. And he was amused by the irony of his – a republican's – encounter with the British Queen's sister, as reported in the *Daily Mail* :

PRINCESS MARGARET HAS HER FIRST LESSON IN RUSSIAN . . .

Princess Margaret got her first lesson in Russian yesterday after she had unveiled a plaque commemorating new extensions to the factory of Sir Isaac Pitman and Sons at Castlereagh, Belfast.

Mr Christian Pitman, a director of the firm, who escorted the Princess on a tour of the factory, introduced her to Mr Charles McCrystal, a reader with the firm. Mr McCrystal, who was reading Russian, explained that the firm sets type in at least six languages.

When Mr McCrystal read: 'I must buy some blouses for my sister,' in Russian, then translated, the Princess insisted on knowing the Russian words for 'blouses' and 'sister', for she is taking a blouse back for the Queen.

Earlier the Princess and her husband, Lord Snowdon, visited Belfast Ropeworks.

By then, my father had taken up German and was working his way through Hermann Hesse's *Glasperlenspiel* and Thomas Mann's short stories, *Der Erwählte*. I couldn't understand how his eyes coped with it: reading all day at Pitman's, and reading well into the evening at home.

'Reading maketh a full man,' he intoned, quoting Bacon.

'But full of what?' I scoffed, sarcastically. 'Dandruff?' A layer of it had settled on his shoulders.

There had been a lull in republican activity following the failure of the 1956–62 terrorist campaign, and I cannot recall many conversations with him on the subject in the eight years preceding the most recent and savage outbreak. In December 1957, the IRA had published a statement that fell largely on deaf ears. It said:

There is no question of Protestant Irishmen being asked to submit to a Catholic Parliament [in a united Ireland]. Irish Republicans are not fighting for the incorporation of the Six Counties in the Southern State. They are fighting positively for Irish freedom. They say neither north nor south can have independence in the full sense of the term while the country is divided and part of it occupied by British forces. The enemy of Irish unity still remains British Imperialism – not the Orange rank and file of north-east Ulster . . . Irish Republicans then want an Ireland with the shadow of Imperialism removed from it forever . . . They want an Ireland where Catholics, Presbyterians, Methodists, Baptists, can live in harmony and peace – as Irish citizens.

But the 'revolt', as the IRA described it, was over for the moment.

Northern Ireland regained an uncertain equilibrium. But fresh legends of republican 'martyrdom' and soldierly 'atrocities' entered the nationalist bloodstream, to be stored as fuel for later. There is, in nearly every nationalist mind – as in every loyalist mind – a scoreboard of wrongs to be avenged; and if not in the mind, then on the bookshelf. In Father Kavanagh's *Popular History of the Insurrection of 1798*, thumbed for years in Ponsonby Avenue, I found this account of the end of the 'battle of Arklow':

The insurgents on their march back to Gorey [in Wexford] carried some hundreds of their wounded comrades with them, leaving, unfortunately, many others on the field, who were slaughtered without mercy by the enemy on their return. Not only did these wretches murder the unhappy and defenceless wounded, but they mangled the senseless remains of those whom death might have protected from all but the vengeance of fiends. Imagination sickens at the contemplation of the horrible deeds perpetrated by the Ancient Britons, who, having fearfully mangled the remains of the Rev. Michael Murphy, tore out his heart, roasted it, and ate it. Does history record another so fiendish deed of the soldiers of any country?

Virtually every nationalist house is a repository for folklore of this kind. For those of a revolutionary bent it heats the blood – especially when boiling blood is needed. After the blood of 1952–56 had been boiled away, the threat of revolution, and the sectarian jitters that accompanied it, subsided. This made the Stormont government nervous, for when contentious men are not at each other's throats, they will lunge elsewhere: by, for example, combining against employers.

Between 1935, when I was born, and 1964, when I left for London, Belfast had avoided serious sectarian strife. Even the IRA's border terrorism failed to cause disruptive ripples. As the historian Andrew Boyd noted in his book *Holy War In Belfast*, 'the loyalists could find no reason for blaming their Catholic neighbours for the IRA's violence.' But while this was good news in one sense, it constituted a threat in another. In other words, in Unionism's mind, Protestant–Catholic relations at street level were becoming a little too cosy for comfort. 'Divide and rule' was an instrument that had proved effective in the past and was not to be cast carelessly aside. In 1959, the trade unions were talking about forming an all-Ireland Irish Congress of Trade Unions – anathema to Unionist politicians. Such a cross-border bond might have happened years earlier, but for the irrepressible sectarianism that crept into almost every attempt at co-operation between North and South, between nationalist and loyalist, between Protestant and Catholic.

In the 1930s, one of my father's students in a National Council of Labour Colleges economics course was Harry Midgely, a little sparrow of a man who later entered active politics. Midgely, a Protestant, and my father were friends, sharing many beliefs, antipathies (not least towards General Franco in fascist Spain), and a dry sense of humour. Their declared faith in socialism was so strong that they used whatever free time they had to distribute NCLC leaflets among groups of workmen in the city – in bars, clubs and on the way to and from work. The 1930–31 winter session leaflet explained why these workmen should attend classes: 'Because Nature furnished you with brains to use in the work of extracting from life the maximum of happiness. Because membership of the Trade Union and Labour Movement imposes upon you the task of assisting your fellows to secure higher wages, better houses, education and more leisure time. Because Capitalist Society is in decay, and the workers must learn how to build a new system rapidly before it collapses . . . Knowledge means power.'

But in Northern Ireland, other things mean power too. My father had belonged to the Irish Labour Party. Midgely was in the Northern Ireland Labour Party, though both organizations had maintained fraternal relations for years. Midgely represented Belfast's Docks Division at Stormont – a constituency with a majority of Catholic voters. But in the 1938 election, pro-Franco Catholics, no doubt stirred up by their clergy, took their revenge on Midgely for his conspicuous support of Spain's legitimate government in the Spanish civil war. They put up a Catholic nationalist, which split the anti-Unionist vote and allowed in a leading Orangeman.

Embittered, Midgely abandoned Labour, joined the Unionist Party and the Orange Order and quickly rose in the loyalist firmament, eventually becoming a member of the Stormont Cabinet. Although my father was disgusted with those Catholics who had spurned Midgely, he concluded that his old friend had put self above principle and should be regarded as a renegade.

'Guess who I ran into on the bus coming home tonight,' he announced one evening in the 1950s. He'd spotted Harry Midgely on the upper deck. But Midgely, my father said, 'ducked his head and pretended not to've seen me, and bolted from the bus like a scalded cat before you could say Jack Robinson.'

When Midgely, a clever and immensely likeable man, joined 'the enemy' he helped devise a formula to confuse his former friends. He demanded that the Northern Ireland Labour Party should either make it clear that it supported the constitutional link with the United Kingdom, or declare itself in favour of a re-united Ireland. Believing that the former course would enable it to harvest most of the working-class Protestant votes, the party opted for it, consequently losing most of its appeal for working-class Catholics. Midgely then pressed ahead with a plan to further split the working class – the setting up of a Northern Ireland Trades Union Congress. 'The enemies of Northern Ireland,' he wrote, 'are working relentlessly through every channel to bring about the reunification of Ireland, and they are not averse to using the trade union movement as an instrument for the consummation of this policy.'

Such fulminations worked for a time. But in 1959, an all-Ireland ICTU finally was formed, viewed with equal hostility by the Northern Ireland Labour Party and the Unionist Party. Attending one of its first annual meetings as the *Belfast Telegraph*'s labour correspondent, I observed delegates from north and south mixing affably in Killarney, supporting each other with crusading speeches and copious amounts of Irish whiskey, singing the praises of the proletariat, damning the excesses of capitalist imperialism, and breakfasting on Alka-seltzer. They sang the 'Internationale' with fervour and in harmony before returning to their home towns north and south of the border. But they never discussed the border itself. Many of the northern union leaders knew my father well and could recall things he had written years before. In his left-wing socialism he was their brother. But in his demands for a united Ireland he was an alien to be kept at arm's length. One of them, Harold Binks, a self-described 'Protestant atheist' and General Secretary of the Clerical Workers Union, got drunk in McGlade's bar in Belfast one night and unburdened himself to me. 'Charlie McCrystal is the smartest man I know,' he said. 'Charlie McCrystal is the most genuine socialist I know, the most open-minded, fair-minded, friendliest man I know. When he has spoken at the [Belfast] trades council, everybody listens and takes seriously everything he has to say, because we know he has no narrow constituency urging him to take this or that line. We all respect the breadth of his knowledge and the way he can make a point cleanly and simply. D'you mind what I'm saying? Will you take one for the road? Now listen . . . your da is all those things and more. But his big mistake is wanting to put us in with the Free State [Irish Republic]. That's his *only* mistake but, I'm telling you, it's a fatal mistake. It's not that I disagree with him, but if I were to say I agreed with him, my members would boot me out of my job. And my union's more tolerant than most. So there you are . . . I hope, as Charlie McCrystal's son, you're not offended.'

My own career benefited from fairly steady promotions and pay rises. At first, I shared a large editorial room with other general reporters and copytakers (typists who took reporters' dictation over the telephone). The copytakers tended to be older and more cerebral than the journalists. The oldest, Charlie Marshall, a grandfatherly type, took pleasure in asking dictating reporters to spell certain words, in the hope of discovering they couldn't. Another, slightly younger, called Stanley, brought a pound of raw tripe, cut in strips, into the office on Fridays, chomping through it with toothless gums, as he typed reporters' copy.

'What's that?' I once shouted into the phone from the High Court, misunderstanding his mumble after I had dictated my first paragraph.

'Tripe.'

'What?'

'Tripe.'

'Oh,' I said, chastened.

The most enigmatic member of the staff was yet another copy-taker, Bob Young, who had a well-ordered mind and a cirrhosed liver. He lived in a bleak loyalist ghetto in east Belfast, yet mocked the Orange Order. Sober, he could have passed for a Mormon; drunk, he would burst into bawdiness:

> We're the bin men, we're the bin men;
> Some of us are fat and some are thin men.
> We go round to yer old back door –
> Rat-a-tat-tat, rat-a-tat-tat on yer old back door.
> 'Are ye in, Mam? We're the bin men,
> We've come to put yer bin agin the wall.
> There's a woman up the Shankill
> With her knickers around her ankle
> When the bin men call.'

Promotion sent me to a smaller room up the corridor, where the specialists resided. There, largely unsupervised, we phoned our contacts and, if lucky, got our 'scoops'. I felt close to my colleagues, except on those occasions when they would arrive with little black attaché cases containing, I assumed, their Masonic regalia. Masonry was a subject unmentioned in my presence. But I have always felt some disappointment on learning that a journalist could bring himself to join a society not famous for its openness. I have always taken the view that a journalist should belong to as few associations as possible. This may strike colleagues past and present as a touch naïve. But how on earth can one even pretend to be objective in reporting, say, ferment in Northern Ireland if one is a member of the Unionist Party, or of Sinn Féin? If you are on a committee of the National Union of Journalists, pledged to negotiate the best deal you can exact from your editor and proprietor one day, how can you reconcile that pledge with giving the editor or proprietor a secret handshake in a Masonic chamber the next day? Perhaps it *can* be done. I have never tried it. There have been occasions when my father had wondered aloud, but without discernible reproach, about where I stood 'on the national question'. I replied, a trifle pompously perhaps, that I stood not *on* it, but aside from it, so that I could get a better look at it.

'Do you mean to tell me,' he said, 'that because you're a journalist, you mustn't commit yourself to anything?'

'No, not really; but I have to distance myself, and not appear to take sides.'

'What does that mean? Let's say you've got republican sympathies, and you believe they could influence you when reporting politics. What do you do? You can't eradicate what you know; what's in your heart or on your conscience. Do you mean you bend over backwards to accommodate the Unionist point of view?'

'All I know is what I ought to try to do,' I said – and I must have sounded lame – 'and that is to repress personal convictions – shove them into a cupboard – so that I can try to see things dispassionately.'

And so we would argue; my father calm in a logic that seemed to him irrefragable, and I increasingly rattled by a subject I had not properly thought through. I do not think he wanted to score points. Rather, he was genuinely curious about the prismatic focus his son might have on the world. Sometimes I would end the discussion with a cutting, 'You're living in the past!' To which he would reply, quoting Burke: 'A nation which does not respect its past will have no future to deserve respect'; or, more enigmatically: 'The chief part of our lives is remembering. Otherwise we'd go mad.'

As he spoke, the future beckoned.

In 1961, after a great amount of legal wrangling, the *Belfast Telegraph* passed into the hands of Roy (later Lord) Thomson, the Canadian newspaper and radio station owner who had earlier bought the *Sunday Times*. Jack Sayers remained as editor, but the Thomson Organization appointed a Welshman, David Thomas, as managing director – a man who was either unimpressed or unacquainted with the sectarian subtleties of Ulster media operations. The *Telegraph's* view of its own role continued to broaden, and Sayers urged that Catholics should participate more fully in public life. Further, he urged that Lord Brookeborough should step down as prime minister, in favour of Terence O'Neill. In 1963, the old bigot did so. The *Irish Times* in Dublin credited Sayers with 'a liberating revolution'. Some Protestant readers complained about 'too much Catholic news'. Sayers's 'Viewpoint' column declared: 'We are at a point of flux more disturbing than any since the war. Social and political evolution is gathering pace and no one can be sure where it will lead or whether new forces of character will replace the old . . . The record of recent times is heavily on the credit side of the ledger. Poverty and bigotry are being cancelled out . . . a natural goodwill is growing up.'

These were promising times in Northern Ireland. The atmosphere in which we journalists worked was at times highly charged, as we sensed change in the air and our role in bringing it about. But none of us imagined that the men of 1798 were about to have a hand in it.

June 1963, however, was the two-hundredth anniversary of the birth of Wolfe Tone, the would-be unifier of 'Protestant, Catholic and dissenter' and organizer of the '98 Insurrection. My father took part in the commemoration without drawing attention to himself, possibly because he was reluctant to do or say anything which might compromise my detached status (I can almost hear him chuckle as I write it), and possibly because of a distracting row among the organizers. The row concerned the Irish tricolour. As a symbol of Irish nationalism it was banned in Northern Ireland under the Flags and Emblems Act (1954). In the Wolfe Tone commemoration parade in Belfast, should it be carried aloft or not? After much acrimonious infighting, the decision was taken not to defy the ban. My father was on the side of defiance, but worried about the degree of rancour the argument had created. A month later, he and my stepmother joined Stella and me and our three boys, Cal, Damien and Kieran (then seven months old) at the summer house in Ballymacormick. 'There'll always be factions,' he said when I brought the subject up. 'There were factions in 1798 and there'll be factions in 1998 and in 2098. Disharmony has split Irish political groups for centuries. Unity and homogeneity are not distinctive notes of our history, and that can be all to the good, you know – catharsis!'

I later heard that, as a result of the bitterness which the Wolfe Tone flag dispute engendered within the republican movement, a more hard-line leadership quietly seized control of the then more-or-less dormant IRA in Belfast.

I attached little significance to it at the time. As the *Sunday Times* stringer, I was filing stories to London about a new mood in Ulster politics. One Saturday, I reached the new Ulster Prime Minister, Terence O'Neill, at his home and got him to talk, for the first time openly, about opening the Unionist Party to Catholics. I wrote about a new civil rights movement struggling to get off the ground with middle-class organization behind it. It was called the Campaign for Social Justice. Its impact on Northern Ireland politics was far greater than any terrorist campaign had until then achieved. O'Neill visited Catholic schools, strolled in Catholic ghettoes, ended Unionist gerrymandering in Derry and, when Pope John XXIII died in 1963, sent condolences to the Irish Cardinal. He made speeches which showed him to be of an entirely different stamp than his predecessor. He was a tall, thin, pale man with a long nose through which he appeared to deliver his speeches. He was good at keeping his temper, not least with the hard-liners in his party. An Old Etonian, he seemed not entirely suited for the ditch-fights of Ulster politics. Yet he did not look down his long nose at either the aggressive Opposition or his sullen backbenchers. He sounded embarrassed when obliged, on occasion, to beat the loyalist drum. In my, albeit brief, dealings with him, he never appeared to be terribly bright. But that part of his mind which was in motion appeared to be surprisingly open for a Unionist. The very fact that his own Unionist colleagues began plotting against him seemed a significant indicator that intransigence in Ulster might be at the point of beginning to wane.

In January of 1964, before I left for London, David Thomas called me into his office and asked how long I planned to stay with the *Sunday Times*. I said I thought three years would be about right.

'Would you be interested eventually in becoming editor here?' he asked quietly.

I could scarcely believe what I was hearing: a Catholic editor of a Unionist organ! Things *were* humming along.

'Oh well, er, hmmm, sure, OK, yes, kind of you,' I said, both thrilled and sceptical.

I was back in Belfast sooner than I had thought possible. In October, just six months after moving my family to Finchley, I returned to my native city to write a front-page story for the *Sunday Times*.

RIOT-TORN BELFAST MAY CALL
FOR HELP FROM THE ARMY
By Cal McCrystal, Belfast, Saturday

The British Army may be called into action if the vicious rioting which broke out here on Thursday night and intensified last night cannot be quelled by the police. Only 12 days before the General Election, the city faced the prospect of civil commotion on a scale which could well equal the bitter and still remembered Troubles in the early Thirties.

It was the first really serious disturbance I had witnessed in my home town. I was appalled at the savagery of the attacks and counter-attacks. Police, backed by armoured cars with wheels blazing from a petrol bomb attack, baton-charged more than 3,000 screaming rioters on the Catholic Falls Road, as a tense and emotional Deputy Police Commissioner said to me: 'we cannot rule out the possibility of having to ask the Army for support.' The rioters directed their violence against the police, private cars, corporation buses and onlookers. I attempted to interview leaders of a gang of about fifty whose ages ranged between sixteen and thirty. Some of them were half-crazed with drink and insisted I was a 'peeler'. Two held my arms and pushed me against a wall while a third punched me in the stomach. A short time later, six sober youths came to my aid. I told my newspaper that what was happening in the nationalist ghetto was far from being an isolated constituency disturbance sharpened by bigotry, unemployment and a traditional hatred for the police. It needed only one shot to be fired by the perpetually armed police to send the city into even worse turmoil.

The trouble started when police removed a banned Irish national flag, the green, white and orange tricolour, from the window of republican headquarters in Divis Street, Belfast. A second tricolour was displayed and, on the orders of Northern Ireland's Minister of Home Affairs, the police seized this too, breaking into the premises with pickaxes. But the rioters placed most blame on Ian Paisley, who had complained to the police about the display of 'an enemy flag' in the first place and had threatened to invade Falls Road with his supporters to remove it himself. At that time, the republican movement in Belfast had given up (or postponed) the idea of a violent abolition of the Irish border, and were preparing to use the ballot box in support of their objective. When I asked rioters who they would vote for in the next election, they cried: 'Republican, republican' .

Ten days later, in a General Election which put the Labour Party in power in the United Kingdom and Harold Wilson into Downing Street, a Unionist was elected in West Belfast, with a majority of 6,000. His first act was to thank Ian Paisley, without whose help, he said, 'it could not have been done'. Twenty-three years were to pass before the West Belfast seat was taken for Sinn Féin by Gerry Adams. In 1964, however, Adams was only sixteen, still a pupil at St Mary's Grammar School, Barrack Street, where Divis Street pokes into Belfast's city centre.

Back in London, I put Northern Ireland out of my mind until early in 1965 when O'Neill, pursuing what Jack Sayers anticipated was 'Ulster's Golden Age', invited Sean Lemass, the Irish Republic's Prime Minister, to Stormont Castle for talks. It was a bold move which astonished everyone – Britain, Ireland and, most of all, Northern Ireland Unionists; the first get-together of Prime Ministers since their island was divided. Some accused O'Neill of treachery. Ian Paisley and his *Protestant Telegraph* (established to counter Sayers's liberalism) thundered: 'O'Neill must go.' In February, O'Neill agreed to see me, and I flew to Belfast again.

'Sit down on the chair that Lemass sat on,' he said in the sonorous public school voice I had liked to mimic while drinking in McGlade's. He seemed happy, if somewhat guarded, about the diplomatic manoeuvre that had made him so controversial and added to his personal stature in London and elsewhere. He had just made a reciprocal visit to Dublin a couple of days before my arrival, and he talked about a 'new atmosphere [which] can make it difficult for the extremists to function'.

But beyond the gates of Stormont the 'new atmosphere' was already – and inevitably – being poisoned, and the promise of a golden age tarnished. The poison was coming from both sides of the Northern Ireland divide. The Nationalist Party had been urged by Lemass to apply for recognition as Stormont's official Opposition – an entitlement it was due from a numerical viewpoint but which it traditionally had declined, on the grounds that to do otherwise would have implied acceptance of partition. Lemass's advice had many grassroots nationalists foaming at the mouth. It was, they said, tantamount to accepting the constitutional fact that Ulster was part of the United Kingdom. That, they added, was treachery. So cries of treachery from the Unionist side were matched by similar cries from the nationalist side. Before catching the London plane, I called at the house in Ponsonby Avenue. I said to my father that I thought O'Neill might have bitten off more than the Unionist Party could chew.

'Yes, I think O'Neill will be able to handle the likes of Ian Paisley,' my father said. 'But I can't see some of his own colleagues forgiving him for it. He'd have to purge his Cabinet and risk repudiation by his party. Did I ever tell you what Sir Henry Maine [nineteenth-century British jurist and historian] said? He said party feeling is a survival of the primitive combativeness of mankind. It is war without the city transmuted into war within the city.'

But my father always had somebody else's words to apply to everything. Years later, after O'Neill was ousted and the Stormont government prorogued, and war was destroying the city, I remembered what he had said back then. I wondered if he was displaying unusual prescience. I concluded that he wasn't, and that it was I who was seizing on a comment that had only accidental significance in the light of subsequent years.

Less visibly, 'primitive combativeness' was being conducted within republican ranks. It was now seventeen years since my father had stood on Napoleon's Nose to harangue the crowds about the ideals of Wolfe Tone and the United Irishmen. The year of his mountain rhetoric was, coincidentally, also the year of Gerry Adams's birth. In an essay published in 1988, Adams wrote about the Belfast Wolfe Tone Society, 'a republican-oriented discussion group' which had 're-invigorated the initiative' on civil liberties. It was an initiative with which, earlier in his life, my father almost certainly would have been involved. I do not know for certain that he was not involved in 1965. But if he was, he never spoke of it to me. It is odd, really, since the groups embarked on the 'initiative' were those which had his sympathy – as Adams put it, 'republicans, communists and unaffiliated trade unionists'. But I would guess that he deliberately may have distanced himself from it on the grounds that the 'initiative' was not all that it seemed. In Dublin, the Wolfe Tone Society was regarded as 'more or less an IRA debating club'. Its leading lights viewed the Belfast branch as having greater potential than that of a mere forum. They wanted republicans associated with it to infiltrate Northern Ireland trade unions, with the naïve idea of creating a revolutionary consciousness attractive to Catholic and Protestant workers alike. That idea, worthy enough in many eyes, was doomed to failure. It had been pursued often before by, among others, Charles McCrystal. He had seen enough, I think, to be convinced that it was 'a hope of worms'. In the end, the idea was dropped in favour of the setting up of a civil rights crusade. To make the crusade seem less *parti pris*, the Wolfe Tone banner was dropped. Many of the crusaders were moderate citizens who wanted only a fair deal for Northern Ireland's Catholic minority, and believed that O'Neill would deliver it if jostled. But its vigour undoubtedly came from a solidly represented republican movement with a grander objective. The surveyors of a road to the violence that lay ahead were adjusting their optics.

I was not terribly keen on being typecast as a writer about Irish events, feeling almost too close to the subject to tackle it as a journalist. I wanted to see more of the world than John Bull's 'other island', all of which came under the heading of 'home news' in Fleet Street (as though the 1920 partitioning of Ireland had never happened). The occasional Irish assignment was an opportunity to see my father and stepmother and to catch up on family news. But I was fast weakening in my intention to return to Northern Ireland to live. Harold Evans, who was to become one of the most inspiring editors in British journalism history, had joined the *Sunday Times* as an assistant editor in 1966, charged with pepping up all its departments before taking over the editor's chair a year later. There was comradeship and loyalty among the staff which I have never since encountered. I don't think Evans, a Yorkshireman, was especially interested in Ireland in 1966. But curiosity got the better of him when rumbles and whiffs of smoke began to drift eastwards across the Irish Sea. And so, I found myself in Ireland again, in March 1966 – this time in Dublin.

The story I wrote caused few alarm bells to ring, and at the time I myself did not foresee anything like the catastrophe that was about to destroy thousands of lives and cost billions of pounds in wrecked and damaged property in Ireland and Britain. Nevertheless, it bore bad tidings. To research it, I talked to people on the republican fringe, who led me to people familiar with the IRA's changing agenda. My telephone calls from my Dublin hotel were monitored by Special Branch. One evening a Dublin officer rang from the lobby asking if he could come to my room for a talk. I declined and met him downstairs. He was polite, showed by his questions that he was aware of the identity of people I'd been phoning, and said that his superior would be 'extremely grateful' were I to go to headquarters at a mutually convenient time the following morning. I agreed, and duly met the avuncular head of Ireland's Special Branch. He was sorry to take up my time, asked me a few seemingly inconsequential questions, then wondered if I had been in touch with members of an organization intent on making mischief, and if so what sort of mischief did I suppose that might be. I told him I had spoken to a number of people whose names I was not at liberty to disclose, but that he could read what I proposed to write on the following Sunday. He seemed satisfied with the conversation and hoped that the rest of my stay in Dublin would be fruitful. The headline on my story said:

IRELAND HEADING FOR EMERGENCY

Underneath, I had written that a new wave of sectarian attacks in Northern Ireland was beginning to push the country towards a state of emergency, and that governments on both sides of the border were anticipating more violence. The lengthy despatch included the following:

While the IRA disclaims any connection with the recent outbreaks, these, if they continue, could easily lead to serious deterioration in the much improved relations between Northern and Southern Governments . . . The IRA not only denies causing the disturbances, but this week contended, through its official mouthpiece, Sinn Féin, that the incidents were caused by agents of both Governments acting in collusion.

Sinn Féin and the IRA have now become virtually one organization and not the loosely affiliated body [sic] they once were. Every member of the Sinn Féin executive in Dublin is an IRA man.

The whole movement is going through a testing time. A membership drive is on – and apparently succeeding . . . Preparations are being made for what may be this generation's final do-or-die effort to wrest the six counties of Ulster from Britain . . . A new left-wing group . . . is now in control of the republican movement.

Until then, the British media, like the British government, had shown little inclination to poke around in Northern Ireland's affairs. In retrospect this may seem surprising, though it shouldn't be. For as long as anybody cares to remember, the English, on the whole, have tended to regard the Irish as ignorant peasants reliable only in laying bricks or digging ditches. My father, useless at telling jokes, nevertheless passed on the following one with enthusiasm:

'A big Mayo man goes to London and asks for a job as a carpenter. The foreman says: "Oh come on, Pat, I bet you don't know the difference between a joist and a girder." To which Pat replies: "I do so. Joyce wrote *Ulysses* and Goethe wrote *Faust*."'

The Northern Irish had the added distinction of being regarded as best capable of laying the bricks and digging the ditches around themselves. Many of the Irish, wrote the second Earl of Clarendon to his brother in 1686, believed that 'this kingdom is the Pope's and the inheritance of St Peter's chair, that the King has no right, further than the Pope gives him authority . . .' Some Englishmen believed that the coming of William III prevented England from becoming 'a wilderness of howling Irish'. Such attitudes persisted through and beyond Victorian times and were immortalized in the cartoons of *Punch*, which showed Irishmen as cretinous beggars, lazy good-for-nothings, or simian scoundrels – images that have proved hard to eradicate totally in modern times. Yet, given the British taxpayer subventions to Northern Ireland, to the tune of hundreds of millions of pounds annually, one would have expected a more probing curiosity to prevail.

In the late 1960s, however, Northern Ireland was becoming increasingly impossible to ignore. The civil rights campaign was directly and vociferously challenging the O'Neill government. Loyalist extremists, led by Ian Paisley, were doing likewise. The civil rights people and the loyalists, far from joining forces to attack their mutual target, began to turn on each other. Gunfire, petrol bombs and an upsurge in overt acts of religious bigotry ended completely the near-lull that had existed since 1935, and the noise could be heard in Westminster and in Fleet Street. In July, 1966 the *Sunday Times* sent me to Belfast yet again. The idea was to try to explain, in terms comprehensible to unreceptive readers in Britain, what had been going on in *their* name, in *their* westernmost province. It was the traditional Orange marching season. More significantly, the Queen was about to make an official visit to the most self-abused part of her realm. The ensuing article was headlined 'JOHN BULL'S POLITICAL SLUM'.

I stayed in the Grand Central Hotel. Journalists from Europe and North America milled about, most of them in Belfast for the first time. Now and again, locals would crowd the hotel lobby to gawp at these foreigners and to wonder what their presence could possibly augur. I was there, with three *Sunday Times* colleagues, for three days, describing, as dispassionately as possible, a part of the United Kingdom where the crude apparatus of political and religious oppression – ballot-rigging, job and housing discrimination, and an omnipresent threat of violence – comfortably co-existed with intense loyalty to the Crown. When the Queen visited Northern Ireland on the day after the article was published, the demonstration of allegiance would, we predicted, verge on frenetic; Protestant Ulster had just survived another bloody crisis and was anxious to know where its heart lay. Within the previous week, the British public had been confronted with the endemic brutality of the Ulster situation where half a million Catholics lived uneasily among a million Protestants. A series of thuggish incidents culminating in the cold-blooded killing of two Catholics had finally galvanized the O'Neill government. The paramilitary loyalist Ulster Volunteer Force was banned, and O'Neill denounced Paisleyism as 'quasi-Fascism behind a clerical cloak'.

Paisleyism, however, was merely the visible symptom of a deep-seated malaise, for which the Westminster parliament bore a large measure of responsibility. When the flags and bunting were pulled down after the Royal visit, we wrote, Mr Wilson's government 'will be confronted with a sharp alternative: whether to use reserve powers to bring elementary social justice to Northern Ireland, or simply allow Britain's most isolated province to work out its own bizarre destiny'. Brought up to despise the 'Scarlet Woman' (Rome) and distrust 'the Micks' (Catholics), many Protestants found the new perspectives repellent. Paisley had not won converts to his intransigent views; he had merely reaffirmed Ulster's traditional bigotries and found that they still had a tenacious hold. The fight was vicious. Many moderate political leaders were bombarded with abusive telegrams and phone calls from the banned UVF. Paisley claimed he had nothing to do with this organization, despite O'Neill's accusations. What was clear, however, was that the UVF hero-worshipped Paisley.

The *Sunday Times* article covered most of the wretched ground. For all its bizarre extremism, Paisleyism was only a symptom of a divided country. Another, most grievous symptom was the injustice of discrimination. It was not just a political tradition in Ulster; it was a way of life. At its most ludicrous it was illustrated occasionally by newspaper advertisements: 'WANTED – reliable cook, Protestant (Christian preferred)'. At its most serious, discrimination was strengthened by the regular misuse of political power. In local government, where discrimination was worst, the local Unionist parties held fearfully to the belief that the more fecund Catholic population would soon swallow them. To extend the influence of an already limited franchise, the Unionist Party had learned to love the art of gerrymandering, or fixing boundaries to wring the last ounce of political advantage. The classic example was Londonderry. There were 14,325 Catholics on the local roll, and 9,235 Protestants; but the wards were so organized to give Protestants a majority in enough of them to win control of the City Council, which comprised twelve Unionists and only nine Nationalists. Derry was not unique.

Dungannon, with a population of 7,500 – 53 per cent of which was Catholic – had fourteen Protestants and seven Catholics on the council. Kilkeel, population 3,000 – 60 per cent Catholic – had returned a Protestant-dominated council ever since 1937, when the existing rural council was made an urban council with new boundaries; these happened to be in areas in which there was a Protestant majority.

The outcome was nakedly partisan politics, not least in the allocation of houses. Catholics did get houses in most Ulster towns in those days, but the location of their estates was usually chosen with loving care by Unionist councils. In Dungannon, for example, there was one housing estate with 192 houses, and all the tenants were Protestants (the estate was known to local Catholics as 'segregation park'). The Unionist council provided houses for Catholics, but only in the single ward electing seven Nationalists, thus preserving the Protestant stranglehold. In employment, the pattern of prejudice was the same. In Londonderry, the heads of all City Council departments were Protestant. Of 177 salaried employees, 145 – earning £124,424 – were Protestant, and only 32 – earning £20,420 – were Catholic. The pattern was even more distinct at national level: the Northern Ireland Housing Trust (generally admired for its 'fairness') had seven Protestant members and no Catholics; the National Assistance Board, five Protestants, no Catholics; and the Northern Ireland Economic Council, sixteen Protestants and no Catholics. A study just earlier completed for the Peace Research Centre at Lancaster concluded that the combined effect of various types of discrimination had been to create something approaching paranoia among many Catholics, particularly in the rural areas, who believed that the state of Ulster was totally corrupt and static. Although Londonderry was badly in need of rejuvenation (I still carry disturbing memories of Catholic families living in squalid, leaking Nissen huts left over from the Second World War, where rats ate the hair of sleeping children), yet the Northern Ireland Government's planned new town – Craigavon – would be built in the prosperous Protestant-dominated area between Portadown and Lurgan. Derry seemed the obvious location, too, for Ulster's new university, yet the government opted for Coleraine, a staunchly Unionist town. Catholics believed implicitly, and often hopelessly, that these decisions by the Stormont government were not coincidental. So did a number of British MPs. But one of the most curious aspects of religious discrimination in Ulster was that the Westminster parliament was prevented by convention from discussing it. Ulster debates in the British House of Commons followed a monotonously predictable routine. A Labour backbencher, say, referred to some form of anti-Catholic religious discrimination, only to be interrupted, on a point of order, by one of the eleven Unionist MPs (now eighteen, plus two Paisleyites). Invariably, the Speaker's ruling was that Ulster's 'internal affairs' could not be discussed unless a British minister was directly responsible for them. Since the Stormont government controlled housing, education, local government, and constituency boundaries – which covered most potential sources of discrimination – the area left to the critical MPs often seemed to stretch from agricultural subsidies to the future of Shorts, Belfast's ailing aircraft manufacturers, with virtually nothing in between.

The *Sunday Times* article warned:

One thing is certain. Any liberalization of the Ulster regime will only come after some vigorous prodding from Westminster. O'Neill may put a brake on Paisley's virulence, but the grass-roots strength of 'Paisleyism' has undoubtedly shaken the Northern Ireland Government, and what little reforming zeal it ever had is in danger of burning out. The loyalist cheers for the Queen . . . should not be allowed to soften a very hard line on John Bull's political slum.

Reaction was mixed, as one would expect. My father sent his congratulations for 'a first-class piece'. A barrister who had been my classmate at St Malachy's College, wrote to Harold Evans the editor to say that over one-third of Northern Ireland's population 'is indebted to your newspaper'. Jack Sayers was less enthusiastic. For years, he had been pressing for change, and was understandably defensive of his protégé, Terence O'Neill, who was trying to bring it about. He wrote to Evans pointing out that 'Capt. O'Neill' had done more to ameliorate the divisions of centuries of Irish history than had been achieved 'in any period since Home Rule first became an issue.' Those who were convinced of the need for further improvements 'will not be assisted by the suggestion that the British government should do their "slum clearance" for them.' Much of what he wrote was low-key and balanced. But I think he was unwise to have seemed to put himself, by his letter, on the side of the slum's landlords. In any case, his much trumpeted 'Golden Age' was over.

13

FAR, FAR AWAY . . .

My father retired in 1970, when I was based in the United States. On my return to London as news editor, I went to Belfast to see him, finding his finances in some disarray, though less drastically than the disarray afflicting my native province. IRA bombs shook Belfast. Paisley had taken O'Neill's Stormont seat. The British Home Secretary, Reginald Maudling, fleeing to London from his first visit to Belfast, remarked: 'For God's sake bring me a large Scotch! What a bloody awful country!' A Dublin Cabinet minister secretly visited Falls Road. Rioting took place on Shankill Road. In Ponsonby Avenue, my stepmother dropped a hint that she and my father were having difficulty in making ends meet. He had adhered, too well, to his principle: spend, don't save. His sole income was the state pension, since he had not bothered to invest in a private one.

'Ach, at my age you don't need much to keep going,' he said. 'You don't thrive on luxuries. Man can survive on beans.' And so on with no audible or visible trace of self-pity.

I was horrified to discover that he had sold most of his beloved books, many of them of great value, to a Galway bookseller for about £100. He'd also sold a violin that had been in the house for as long as I could remember. It had a label which said 'Stradivarius'. He got rid of it for a few pounds. Even if it was a fake – and I sincerely hope that it was – it must have been worth considerably more than that. Against his protestations, but with Theresa's whispered gratitude, I arranged for a modest sum to be transferred monthly from my London bank account to his. The arrangement lasted only for a year or so. His friend Paddy Devlin, who was then Northern Secretary of the Irish Transport Workers' Union, offered him a part-time job in the union's offices, which were on Antrim Road, a few hundred yards from the house in Ponsonby Avenue.

Northern Ireland was collapsing in on itself. I am glad I did not have to witness the worst of it. Since 1972, my journalism was focused, not on Ulster, but on a wider world. In the following year, when I was in the United States working on a book about the Watergate scandal, my father reached me on the phone. 'Mammy has cancer. She's dying. She doesn't know she's dying. I've told her she's going to get better, and she believes me. She trusts me to tell her the truth, because I always have. But when I look at her fading away, I . . . just . . . can't. It's something for her to hold on to. She hasn't long to go. When can you come?' At that point, I think, Northern Ireland politics lost all personal significance for both of us. As the Troubles claimed their 200th British Army fatality, and a Protestant–Catholic power-sharing executive started out on the road to its inevitable doom, neither of us would be able to revive, to any great extent, our interest in Ulster's future.

She died before I reached Belfast. I found my father in an armchair, before an unlit fire in Ponsonby Avenue. He had shrunk, it seemed to me, to half his normal size. His old friend Eddie Nolan was with him. Both were staring into the dead hearth when I entered the room. My father struggled out of the chair and turned to face me, saying nothing. His legs trembled and he reached out a hand to steady himself against the back of the chair. The veins on the back of his hand stood out large and dark. As I went forward to embrace him, he made quick little gasping sounds. Something like a moan rose from his chest, tapering to a throttled squeak. As I put my arms around him, he finally said: 'Ah, Cahal óg . . .' Eddie Nolan turned his head away. I noticed that my father had cut himself shaving, and that dandruff had accumulated on the shoulders of his dark suit jacket. I felt pity, guilt, impotence. My stepmother's coffin had been sealed some hours before my arrival.

That December night, I slept alongside my father, in the bed he had shared with two wives. The blue-metal alarm clock still ticked beside us. I tried to pick out things that I could identify specifically with my stepmother, but, aside from some of her clothes visible through the half-open wardrobe door, couldn't. The room was very cold, for the house did not have central heating. He did not believe in central heating ('dries out the skin'), just as he preferred linoleum to carpet ('germ-gatherers'), and a cold bath to a hot one ('builds character'). The bed was extremely hard, because of wooden planks he had placed beneath the mattress ('good for the spine'). We did not talk much. After I switched out the light he was asleep before I was. I lay on my back, staring out through a chink in the window-blinds into the dim, lamp-lit night. I wondered what would become of him now, with no woman to warm his planks. It was around then that I decided it would do both of us good were he to accompany me on short summer trips whenever I could contrive them.

On the last of these, my father and I travelled most of the circumference of Northern Ireland, taking in Donegal. I thought by then there was little about him that I had yet to discover. But I was wrong. Many landmarks on the road we travelled reminded him of events of varying significance. Driving north out of Belfast in the shadow of Napoleon's Nose, his eye was caught by an advertising hoarding with a young woman's face on it. The face reminded him, he said, of a girl he'd known before he met my mother. Her name was O'Prey. She was warm and pretty and cerebral, an attractive combination. She invited him to her home to meet her father who was in shipping – and quite prosperous. The relationship edged towards marriage, but foundered when my mother came into the picture.

'Did you lose contact with Miss O'Prey?' I asked.

'Oh, of course! I think she was terribly hurt. I was remorseful for that. I think she was one of those women who loved with their every fibre, you know? No half-measures. She loved me to distraction. I heard she rose quite high in the civil service. But she never married.'

Driving along the Antrim coast road, he would point out little coves, promontories, hills, hamlets, give their names and explain each derivation using anecdote. He retained much of the ancient folklore, some of it predating British interest in the island of Ireland. I asked him if he had ever thought of writing a book.

'I did start one once,' he said. 'It was about Belfast before you were born, a factual account with fictionalized characters.' He talked about 'the life of the imagination' with its apprehension of individual wholes, and 'the life of intelligence' which consisted of classification and abstraction. The novel's theme, I gathered, was about the power of intelligence pitted against the power of the imagination in the context of the Northern Ireland he'd grown up in. It sounded like an interesting theme.

'What happened to the book?'

'I didn't finish it. I lost interest.'

That didn't sound quite right. When I probed, he said he had written 87,000 words before abandoning the project. Whew! Where were they?

'Oh, I destroyed it; burnt it. I'm not a natural writer. I'm a natural teacher. I think old man vanity made me think I had a book in me!'

Near Ballycastle, in County Antrim, is a little hamlet called Corrymeela. There is a compound containing low-rise buildings, named 'the Corrymeela Project', dedicated to bridging the religious divide and enabling people to come to terms with grief. A place of mediation and meditation, it prompted my father, as we drove past it, to meditate on his own role as mediator shortly after the present Troubles began. The IRA had split into two factions: the 'Official IRA' which wanted a socialist Ireland without violence, and the 'Provisional IRA' which saw violence as the only way. My father sided with the 'Officials', but being an elderly man with cool judgement and proven negotiating prowess he was asked to help mediate between the two. This was all news to me. His secret role involved trips to hotels south of the Irish border and conversations conducted partly in Gaelic, sometimes late into the night. His efforts came to nothing.

In Donegal, his favourite among all Irish counties, he told me that summer that, in the first years of the latest Troubles, he had met a couple of British Army officers whom he found 'engaging enough'. Both had been in charge of patrols in the Newington district. One, a young captain, had come to the door of the house in Ponsonby Avenue as part of a routine check on households. 'We had a bit of a yarn,' my father said, as we bumped over a rough bog-road to the isolated valley of Glencolumbkille. 'He had a clipped Oxford accent, obviously born with a silver spoon in his mouth, but he said he had Irish blood in him, from Waterford, I think. As a teenager he'd been to Yeats country in Sligo, and he'd read Yeats's *The Celtic Twilight*. I said to him: "What's a chap like you doing in the British Army?" He said he was there to defend his country. So I said: "Well then, you'll understand us wanting to defend ours!" He laughed at that. He reminded me of one of my students in the Ard Scoil years ago. We had a chat about politics, and I got the impression he would have been a Labour voter, though he didn't say it exactly. But he was well-read, and I found myself taking a liking to him.'

Glencolumbkille is where the legendary Irish saint, Columb (or 'dove'), built his church, before going off to found Derry and Christianize much of Scotland and northern England. We were there as a result of a conversation we'd had before leaving Derry.

'I wouldn't be at all surprised,' my father had said, 'if we were descended from one of the sixth-century Irish missionaries who went to Scotland with St Columb?'

'How so?'

'The name "McCrystal" doesn't just mean "son of Christopher", which is a Greek word. The Gaelic, *MacCríostáil* means, literally, "son of the Christly one". Can't you imagine one of St Columb's holy men travelling beyond the Grampians 1,500 years ago, and settling down with a Pictish tribe?'

'Wouldn't he have been celibate?'

'Mmm . . . everyone's allowed one mistake, I suppose. But he'd still be the Christly one as far as the Picts were concerned.'

'So we're Irish first, then Scottish, then Irish again?'

'It's not an unreasonable theory', he said, coughing into his handkerchief.

Glencolumbkille is a place of great beauty if you are a tourist, and of great bleakness if you are not. Its towering cliffs are gnawed by the Atlantic, and there is far more bog than arable land. The portal dolmens marking the burial places of Stone Age farmers add to one's sense of desolation. We called on Father James McDyer, who founded the first 'people's commune' in western Europe, in the face of local conservatism, civil service suspicion and allegations that he was either a communist or a fascist. To introduce new ideas, or even to borrow old ones for new purposes, can be an uphill task in Ireland. His commune was about to go into liquidation when we talked to him. Father McDyer was a tall, ascetic, courteous man whose eyes twinkled when he discovered that he and my father, five years his senior, shared a passionate love for Donegal and its strangely accented Gaelic. After wandering through the surviving co-operative ventures – a crab- and fish-processing plant and a machine-knitting enterprise – I returned to find them in animated discussion. Between them was a book my father had spotted on the priest's office shelves. It was called *The Year of the French*, by Thomas Flanagan, a novel about the 1798 Rebellion and the failed French attempts to support the United Irishmen. My father was virtually on home ground here, and I marvelled at how frequently the fate of the United Irishmen had dogged his life.

My father and the priest also talked about an ancient custom of stone-throwing, in honour of a saint. This ceremony has taken place at Glencolumbkille every June for hundreds of years. It involves a pilgrimage to cairns – or monumental mounds – marked by great stones, reputed to be sepulchral pillars. Each pilgrim was expected to throw a stone on to each cairn while intoning prayers to St Columbkille. The practice, I think, is rooted in pre-Christian times. It has been compared with the habit of Greek warriors who would fling a stone upon a pile before going into combat. The battle over, each survivor removed a stone from the pile. The remaining stones commemorated – and recorded – the numbers killed in battle. In Ireland, stones have become part of religious expression, both in veneration and in street warfare. They frequently accumulate in the human heart.

There was one other thing I learned on that trip. We were in Ballyshannon, a small, raucous town where the River Erne flows into Donegal Bay. My father talked about William Allingham, the Anglo-Irish customs officer who was born there in 1824. Allingham, a friend of Carlyle, had written lines of such moving simplicity that for them alone, he rated him as one of the greatest poets to have lived in Ireland.

> Four ducks on a pond,
> A grass-bank beyond,
> A blue sky of spring,
> White clouds on the wing:
> What a little thing
> To remember for years –
> To remember with tears.

'I can think of nothing more evocative, more saddening, yet elevating – or more pacifying that those simple, unembellished words,' my father said after reciting them for me – yet another gem from his vast memorized treasury.

On the trip through Donegal and along the shores of Lough Erne in County Fermanagh, it was hard to reconcile contemporary Ireland with Allingham's vision. And when 'peace' suddenly (and temporarily) broke out, the 'four ducks' – if seen as a metaphor for the island's four Provinces – were still swimming on a pond, though a pond of tears – the tears of 3,000 bereaved.

In the 1994–96 break in the Troubles, I again walked Belfast's coffin route to visit the grave of my father and his two wives. Having walked up Falls Road, I then strolled down Shankill Road. Because all streets connecting the upper part of Falls Road with the Protestant thoroughfare were blocked by a 'peace line' – in reality a wall to prevent Protestants and Catholics murdering one another – this was not easy to accomplish. It rained as I went up 'the Falls', and brightened a bit as I went down 'the Shankill'. These were deceptive omens. Halfway up 'the Falls', a pale young man who had popped out for a newspaper, told me: 'The Protestants will be defeated if they insist on carrying out sectarian killings. They don't have as many volunteers as our side. And they're not as well armed.' Halfway down 'the Shankill', an alert octogenarian grabbed my arm and shook it urgently. 'I think there will be civil war,' he said. 'There's no one can stop it. It's an awful thing for my seven great-grandchildren to have to face.' Another man, about my own age, said: 'We ought to be able to live together. But the Catholic Church will always be the same, wanting to control everything.'

Since then, as they invariably do, Northern Ireland's politicians helped talk trouble back to the streets again. Moderation yielded to vituperation as ancient slanging matches were resumed. They seemed unaware that, in Ireland, words are missiles. They also seemed unmoved – perhaps imperilled – by other words, in this case penned (by Matthew Prior) in England:

> No harsh reflection let Remembrance raise,
> Forbear to mention what thou canst not praise.

It is hard to take comfort from a rejection of that sentiment – or, indeed, even a rejection of the consideration of it. In his *Outline of History*, H. G. Wells addressed the subject, 'Why Life Must Change Continually'. He wrote: 'We do, however, find certain creatures of a lowly type which early adapted themselves to widespread simple conditions so completely that they have never been greatly modified or exterminated or replaced.' That does not leave a great deal of room for hoping that Northern Ireland's 'lowly creatures' are capable of modification.

There were flowers on the grave, though nothing to show who had put them there. A surprisingly large number of people wandered among the burial plots, some stopping to kneel on bits of plastic and murmur incantations. I remembered that my father had once confessed to me that he was naïve on the matter of his own churchgoing. A religion, he acknowledged, had magic origins, with rites and symbols that belonged to the crudest Nature-worship (to agriculture and the reproductive organs, for instance). It gradually developed and absorbed higher ideas, till it might achieve for the worshipper the unity of the godhead and the immortality of the soul. But could the achievement be celebrated without continual recourse to its primitive antecedents? Can it – will it wish to – cut itself clear from its past?

In the Northern Ireland where I grew up there seemed little or no inclination to make such a break. Since leaving it in 1964, I have seen no compelling evidence that the future – the foreseeable future at any rate – will be much different, whatever new structures evolve, are voted for, or are imposed. The ancient rites and symbols still work their old magic on the people as though no higher ideas had been absorbed. Year after year, mouths intone and missiles fly with numbing monotony, all in the Christian God's name. Life is a terror, as fears are crowned, and minds are cramped and dwarfed. There is nothing that I have observed so far that convinces me, living as I do on the larger island which is often referred to as 'the mainland', that religious Ulster is cutting itself clear of primitivism.

A few months after the 1994 IRA ceasefire, Tim Deal, then the Minister – deputy to the Ambassador – at the American Embassy in London, and a long-standing friend, invited me to talk informally to members of the embassy staff on what might lie ahead for Northern Ireland. When Tim showed me into an embassy conference room in Grosvenor Square, about two dozen staffers were seated around a long table, with the Ambassador, Admiral William Crowe, at its head. I spent the next half-hour explaining why I was so pessimistic; why the Irish republican will to achieve a British withdrawal would never be overcome by either might or right; and why Ulster Protestants would never bend to that republican will, however great their hunger for peace. I was heard in polite silence. I knew they didn't believe me, because they had put all their efforts and all their trust into believing otherwise, perhaps even after it started to become clear later that the peace was crumbling. But, as my father used to observe, to relinquish the smallest spark or sliver of hope is to surrender to the forces of darkness. He himself never did, always clinging tenaciously – against historical and contemporary evidences – to his conviction that Protestants and Catholics would one day unselfconsciously enjoy each other's company. He tended to seize on any scrap that might fit into his dream of things. He was moved, for example, when a Protestant magazine commissioned from him a poem which he called 'Humility'. Republished in another Protestant publication in 1990, just twenty months before he died, it said:

> We cannot afford to be rash,
> Meeting the sneers
> That hurt like the sting of a lash,
> Bringing the tears;
> In heeding the scorn of the rude,
> The glance of the snob,
> The mean slavish tricks of the prude,
> The curse of the mob.
>
> Nor can we afford to linger
> In cloisters of praise,
> Our vanity urging the singer
> To lengthen his lays.
> We cannot afford to be other
> Than humble and true,
> Making humility mother
> The virtue in you.

He was always going on about 'old man vanity' being responsible for his own lack of virtue. But in his quiet, almost self-effacing rebellion against the order established in his Province, and the limits it imposed on freedom to move, to associate, to change, I cannot recall him being rash in response to sneers or untrue to his beliefs.

And when I left O'Kane's funeral parlour in Donegall Street, my eyes perplexingly dry, my thoughts dwelt on one of the many aspects of his life that were to his credit: that he had never succumbed to the curse of the mob. I walked up one side of the street and down the other, past the churches, the newspaper offices and the pubs. I stopped at a shop window and studied my reflection, seeing traces of him in myself, wondering why I felt no pain. Later, at Charles McCrystal's funeral, a stinging wind swept up the slope of Milltown Cemetery, bringing to my eyes the only tears I shed that day. Since then, wherever I happen to be, I have never felt him to be far, far away.